# Transforming
# Capitalism and Patriarchy

# Women and Change in the Developing World

**Series Editor**
Mary H. Moran, Colgate University

**Editorial Board**

# Transforming Capitalism and Patriarchy

## Gender and Development in Africa

April A. Gordon

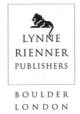

LYNNE
RIENNER
PUBLISHERS

BOULDER
LONDON

Published in the United States of America in 1996 by
Lynne Rienner Publishers, Inc.
1800 30th Street, Boulder, Colorado 80301

and in the United Kingdom by
Lynne Rienner Publishers, Inc.
3 Henrietta Street, Covent Garden, London WC2E 8LU

**Library of Congress Cataloging-in-Publication Data**
Gordon, April A.
   Transforming capitalism and patriarchy : gender and development in
Africa / April A. Gordon.
      p.   cm. — (Women and change in the developing world)
   Includes bibliographical references (p.  ).
   ISBN 1-55587-402-9 (hc : alk. paper)
   ISBN 1-55587-629-3 (pb : alk. paper)
   1. Women in development—Africa.  2. Capitalism—Africa.
3. Patriarchy—Africa.  4. Feminist theory—Africa.  I. Title.
II. Series.
HQ1240.5.A35G67   1996
305.42'096—dc20                         95-41235
                                              CIP

**British Cataloguing in Publication Data**
A Cataloguing in Publication record for this book
is available from the British Library.

Printed and bound in the United States of America

      The paper used in this publication meets the requirements
∞  of the American National Standard for Permanence of
      Paper for Printed Library Materials Z39.48-1984.

5  4  3  2  1

# ▲
# Contents

▲

# Preface

Lila Abu-Lughod (1993:36, 40) writes that it is important for scholars to recognize the "positionality" of their work. She criticizes the notion of the "objective" observer who supposedly stands outside the reality or objects being observed. In actuality, what we call the outside "is always a position within a larger political-historical context." In the course of conceptualizing, researching, and writing this book I became more aware of my own positionality both as a scholar and as a relatively privileged white Western woman who has benefited in many ways from the global capitalist economy.

As a social scientist, I work within developmentalist and feminist scholarly traditions that have significant influence as discourses about Third World people, development, and gender relationships. These discourses, conceived mainly by Western scholars, inevitably reflect Western experiences, perceptions, and biases. Admittedly, the development process I discuss in this book is part of the capitalist transformation of the world, a transformation that involves reshaping non-Western societies and cultures in ways that will make them more like the West. Western feminism also assumes conceptions of gender equality and inequality that reflect Western values, although many of these values resonate with many non-Western women as well.

My approach to studying capitalist development in Africa is critical. I include the ideas of many African as well as Western scholars to show how the development project in Africa has benefited mostly a small stratum of African elites, while most Africans—especially women—have seen few significant benefits. Nevertheless, I do not reject the idea of development per se. My focus is on the need to make capitalist development more beneficial to women. This does not mean that I valorize capitalism or development as unproblematic and nonsexist and view precapitalist African societies as backward and sexist. Western and Third World capitalist societies and "modernity" have their own distinctive problems—and forms of gender inequality. And there are many positive aspects of African cultures, which can be useful to Africans in developing better lives for themselves. My focus, however, is on those aspects of African cultures that result in the unequal and exploitative gender relations that are now an obstacle to capitalist development in Africa. I maintain that, regardless of the problematic aspects of capitalist development, the expansion of capitalism is inevitable, and efforts to improve Africans' material living standards through more-productive agriculture, industry, education, science, and technology must occur if Africa is to escape a future of incalculable human misery. It is also my view that if capitalism cannot be avoided (at least in the near future), the challenges it poses must be met head on and, as much as possible, directed to maximize human welfare.

In my examination of capitalism and patriarchy in Africa, I rely largely on structural analysis. Structures are relatively patterned and stable complexes of institutions, relationships, and behavior. But, as I try to demonstrate, capitalism and patriarchy are not all-determining structures that produce uniform effects. Both women and men create, consent to, and struggle against these social arrangements. Moreover, not all people fit the patterns we use to characterize them and their societies, nor do they always do what we expect on the basis of our theories and generalizations (see Abu-Lughod 1993:6–10). This does not mean we should abandon as a fatally flawed modernist[1] enterprise the effort to theorize or develop generalizations. It is important to theorize the relationship among structures such as capitalism, patriarchy, modes of production, and class. This helps us to grasp the broad outlines of macrolevel social processes that provide the context for people's actions and beliefs, and how and why they change. At the same time, and despite the fact that I use examples of many African societies and women to support my arguments, I recognize that my analysis of capitalism and patriarchy will not fit all African societies equally well. Undoubtedly, Africanist and other Third World scholars will be able to show in future research where my analysis is applicable, and why it does or does not fit different societies and women's realities.

Although modernist scholarly exercises can result in hegemonic discourses that reinforce power arrangements and differ from ordinary people's representations of their lives, they can also dissect and unmask power arrangements, arrangements about which ordinary people have little awareness. This unmasking is a major goal for me in this study. While it is impossible to avoid ethnocentric or masculinist assumptions and biases when doing any research, these flaws can be and are being exposed and corrected by including the perspectives of Third World people, women, and other oppressed people. In the long run, as the history of ideas shows, hegemonic discourses often are discarded and transcended by new discourses and paradigms. This is perhaps modernist scholarship's greatest virtue: it views knowledge as always tentative and subject to critical scrutiny and change. My analysis of capitalism and patriarchy in Africa is essentially a modernist discourse, although it encompasses a wide range of theoretical perspectives and empirical research to indicate difference as well as universality. It also inevitably reflects who I am as a social being, as well as a scholar. Its merits and flaws are for the reader to judge.

## ▲ Note

1. See Smith 1987; Rosaldo 1989; Mohanty 1991a, b; Scott 1995; and Said 1978 for critiques of modernist scholarship.

▲

# Introduction

## ▲ The Global Capitalist Economy

For several decades, the world has been witnessing major transformations in the global capitalist economy, affecting industrial and developing countries alike. International capital has deepened the integration of nations into the global economy, a process furthered by the recent breakdown of international socialism due to the dissolution of the Soviet Union. A new international division of labor is emerging as the industrial nations that dominate the global economy attempt to promote growth and profits through shifting investments and restructuring. Many labor-intensive industries, such as textiles and electronics, are being relocated to selected developing countries, with a resulting loss of manufacturing jobs and a shift to service sector employment for industrial nations' workers. In the countries that are recipients of new manufacturing jobs, the hope is to join the ranks of the so-called NICs (newly industrializing countries), such as South Korea, Hong Kong, Taiwan and Brazil. Other developing nations, including those of sub-Saharan Africa, are still primarily producers of agricultural commodities, minerals, or fuels exported to more-industrial areas. Both NICs and producers of primary products make possible another major economic role of industrial nations—that of primary consumers of the world's output of goods and services.

The restructuring of the global economy has not been quick or painless. Recession, unemployment, slow or no growth, and balance of trade disequilibrium have plagued both more-affluent and poorer nations. As Elson (1992:26–27) notes, we are in a transitional period of instability and stagnation. Not yet born is a new mode of capital accumulation that will produce a return to high and stable growth rates. One factor preventing this return to growth is the huge debt in developing countries that inhibits their productivity, investment, and purchasing power.

It is ironic that most of the world's poor nations, which were initially integrated into the global capitalist economy through colonialism and neo-colonialism, are now so mired in poverty, debt, and economic malaise that

1

they are a major drag on the whole system. After decades of development and modernization, there is little cause for optimism that the situation will improve much in the near future. Development and modernization are for most poor countries an elusive and remote dream, Joekes (1987:138) concludes.

> The present international economic climate is fundamentally inimical to development. Employment prospects in general and particularly for the younger generation and for women have deteriorated drastically since 1980. Real interest rates are unprecedentedly high; the flow of external finance for development investment has almost dried up; and prices of commodities have either fluctuated widely or fallen in a sustained way. Instability and uncertainty are the order of the day for the majority of countries. With unemployment at record levels, industrialized countries have pursued nationalistic trade and monetary policies, which only worsen the situation. Heavily indebted developing countries and those still dependent on exports of primary commodities are struggling through times of domestic austerity, which are damaging to their productive capacity in the long run as well as immediately harmful to the standard of living of their populations.

The austerity measures Joekes refers to result from the direct or indirect pressure of capitalist industrial nations and the international financial institutions they dominate, such as the World Bank and International Monetary Fund (IMF). These agents of international capitalism are, in essence, attempting to more profitably integrate the indebted, poor countries into the global economy through a mixture of neoclassical capitalist free trade policies and an attack on state intervention in the economy. Developing nations are expected to liberalize their economies by cutting government spending, such as food subsidies and civil service employment; privatizing state-owned industries; devaluing currencies; encouraging entrepreneurs and the private sector; and basing production decisions on comparative advantage and an export-oriented development strategy.

The overall economic goal, defined largely by the United States and Great Britain and manifested in such pacts as the North American Free Trade Agreement and the Global Agreement on Tariffs and Trade, is the construction of a new world order of markets, multinational corporations, and banks in which the international division of labor is connected and conditioned by international trade (see Harris 1988:314–315, 325). The tendency is toward capitalist relations of production, the "complete freedom of movement of the factors of production," and "the commoditization of the world" (Mahjoub 1990:160–161). What all this means is that the logic of the market—rather than, say, national development goals and planning—would largely dictate national economies. In this schema, the role of the state in each country is primarily to facilitate market forces and the private sector rather than as in the past, to lead national development drives.

## ▲ Concern for the Poor and Women

According to the new capitalist development orthodoxy, another essential element in better integrating poor countries and their people into the global economy is expanding the benefits of development to the poor. Development is no longer measured simply by such gross indicators as GNP (gross national product) or rate of economic growth, since so often these mask the reality of mass poverty and unequal development. Capitalist institutions like the World Bank have, since the early 1980s, expressed a growing commitment to equity and providing more resources to the poor and disadvantaged.

But many experts doubt the Bank's sincerity. For instance, as Payer (1983:89–90) sees it, concern for the poor is motivated mainly by a desire to tie the poor to the market economy, even if this entails loss of autonomy and self-sufficiency and little or no betterment of standard of living. Making the poor more productive means enabling them to produce a surplus for local markets or the international market. Or, as Mies (1988) puts it, the goal is to utilize all underutilized and nonutilized labor in a productive way—that is, to promote the process of capital accumulation. All too often the resulting development projects do little to eliminate poverty or promote equality and self-determination; motivated and guided by the dominant capitalist-oriented development paradigm, they give government and international agencies more control over peasant subsistence resources and labor (through small business loans, agricultural projects, income-generating projects, etc.). Another motivation for investing in the poor is that it is politically beneficial. As Robert McNamara cautioned in a 1973 speech, the growing inequality between the rich and the poor gives rise to political instability (in Mies 1988:7). Therefore, some development for the poor is in the interest of the privileged as well as the poor.

In a somewhat different vein, Becker (1987) argues that today's international capitalism is genuinely less rapacious than in the past, and more people-oriented. In the early stages of capitalism, capitalists were forced by competition to squeeze their workers for surplus value, but this is no longer the case. We have entered a new, postimperialist stage, in which mature oligopolistic capitalism can afford and indeed benefit from a more humane treatment of workers and concern for the poor. Moreover, capitalism's interest in system stability is better served by ideological, noncoercive hegemony than by force and blatant exploitation. The result is a growing bourgeois humanitarianism including a renewed support for democratic reforms. It is believed that democracy rather than authoritarianism will help promote bourgeois hegemony by compelling competing elements of the bourgeoisie to enlist popular support in intra- rather than anti-bourgeois conflicts. In other words, capitalism and capitalist elites can gain more legitimacy and systemic stability by being to some degree accountable to the masses.

One component of the effort to better integrate developing nations into the global economy by helping the poor is a growing concern for integrating women in development. The concern for women was initially generated by Boserup's pioneering work on women and development. Boserup's research (1970) revealed the fact that most women were receiving few benefits from development. She also demonstrated the negative consequences of denying women access to productive resources. These revelations helped spawn the women in development movement among the world's governments and development organizations. The U.S. Agency for International Development (USAID), the United Nations International Children's Emergency Fund (UNICEF), and the World Bank are now devoting increasing attention in both their publications and funding to the needs of women. In Africa the problems of women have been especially acute and closely tied to the continent's economic and political malaise as well as to the economic liberalization policies designed to address them.

## ▲ Africa's Economic Crisis, Structural Adjustment, and the Status of Women

Sub-Saharan Africa is the poorest region of the world, and many countries are now as poor as or poorer than they were at independence. Although many areas registered positive growth in their economies in the 1960s and early 1970s, after that time most African economies began experiencing a downward spiral. Stagnating agriculture, declining foreign investment, meager industrial growth or even deindustrialization, spiraling population growth, balance of payments difficulties, and debt were symptoms of the growing crisis. By the 1980s most African countries had implemented structural adjustment programs (SAPs) under the auspices of the IMF and the World Bank in an effort to reform and liberalize their economies. In analyzing the causes and cures for the continent's woes, the vital roles of African women in their nation's development efforts received greater recognition by the international donor community, scholars, and many African governments as well. Symbolically important, the 1985 United Nations Conference that ended the UN Decade for Women was held in Nairobi. Women delegates from all over Africa as well as the rest of the world formulated the multifaceted "Forward-Looking Strategies for

Improving the Status of Women." Many legal, political, and economic reforms have been passed, and many African governments now include women's ministries or bureaus. Nongovernmental organizations serving women's needs, and informal women's groups have grown by the thousands. Women in development (WID) components of development projects have been expanded.

There is cautious hope that economic liberalization and better-devised and implemented development policies will provide the needed stimulus for a renewal of economic growth on the continent. Such reforms as privatization of land and wasteful parastatal industry, support for indigenous entrepreneurs, less government regulation, and getting prices right to encourage agricultural production are touted as the ingredients for a transformation of economies that have been crippled by statist policies and mismanagement (see World Bank 1989b). Even if liberal economic reforms do ultimately result in overall growth in African economies, a major unanswered question remains: can a more liberal capitalist economy and integration into the global economy develop Africa so that rich and poor, men and women benefit? Or will a capitalist transformation of Africa simply produce greater class stratification, neocolonial exploitation, and patriarchal oppression?

## ▲ Capitalism and Patriarchy in Africa: An Argument for Contingency

My concern is not primarily with the effects of capitalism on economic development in general, but its effects on the status of women and on gender inequality. Too often development is measured by such indicators as economic growth rates, employment or unemployment statistics, and per capita income without reference to gender. This obscures the fact that the impact of capitalism on males and females is different and unequal. Economies may be developing even though large numbers of people, especially women, find their lives worse or improving only marginally.

It is my contention that the differential impact of capitalism on women and men reflects the particular ways capitalism intersects with patriarchy within each society and is therefore conditioned by both historical and contemporary forces. Before colonial capitalism, African economic, social, and political institutions were to varying degrees patriarchal, and promoted male-dominated societies. Although women often held considerable influence and status within their communities, land tenure systems, formal political institutions, and cultural norms typically accorded more authority, status, and control of wealth and other resources (including women) to men. Therefore, we cannot claim, as some Marxist feminists do, that capitalism created patriarchy in Africa. But the collision of colonial capitalism with African political economies did result in a modification of African gender relations to further colonial economic objectives and to give men more authority and opportunity. Colonialism also introduced and sometimes imposed European forms of patriarchy in Africa. Since independence, many of these modified precapitalist and colonial forms of patriarchal gender relations have been perpetuated in societies undergoing capitalist transformation.

At issue is whether these patriarchal patterns are necessary and beneficial to capitalism or whether they persist for other reasons. Understanding the relationship between capitalism and patriarchy is important for feminist theory in general as well as for those seeking to better African women's lives. Is capitalism a force for the development of women, as its advocates claim, or does capitalism inevitably and necessarily promote the subordination and exploitation of women, as critics charge? Are capitalism and patriarchy inextricably linked by a mutuality of interests, or is the apparent linkage between the two historically based and contingent? Can women to some extent ally themselves with capitalism to promote greater gender equality, or must capitalism and patriarchy both be unequivocally opposed? Is gender equality possible in a society with class, race, or other forms of hierarchy, or is only a radically egalitarian socialism compatible with gender equality? The answers to these questions are vital for women everywhere; although every society is to some extent unique, examining these questions both theoretically and empirically in the African context may provide useful insights with applications to other areas of the world.

Much of the feminist scholarly literature argues that patriarchy and capitalism are inextricably linked; the direct or indirect conclusion is that capitalism is antithetical to women's interests and gender equality. On the other hand, paradoxically, much of the policy-oriented research literature (also feminist) on women and economic development argues for ensuring that women benefit from development by integrating women in development planning and implementation, development that is typically market-oriented (i.e., capitalist). These differences in perspective reflect in part the lack of consensus among scholars in general as well as feminist scholars on the desirability of the capitalist development path in the Third World. Unlike feminist scholars who see patriarchy and capitalism as inextricably linked, those doing policy-oriented work on women in development treat the inequality of women as a result primarily of patriarchal institutions and customs or inadvertent policy mistakes rather than as an inherent systemic problem of capitalism.

In my analysis, I use insights from feminist theory, political economy, and the voluminous studies on women and development in Africa to argue that patriarchy and capitalism are interrelated, but the relationship is contingent and variable. Rather than being ahistorical, unchanging social structures, patriarchy and capitalism are dynamic and variable. More specifically, patriarchies associated with precapitalist societies are likely to change as societies enter the earlier stages of capitalist development and to change again or be different in mature industrial or postindustrial societies.

Although patriarchal elements in societies undergoing transformation from precapitalist to capitalist may attempt to preserve traditional patriarchal institutions in order to control and limit women to their proper place, at some point these institutions become an obstacle to further capitalist development. Among the agents for change in gender relations are foreign donors and development agencies, national governments, and transnational corporations (at least those who hire women). Through paid employment, political participation, and education, women become more involved in the public arena. Capitalism also creates new groups and classes in society who would benefit from deepening the capitalist transformation under way; these include some members of the state and private bourgeoisie (such as the Westernized professional, technical, and business middle-class elites), some workers and small business people, and commercial farmers. Especially among the middle class we find not only more participation of women in the public arena but support for more-egalitarian relationships in the family (e.g., legal reforms in marriage, divorce, and inheritance, and more shared decisionmaking).

Patriarchy as it currently exists in Africa must be understood within the context of Africa's peripheral and dependent position within the global capitalist economy. Most African men and women are struggling to survive, and in some cases prosper, within constraints global capitalism imposes on their societies. But women typically face more disadvantages and exploitation than do men. They must cope not only with poverty and underdevelopment; they are also limited by patriarchal attitudes and practices, some predating capitalism, others established during the colonial period. These patriarchal attitudes and practices, which privilege men, continue to permeate African societies from the level of the family up to the state. Added to this are forms of patriarchy from Western capitalist nations that dominate the global economy. Western ideas about the sexual division of labor and gender relations are being introduced in Africa by transnational corporations (through their hiring and wage policies), by advertisers and the media, and by the policies and prejudices of the donor and development community. Together these are powerful—but often conflicting—forces for gender-biased changes in Africa.

The historical association between capitalism and patriarchy is undeniable; the links between them from the colonial period to the present are well documented in the literature. But this does not mean that patriarchy and capitalism are necessarily and uniformly mutually reinforcing and compatible. My position is that the exploitative (to women) collaboration between patriarchy and capitalism fostered in Africa up to now has out-lived its usefulness in important respects. It is, in fact, a significant factor in Africa's current economic stagnation. There is widespread agreement among Western, capitalist-oriented policymakers that deepening of the capitalist mode of production in Africa and integration of Africa into the global capitalist economy will necessitate new socioeconomic and political arrangements in Africa; among these are more-equitable gender relations and changes in the sexual division of labor.

Patriarchy in Africa has its roots in African extended family systems and precapitalist familial modes of production that controlled both women's productivity and reproduction. These precapitalist systems were not replaced by capitalism but have been utilized and reinforced by capitalism and the postcolonial African state to promote quasi-capitalist[1] development. But, as Africa's current economic crisis and the efforts to solve it with structural adjustment and economic liberalization show, quasi capitalism is a distorted and inefficient form of capitalism. One reason for the failure of quasi capitalism is the exploitative sexual division of labor, and the unequal gender relations on which it is based. The growing incompatibility of African patriarchy with capitalism is reflected in the fact that gender issues are gaining much more attention from such Western agents of capitalism as the World Bank and USAID. And after decades of discrimination against women, many African states are enacting reforms that are designed to provide women with greater legal, economic, and political rights and opportunities. Both the international community and African states are directing more of their efforts and attention to the problems and potential of African women. The constraints on women's productive potential as farmers (of both food and commercial crops) and in the informal sector (as entrepreneurs in mostly microenterprises) are especially noted. There is growing awareness that women's lack of secure access to land and other productive resources, along with other forms of sexist discrimination, are not only inequitable but lower the overall productivity of the economy. Other impediments to development, such as high rates of population growth, high infant and childhood mortality, and overall poor health and nutrition, are attributable to a significant degree to gender bias and the subordination of women. Finally, discrimination against women in marriage, divorce, and inheritance has a negative impact on class formation and capital accumulation.

That the attention being given to women's issues and gender inequality signifies a growing recognition of the negative effects of African patriarchy does not mean that capitalism is against patriarchy per se. We need to examine specific patriarchies or aspects of patriarchy to see whether they benefit capitalism. Conversely, we need to examine how and to what extent different patriarchies benefit from capitalism. It is my view that, in the context of Africa, it will be difficult if not impossible to bring about a capitalist transformation unless the overall status of women improves.

There are important implications of these arguments. One, relating to feminist theoretical claims about the need to oppose capitalism, is that the current political-economic environment globally and in Africa over-whelmingly favors capitalist expansion and integration into the global economy. Most Africans (as well as the global community) are fed up with the bankrupt statist policies that have stifled initiative and expropriated much of the returns on the labor of Africa's rural and urban producers. For the time being, therefore, it would be politically unwise for women to em-brace a dogmatic radical or socialist feminist ideology and agenda that is in principle opposed to economic liberalization and market-oriented re-forms. Such an anticapitalist stance also overlooks the potential benefits and opportunities for greater gender equality capitalism can offer. For ex-ample, African women and their advocates are in a favorable position to push for the expansion of rights and opportunities for women that coincide with liberal capitalist ideology. That is, capitalism's support for individu-alism, entrepreneurial effort, meritocracy, and innovation are, with some adjustments, compatible with feminist goals of freeing women from eco-nomic, cultural, and political discrimination. And given the vital role women play in both production and reproduction, investing in women is obviously economically rational from a capitalist standpoint, as I will show.

This does not mean that women can rely on capitalism alone to spur greater equity. In part this is due to both external as well as internal con-straints on the expansion of capitalism in Africa. The success of capitalist reform in Africa will depend heavily on financial and technical support and investment from the international capitalist community. So far, that support has been very limited Africa's contribution as a producer or mar-ket for international trade and investment has become minuscule, its pri-mary products are increasingly substitutable, and industrialization is still rudimentary and uncompetitive, as is Africa's labor force. Even Africa's debt is comparatively small. Therefore, whether Africans can count on much future foreign investment, loans, or aid for capitalist transformation is an open question. The same can be said for the prospects of international pressure or commitment of development resources targeted for women. The ability of Africa's indigenous bourgeoisie to promote capitalist devel-opment is also variable and uncertain, as is the impact such support would have on gender relations and gender equality. Finally, capitalism tends to promote growing class inequality, which can leave many women subject to class as well as patriarchal oppression. So, while capitalism's liberal ide-ology and support for women in development hold some promise for women, there are limits to what kind of and how much gender equality capitalism will support. For these reasons, activism on the part of African women is vital to assure that efforts to promote equity for women under a capitalist regime include minimizing class inequality, as socialist and radical feminists have argued.

There are other caveats in an alliance between capitalism and feminism. Women and women's advocates will have to contend with several opposing or divisive forces. Social forces that defend African patriarchy, for instance, will certainly continue to oppose many changes that favor women at the expense of male dominance—even if male dominance undermines economic development and capitalism. Among these oppositional forces to both capitalism and gender reform are many Africans, including some sectors of the poor and the petite bourgeoisie who stand to lose, in a more open economy, from foreign penetration of the economy and society and from a loss of control over women. They may attempt to maintain patriarchal control over women using religious, nationalist, and anti-Western cultural ideologies. Members of the state bourgeoisie who fear losing control over the economy and its resources to the private sector bourgeoisie may also use gender issues, in the guise of preserving tradition, to appeal to conservative patriarchal elements in the population. Such divisive factors as class, ethnicity, and religion often undermine efforts to unite women and weaken patriarchy, since these factors influence how patriarchy or capitalism affects women's lives. These confounding variables can make a unified feminist ideology or program with regard to patriarchy or capitalism at least problematic, if not impossible.

While the divisions among women are often downplayed in the struggle against patriarchy, the grounds for united action of men and women is often ignored entirely. To assume that opposition to patriarchy always pits men against women overlooks the positive role men can and do play in support of women. It is often men, for instance, who head developmentalist modernizing regimes that have led the initial movements to expand women's rights in the Third World. Mustafa Kemal of Turkey, Habib Bourguiba of Tunisia, and Samora Machel in Mozambique are three such leaders. Men may join women of the same class or ethnic group in promoting such women's interests as greater access to productive resources, health care, education, or birth control, especially if benefits for women are seen as benefiting men also. In other words, just as the sisterhood of women may be issue-specific or class-based, women's interests are not always advanced by opposition to "men," conceived as an undifferentiated category. Feminists need to explore these possibilities and perhaps give greater attention to how and in what areas men can be approached and their help enlisted in the struggle for women's rights and opportunities.

These issues are obviously complex and variable across societies. It is important to keep in mind that patriarchy in Africa is not a monolithic reality nor is it divorced from class and cultural influences. The same is true for women and women's interests. Ultimately, future gender relations in Africa will depend on what happens to African economies, which in turn depends to a large extent on the global economy and the internal dynamics of political and economic reform under way in many countries of the continent. But these powerful structural forces can be influenced by how African women define their interests and roles and what actions they take to confront the economic, political, and social forces around them. In other words, the relationship between capitalism and patriarchy is not a given; it is constructed and subject to change. While the obstacles are formidable, the current climate of reform does present a window of opportunity for women to improve their lives. It is my hope that this book will bring together important theoretical perspectives and research that can be used in assuring that the future will be better for African women—and African men as well.

## ▲ Note

1. In the chapters to follow, quasi capitalism is discussed as underdeveloped capitalism. African economies tend to be dependent economies that are a mixture of precapitalist and capitalist modes and relations of production that have failed to produce significant economic development in most countries.

# ▲ 1
# Feminist Theory and the Patriarchy-Capitalism Nexus in Africa

The relationship between capitalism and patriarchy is one of the most contested issues in feminist scholarship. Much of the theory and research on this issue has been developed by Western feminist scholars and reflects Western experience and perspectives. In the past twenty-five years or so, however, a great deal of attention has been turned toward women in the Third World, and the voices and insights of Third World women have been added to Western feminist perspectives. Some of these voices have challenged mainstream Western feminism, as well as the whole approach to development and women in development associated with capitalism. In the discussion to follow I examine selected ideas from the major schools of Western feminist thought—liberal feminism, Marxist-socialist feminism, radical feminism, and postmodernism—on the basis of their relevance to my analysis of the relationship between capitalism and patriarchy in Africa. Postmodernism is discussed separately and last because it is in many respects a critique of feminist theory and research. It is important to outline some of the major issues postmodernism raises and to show where my views and postmodernism do and do not coincide.

## ▲ Capitalism and Patriarchy in Feminist Theory

Liberal feminism is perhaps the most politically acceptable version of feminism. It originated among mainly Western, white, middle-class women, and its focus on individualism, freedom of choice, and equality of rights and opportunities for women and men is, at least in the West, generally seen as moderate and consistent with the liberal ideology of capitalist democracy. Therefore liberal feminism enjoys more political and popular legitimacy than its major competitors (Marxist-socialist and radical

13

feminism); it influences Third World feminism with its emphasis on women's rights, legal reform, and the expansion of women's political participation. However, since liberal democratic rights are seldom accorded to men in many Third World countries, and traditional precapitalist forms of patriarchy remain strong, liberal feminism's demands for equal rights are often given no more than lip service, if that. Nonetheless, liberal feminism's reformism inspired the UN Decade for Women and influential women in development (WID) efforts (Stamp 1989:8–9) of such international agencies as the World Bank, the United Nations, and the U.S. Agency for International Development (USAID) (which will be discussed in Chapter 5).

Despite its influence in the Western development community, liberal feminism has come under considerable attack both within the West and from Third World women. A basic criticism is that liberal feminism uncritically accepts the capitalist system, assuming that patriarchy and sexism are not intrinsic to it. For example, Eisenstein (1981:231) contends that liberal feminism ignores the reality that within the capitalist class system equal opportunity does not exist for men or women because of structures of inequality based on race, class, and sex. Socialist feminists add that gender as well as class exploitation are functional, even necessary, for capitalism. As Mies (1988:2–5) argues, women are a means of production and reproduction to be controlled in capitalism (they reproduce labor power); therefore, sexism is not a vestige of backwardness or patriarchal history that can be overcome by the reformist measures advocated by liberal feminists. In her earlier work, Eisenstein (1979) considered capitalism and patriarchy so inextricably linked that they comprised not two systems but one, which she called "capitalist patriarchy." Eisenstein (1981:42–49, 81, 187–188) also asserts that the liberal ideology of equal opportunity in the marketplace is inherently patriarchal. In reality, this applies to men only; the ascribed status of women as child rearers remains intact. This ascribed status is then used to relegate women to the "private arena" of the family. While stressing the importance of the individual, merit, and so on, the patriarchal family that needs to keep women passive and dependent goes unchallenged. Furthermore, the sex-class oppression of women rooted in the sexual division of labor within the family is protected by government, which sees the family as private rather than public. As long as the notion of equality before the law fails to address the problems of inequality in everyday life within the family, legal reform by government is no solution to patriarchy.

Other socialist feminists add to Eisenstein's analysis that women are not just reproducers in capitalism. They are a cheap reserve labor force or sex-segregated labor force for capitalism. Women's free labor in the home as housewives allows capitalists to pay men less for their labor and provides for the reproduction of the labor force. Women are also major consumers of capitalist-produced goods. Ideologically, by propagating self-serving

notions of family, childhood, femininity, and sexuality, patriarchy and capitalism work together to reinforce the power of bourgeois man (Ollenburger and Moore 1992:20–21).

There are other ways capitalism and patriarchy are said to be mutually
reinforcing. Patriarchy seeks to consign women as primarily mothers and
housewives to the home, where they are isolated and can be subjugated to
men. Capitalism reinforces this goal through occupational discrimination
and low wages, which force most women to labor in the home because
they have no way to support themselves otherwise (Hartmann and Markusen 1980:92–93).

Western feminism of all types has been viewed with suspicion by
many Third World women (and postmodernist feminism). Some view
Western feminism as a white, middle-class agenda that promotes opportunities mostly for the already advantaged. In addition, some Third World
feminists resist what they perceive to be Western feminists' emphasis on
gender as the basic inequality in women's lives. For many Third World
feminists, gender discrimination is not viewed as the sole or even the main
source of women's oppression. Third World feminists often see their main
struggle as being alongside their men and communities against racism,
economic exploitation, and poverty. Mainstream liberal feminism especially fails to define racism or imperialism as feminist issues. While universal sisterhood is a lofty feminist ideal, Third World women feel they
have as much or more in common with Third World men (in terms of oppression) than they do with white women (Johnson-Odim 1991:315–318).
As Valverde (1985:198) wryly observes, the notion of a universal sisterhood of women obscures "the conflicts of interests between the women
who pick coffee beans for fifty cents a day in Brazil and the white American feminist who sips coffee as she writes about women in general."
Moreover, women and men are not homogeneous groups affected in the
same way by structures of dominance (e.g., race, class, ethnicity). Development does not affect all in the same way either; therefore, it is not always easy or valid to dichotomize oppressor or oppressed along gender
lines (Mohanty 1991b:53–55).

As long as the international economy relegates their societies to a peripheral position, Third World women charge, equal opportunity often is a
formula for sharing poverty. It is inequalities of race, class, and imperialism in addition to patriarchy that undermine most women's potential for
success. Therefore, the central issue for many Third World women is, as
Johnson-Odim (1991:320) states, "not just a question of internal redistrib
ution of resources, but of their generation and control; not just equal opportunity between men and women, but the creation of opportunity itself;
not only the position of women in society, but the position of the societies
in which Third World women find themselves."

Although much of the criticism against feminism has been directed toward liberal feminism, Africanist scholar Stamp takes radical feminism to task. Stamp (1989:10) contends that the resistance to feminism of many planners, policymakers, and Third World women is based on confusing it with radical feminism: "the [radical feminist] argument that all women have been oppressed by all men throughout time and across all cultures is pessimistic, politically unpalatable, and scientifically unsound; it has created an easy target for a sexist backlash against more reasoned feminist positions." Stamp faults radical feminism for being ahistorical, ideological, and ethnocentric, especially in its understanding of the oppression of Third World women. For example, the condemnation of female circumcision as a barbaric patriarchal custom offends many African women. Moreover, the very concept of patriarchy is seen by Stamp as problematic. Patriarchy, according to Stamp, is one of a number of "sex-gender systems" (a more neutral term, she believes, than *patriarchy*) that range from patriarchy to egalitarianism. Stamp (1989:5–16) also rejects what she sees as the radical feminist premise that patriarchy is universal, preceding and superseding all other forms of oppression.

Stamp (1989:17–23) proposes instead a "feminist political economy" that appears to combine elements of liberal, socialist, and radical feminism. This feminist political economy combines Marx's rigorous, historical, materialist method with radical feminism's ideas that the personal is political and that gender oppression cuts across class lines. Gender relations are viewed in their specificity—taking into account the effects of such things as class and race. Stamp roots gender oppression in the way societies are organized to produce and distribute the necessities of life. Although economics is essential to understanding women's status, there is a complex interaction between the economic, political, and ideological aspects of society. For instance, the ideology and practices of kinship are not merely the superstructure determined by relations of production; they help shape productive relations. Economic work and the fulfillment of kinship obligations become inseparable, as are the often dichotomized public and private spheres. In other words, the sex-gender system is closely related to the relations of production but is separate from them and not reducible to them.

Stamp's arguments about the historical and cultural specificity of gender relations and their irreducibility to economic modes of production are compelling and are the basis of my own analysis. However, I disagree with her about the lack of utility of the concept of patriarchy. While admittedly abstract, the concept of patriarchy is not ahistorical. As Eisenstein (1981:22) argues, the concept of patriarchy reflects the durability of the hierarchical sexual organization of society. Patriarchy is intermeshed with particular historical frameworks and economic systems, but its universal qualities are maintained however redefined in specific sociohistorical formations. Both the continuity (universality) and specifics must be understood. Similarly, Walby (1986:243) argues that "gender inequality cannot be understood without the concept of patriarchy. Criticisms of the concept for its inability to grasp historical variations are misplaced; on the contrary, the notion of changing forms of patriarchy is indispensable to the understanding of historical and empirical interlinkages."

Eisenstein's and Walby's position is not necessarily incompatible with Stamp's idea of a feminist political economy. According to Eisenstein (1981:14–16), patriarchy seeks to keep the role of women as childbearers and child rearers primary. To achieve this end, women must be controlled and subjugated "so that their possibilities for making choices about their sexuality, childrearing, mothering, loving, and laboring are curtailed." Women's sexuality, reproduction, and labor are thus appropriated by individual men and society as a whole. As part of the subjugation of women, variable forms of patriarchal organization are developed, such as the sexual division of labor, the division of public and private life, and motherhood ideologies, which define women as emotional and dependent. Capitalism reinforces patriarchy by paying women less than men and limiting the jobs open to them (e.g., through a sex-segregated labor market and part-time or temporary work). Women's second-class status in the labor market (along with motherhood ideologies) promotes their dependent position in the home. As long as we avoid any a priori assertion that the above relationship between capitalism and patriarchy is necessary for capitalism to operate, it does not seem to be an insurmountable task to accommodate Eisenstein's and Walby's notion of patriarchy with Stamp's view that sex-gender systems are historically and culturally specific and closely linked with but not reducible to specific modes of production such as capitalism.

Eisenstein can be criticized, however, for her definition of patriarchy. To insist by definition rather than empirical investigation that patriarchy's main characteristic everywhere is the desire to make women's primary role childbearing and child rearing is problematic. While this may be true in some societies, it may not be true everywhere. Also the content of these roles is quite variable, so that such a label as "mother" misleadingly implies nonexistent similarities in what women do throughout the world. For instance, in much of non-Islamic Africa childbearing means that women often have six or eight children, while the child-rearing role may include providing financially for children and producing most of the family's food. In Western industrial nations, by contrast, women usually bear only one or two children, and child rearing has no such productive component. Indeed, in the West child rearing is viewed by some as a full-time job that disqualifies women from taking on productive responsibilities; instead, men are assigned the role of provider and women often become economic dependents.

A preferable definition of patriarchy, one that does not presuppose the primacy of any one role assigned to women, or a dichotomy between the public and private spheres, is provided by Walby (1986:51): patriarchy is "a system of interrelated social structures which allow men to exploit women." Walby's definition allows for the variability and changes in women's roles and in the order of their priority under different patriarchal systems. It also recognizes that it is the institutionalized subordination and exploitation of women by men that is the crux of patriarchy; this can take many forms. It is even theoretically possible that patriarchy could express itself through a deemphasis on motherhood in favor of women as wage earners or some other role. The emphasis Eisenstein places on the subjugation of women to the private arena of the family in patriarchy is understandable when dealing with Western societies, but it obscures the fact that the fundamental goal of patriarchy is to maintain women's subordinate and exploited relationship to men in all social institutions. Since not all societies, especially non-Western societies, have a clear-cut dichotomy between family and nonfamily roles, productive or reproductive work, or public versus private arenas, it makes little sense to assert that patriarchy is based on such dichotomies.

Another view of patriarchy is that it is an ideology to protect sexual hierarchy. Patriarchy is inseparably linked to capitalism or other modes of production. This position is essentially reductionist (e.g., patriarchy is an ideological manifestation of capitalist patriarchy; Courville 1994:40–41; Marshall 1994:84). While patriarchy has ideological components, conceptualizing patriarchy as not just ideology but institutional arrangements and practices that support and reflect male dominance allows for the possibility of some autonomy of patriarchy from the economic base of society. This allows for other causal interpretations of some forms of gender relations that have no obvious or direct link to the mode of production (e.g., female circumcision).

If patriarchy and the economic mode of production are closely linked but not reducible to each other, understanding the nature of this linkage is important. Walby (1986) examines these issues in her book on patriarchy and capitalism in England. She argues persuasively that, although capitalism and patriarchy are historically and empirically interlinked, they are not one system. They are analytically independent systems and operate in relative autonomy. Walby also rejects the socialist and radical feminist claims of a harmony of interests between capitalism and patriarchy. Instead, the relationship is often one of tension and conflict. This notion of harmony too easily lends itself to reductionism. For instance, socialist feminists tend to see capitalism as the main problem, with patriarchy a convenient

tool for capital accumulation that benefits capitalists primarily. This reduces gender relations to economics (i.e., the needs of capitalism) and
downplays precapitalist gender inequality and the benefits gender inequality provides men. Similarly, radical feminists tend to reduce all oppression
to patriarchy and to see all economic modes of production as inherently
patriarchal and oppressive to women.

The assumption of a harmony of interests between patriarchy and capitalism involves another fundamental error. It assumes two ahistorical,
nonchanging entities—patriarchy and capitalism—that are both in reality
evolving, contested, and dynamic systems. It would make little sense to
discuss nineteenth-century capitalism as though its needs were the same as
postindustrial, global capitalism's today, since capitalism has changed dramatically. So why would we expect that patriarchal relationships that may
have been compatible with capitalism in the nineteenth or early twentieth
centuries would remain so today? Conversely, if patriarchy and capitalism
are relatively autonomous, is it not reasonable to hypothesize that precapitalist patriarchal relations could be threatened by the introduction of capitalism? By the same token, the penetration or expansion of capitalism and
capital accumulation could be impeded by the extant patriarchal relations
found in a society. If so, in the process of transforming the means and relations of production, capitalism could be a force for modifying or even
undermining that patriarchy.

Walby (1986:46) gives several illuminating examples of the conflict
between patriarchy and capitalism in nineteenth and twentieth-century
England. Generally, she claims that capitalism and patriarchy have different interests. Capitalism seeks to exploit labor; patriarchy seeks to exploit
women. In their desire to exploit cheaper, more-docile labor, manufacturing employers often actually preferred women employees. In some occupations, like clerical work, women were preferred also because employers
found they were better workers than men. In pursuing their business interests, capitalists often opposed efforts to pass legislation that would limit
women's access to paid work (Walby 1986:122, 145, 167, 245). The social
forces seeking to relegate women to the home and limit their employment
in favor of men are not capitalist, claims Walby (1986:77), but patriarchal.
For example, male unions played a major role in efforts to exclude women
from paid jobs after World War II even though employers wanted to keep
their female workers.[1]

An important point Walby (1986:110) makes, one relevant to growing
female employment in Third World industries, is that initially the prefer-
ence capitalists have for female workers is not incompatible with patriarchy. In fact, it reflects patriarchal gender relations in which females are
cheaper and more docile in regimented work environments. But at some
point, more women getting paid work becomes a threat to patriarchal

(male) dominance over women. Paid work becomes a source of power for women from which males may be relatively excluded. Men fear losing control over their women and seek to restrict their employment. At this point, capitalist and patriarchal interests conflict.

Often, however, a modus vivendi between patriarchal and capitalist interests is reached that has given the impression that capitalism and patriarchy have common interests. For example, Walby (1986:152–154) relates that, although English employers preferred employing women clerks to men, they bowed to pressure from males, resorting to job segregation (with men getting the better jobs and no longer competing with women) in order to pacify the men. This compromise satisfied both patriarchal and capitalist interests because it undercut the move to equalize men's and women's wages.

There is another way capitalism can ultimately threaten patriarchy. Initially, Eisenstein (1981:203–204) notes, women's wage work is not necessarily a threat to patriarchal relations in the family if it is justified as work to help the family, not work to achieve personal independence. The woman is still subjugated to the family in her primary role. But the market can eventually promote equality of opportunity for women despite efforts to accommodate patriarchy in the workplace. For as Walby (1986) concludes, the patriarchal pressures that result in discrimination against women, such as unequal pay, sex-segregated jobs, and "the double day" at home, can arouse potent opposition from women. Such discrimination, continues Eisenstein (1981: 209–212), contradicts capitalist, liberal ideology, which supports free markets (including labor markets), competition, equal opportunity, and individual achievement. The contradiction between liberal ideology and gender discrimination shows women their true second-class status. Women increasingly expect the ideology of equal opportunity to apply to them. The implications of Walby's and Eisenstein's arguments are that employment and wages for women as individuals outside the family, along with the acceptance of liberal ideology, can result in capitalism's becoming a powerful threat to patriarchy in the family and in other social institutions as well.

Liberal feminist ideology has a useful role to play in women's struggle at this point. Eisenstein (1981:4) points out that all feminism is at root liberal feminism in that it is based on the claim that women as well as men are independent and autonomous selves (albeit within a social collectivity). This claim to individuality is not to be confused with the doctrine of individualism based on a masculinist, competitive, atomistic view of the individual. Important to points I will develop later, Eisenstein's argument suggests that the liberal assertion of personhood is a prerequisite for more-radical transformative feminist theory and politics. If so, it is a mistake to cavalierly dismiss liberal feminism as bourgeois, or ethnocentric, as some feminist thinkers do (see the following discussion of postmodernism).

The role of the state in promoting capitalism and patriarchy must also be considered. The state is not just a tool of capitalism and patriarchy, representing their interests. Both gender and economics are often contested arenas among groups with different perspectives on their interests. As Eisenstein (1981:57–59) shows, the state must mediate these conflicts and aid negotiations. In addition, women's resistance to both capitalist and patriarchal oppression must be entered into the equation. Indeed, women's political struggles have been important in opening up the state to women and changing state policies that patriarchal interests have supported to exclude or limit women's opportunities and rights (Walby 1986:245; Pringle and Watson 1992:62).

The resolution of these struggles among patriarchy, capitalism, and women's resistance determines actual gender relations in a particular society. But since patriarchy and capitalism are both dynamic systems, linked but operating in relative autonomy from each other, any harmony of interests achieved at one point in time may break down at a later point. New gender relations become necessary or, as Walby (1986:245) observes, at each new phase of capitalist development new struggles with patriarchal relations produce a new set of gender relations.

It is my argument that in Africa a point of disjuncture between capitalism and patriarchy has been reached that requires changes in gender relations. I here briefly outline my main points, which will be developed and supported in the remainder of this book. The articulation of precapitalist forms of African patriarchy embedded in familistic modes of production with colonial and neocolonial capitalism produced a fragile harmony of interests between African patriarchy and capitalism that has lasted until recently. African patriarchy was for the most part preserved and enhanced by capitalism, and patriarchal relations promoted some capitalist expansion and accumulation in Africa—to a point. But the accommodation capitalism reached with patriarchy in Africa has two fatal flaws: it creates excessive market distortions and inefficiencies that undermine capitalist expansion; and it results in such overexploitation of women that both production and reproduction of the labor force are threatened. Both of these flaws are generating growing resistance from women (the forms of resistance varying by such factors as class, ethnicity, and religion). The failure of the accommodation between patriarchy and capitalism is reflected in the economic crises, political problems, and development failures confronting almost every African country.

To understand the role African patriarchy plays in the limited capitalist development of Africa necessitates a brief analysis, which will be elaborated in the remainder of the book, of the changing roles of African women in capitalist development.

## Capitalism and Patriarchy in Africa

Much of the Western feminist theoretical analysis of women and development in Africa echoes the work of Marxist-socialist feminist scholars. For example, in Mies's influential work on women and global capitalism (see, e.g., 1986:38–40), she argues that "capitalism cannot function without patriarchy." Capitalism requires never-ending capital accumulation; therefore, it requires patriarchal man-woman relations. Mies (1986:170–171) also believes that capitalism and patriarchy are not two separate systems, but intrinsically connected as capitalist patriarchy:

> Violence against women and extracting women's labour through coercive labour relations are, therefore, part and parcel of capitalism. They are necessary for the capitalist accumulation process and not peripheral to it. In other words, capitalism has to use, to strengthen, or even to invent, patriarchal men-women relations if it wants to maintain its accumulation model. If all women in the world had become "free" wage earners, "free" subjects, the extraction of surplus would, to say the least, be severely hampered. This is what women as housewives, workers, peasants, prostitutes, from the Third World and First World countries, have in common.

Mies (1986:40) concludes from this analysis that capitalist patriarchy is the system of all social relations the feminist struggle is directed against.

Mies's conception of a unified capitalist patriarchy leaves no possibility for any general improvements in equality for African women within capitalism. As one might expect, Mies rejects the liberal feminist agenda, which is based on the conviction that education, socialization, propaganda, and legal rights will liberate women. This means that liberal-inspired WID initiatives and women's rights movements within Africa are futile efforts. On the contrary, "if the emancipation of men is based on the subordination of women, then women cannot achieve 'equal rights' with men" (Mies 1986:23, 76).

Mies's premise that capitalism is inherently patriarchal is found in many other feminist scholars' writing on the impact of global capitalism on women in general and in Africa. For instance, von Werlhof (1988b: 17–18) writes that it is women's nonwage labor that makes male wage labor or extraction of surplus possible (especially when wages are low or little wage labor is available). Similarly, Africanist Robertson (1988:185) maintains that the profits of capitalism globally come increasingly from the exploitation of women as unpaid labor or working for subsistence or lower wages in factories, in putting-out systems, and as unpaid agricultural labor whose work is seen as an extension of domestic labor. Bernard

(1987:202) contends that global restructuring is bringing women into the global economy regulated by "market norms of the Western male world." Both Bennholdt-Thomsen (1988) and Mies (1986) describe the housewife role as the norm in countries undergoing capitalist development. The housewife is paid the least or is not paid at all for most of her work. "The housewife," according to Bennholdt-Thomsen (1988:166), "is female labor power in capitalism." Referring specifically to Africa, Mbilinyi and Meena (1991:847) assert that structural adjustment policies designed to promote capitalism "depend upon the deepening of women's subordination within peasant agriculture under male heads of household and village and the intensification of women's labor as unpaid family workers as well as low-paid casual farm workers."

In another recent thought-provoking critique of capitalist development, Scott (1995:23, 84) argues that capitalism is inherently patriarchal because it is based on "masculinist" and "gendered" premises that inevitably result in the exclusion or subordination of women. Modernization and development stress the importance of autonomy and separation of individuals (i.e., men) from the household and familistic relations (represented by women). The traits of the individual constructed within capitalism include risk taking, innovativeness, rationality, acquisitiveness, competitiveness, and independence. These traits "join liberalism and constructions of masculinity." While this is true, the problem I have with Scott's analysis is that it appears to me to do what she claims we must not do: essentializes and dichotomizes masculinity and femininity. It is patriarchal ideology that constructs masculinity and femininity as polarities, and men and women as "opposite sexes"; in reality this polarity does not exist. Risk taking, rationality, and so on are acquired traits that reflect the status and roles people hold in society, but they can be found in many women and are not necessarily found in all men. While originally the notion of the individual, the modern man, and the entrepreneur were masculinist, why should we conclude that such constructions cannot be changed to include women? In fact, as more women enter the market economy in the capitalist West and in the Third World, women often exhibit these traits as much as men do. The resistance to women's "acting like men" and "losing their femininity" are reflections of patriarchal backlash and male (and sometimes female) anxiety over the breakdown of familiar patriarchal gender relations; they do not reflect inexorable needs of capitalism to maintain a specific gendered division of labor.

While I agree that the foundations of capitalism are masculinist and that women have been exploited by a sexual division of labor that dichotomizes the public and private, the masculine and feminine, modern and traditional, I find these dichotomies only part of the picture. I intend to show that the relationship between capitalism and patriarchy in Africa is

conflictual in many respects and produces different impacts on and responses from men and women, countries, regions, and ethnic groups.
Thus, the actual articulation of the two systems, while seemingly necessary or beneficial for capitalism and patriarchy, is fraught with contradictions and problems as well. In some ways, for example, African patriarchy
is threatened by capitalist relations of production and liberal ideology, and
has successfully undermined them (e.g., through laws that deny a woman
the right to work or run a business without her husband's consent). On the
other hand, capitalism, while often using or accommodating patriarchal social relations, can intentionally or inadvertently undermine them by promoting rights and opportunities for women more expedient for capitalism
(e.g., through wage employment or business opportunities for women or
by advancing female education to upgrade women's skills, women also become more concious of their rights and more independent). Another possibility is that even the hardships and inequities capitalism engenders can
be a force for undermining precapitalist patriarchal productive and social
arrangements by compelling people to adopt new survival strategies that
alter gender roles and perceptions (e.g., women start businesses to add to
family income, thus promoting their status as providers; this in turn improves their self-esteem and authority in the family).

Within the context and constraints of underdeveloped capitalism,
African women's efforts on their own behalf are likely to differ depending on their different situations and perceptions of what their needs and interests are. In some instances, women perceive their interests as best
served by strengthening their rights and prerogatives as women (i.e.,
wives, mothers, sisters, daughters) within African patriarchal systems. This
may be in opposition to capitalism or to the African bourgeois classes capitalism has spawned. In other circumstances, women react against patriarchal gender relations while embracing new opportunities or rights fostered
by capitalism. Some women (including many African feminists and intellectuals), likely to be labeled "radical," reject both African patriarchy and
capitalism as enemies of women and gender equality. Given the nature of
capitalist development in Africa, most women have the difficult task of
trying to minimize simultaneously the male control and exploitation found
in patriarchal structures as well as the exploitation of capitalism.

Male-dominated African states do not always have an easy time me-
diating conflicting patriarchal, capitalist, and women's interests. In some
cases, as will be discussed in Chapter 4, the state acts to promote capitalist transformation and bourgeois class interests, thereby weakening African
patriarchy. However, where patriarchal pressures are stronger and bourgeois hegemony weaker, the state may respond to patriarchal pressures in
ways that undermine capitalism in order to maintain political support. On

the other hand, the state may yield to some demands for women's rights in response to international or domestic pressure from women's groups or donors.

This dynamic process of tension, accommodation, and change does not support the picture of some unequivocal, unified capitalist patriarchy with an ironclad grip on women's labor and reproduction. Instead, what we see in Africa are quasi-capitalist societies that have resulted from the articulation of capitalism with precapitalist patriarchal modes of production. Beginning with colonialism, capitalism and patriarchy have attempted to use each other for their own ends. Both have been modified in the process in ways that produce new tensions. If feminists deny the possibility of the analytical as well as empirical autonomy of patriarchy and capitalism, they are forced to maintain that any tension between them does not exist and that capitalism in Africa depends on maintaining the current familial mode of production and gender relations. I disagree with this, for reasons that will be explored in more depth throughout this book.

## The Postmodernist Critique of Feminist Theory

Postmodernist feminists have offered some valuable insights and critiques of earlier feminist theory and contemporary social science in general. Postmodernist thinkers have influenced my positions on many issues discussed here. I do not agree with some postmodernist positions, however,[2] as I will indicate below, and I limit my focus to issues directly relevant to my research rather than attempting an exhaustive survey of postmodernism.

Postmodernist feminists have concluded that the three mainstream feminist theories are based on flawed, patriarchal, modernist conceptions. These flaws include an emphasis on grand theories (e.g., Marxism) and abstract social structures (e.g., capitalism) to explain human behavior. This results in reductionism and essentialism, as differences based on ethnicity, gender, race, or class go unrecognized and untheorized. Marxist-socialist feminists, for instance, reduce gender inequality and exploitation to class or the capitalist mode of production. Radical feminists, by contrast, erroneously see women as sharing a common sisterhood based on their oppression by patriarchy; other forms of oppression and the differences among women are ignored. Postmodernists see all such abstract concepts as *women, capitalism, patriarchy, class,* or *women's interests* as attempts to impose a false uniformity on reality. This denies the differences in experiences and systems of meaning of those who are observed as object by (usually) white, Western, middle-class feminist theorists. To focus on these differences, postmodernist feminists are turning away from an examination of structure or causality in favor of studying culture, sexuality, political agency, processes of symbolization and representation (i.e., discourses and social constructions of reality), and women's experiences and perceptions (see Barrett 1988, 1992:205–206).[3]

Postmodernists also tend to reject modernist, universalist concepts of equality and individualism because they are modeled on men while ignoring the difference between men and women. Thus the liberal feminist agenda, based as it is on equality between the sexes and respect for the rights of women as individual persons, becomes suspect. As Pateman (1989:14) argues, equality, as it is usually understood, requires women to deny aspects of themselves and conform to a unitary model based on male characteristics and experience. Gatens (1992:124) exposes the negative consequences for women of pursuing supposedly gender-neutral equality with men.

> What this involves, for women, is the difficulty, if not impossibility, of occupying the public sphere on genuinely equal terms with men. Put simply, given that the public sphere has historically been an almost exclusively male sphere, it has developed in a manner which assumes that its occupants have a male body. Specifically, it is a sphere that does not concern itself with reproduction but with production. . . . This is to say that liberal society assumes that its citizens continue to be what they were historically, namely male heads of households who have at their disposal the services of an unpaid domestic worker/wife/mother.

Women can achieve equality on these terms only if they deny their own bodies or juggle their "traditional" role in the private sphere with their "newfound equality" (Gatens 1992:125). Understandably, postmodernist feminists conclude that gender equality is realizable only if sexual difference is acknowledged—and also the differences among women (Phillips 1992:12–13; also Eisenstein 1989).

These are valuable insights, many of which I have tried to accommodate in my analysis. Feminists do need to avoid the often ethnocentric assumption that all women's experiences of patriarchy—or capitalism—are the same, or that all women experience oppression in the same way. Race, class, ethnicity, and subjection to imperialism are other forms of oppression that can combine with or supersede in importance women's experience of patriarchy. We also need to recognize that much supposedly gender-neutral discourse on equality, development, or the workings of capitalist free markets obscures and reinforces the reality of gender hierarchy and unequal power.

Nonetheless, I do not accept postmodernist claims about the theoretical or practical bankruptcy of modernism, as is obvious from the essentially structural perspective I have taken. Many feminist theorists influenced by postmodernism also back off from some of the extreme antistructuralist conclusions of postmodernist thinking. Barrett (1992:216), for one, concludes that while postmodernist critiques of liberalism and Marxism have exposed their flaws, whether postmodernism promises "a more useful alternative is a much more vexed question"; moreover, there are real losses in "a wholesale abandonment of the areas of study denoted by the academic disciplines of sociology, political economy, economics, and politics." Others argue that universality is essential to feminism's goal of gender equality and social justice. Phillips (1992:28), echoing Eisenstein (1989), adds that we need a balance between the search for universality and the appreciation of differences in feminist theory and practice. In rejecting universality there is the danger of losing the concept of equality itself. "Feminism," she concludes, "cannot afford to situate itself *for* difference and *against* universality." Feminist aspirations toward universality are necessary "to take us beyond our immediate and specific differences" in order to promote "radical transformation." On a similar note, Johnson (1994) contends that feminism must recognize its roots in humanism (rather than rejecting humanism as masculinist) and the necessity to universalize its claims for social justice for women.

My view is that we need to incorporate both the diversity of women's experiences and perceptions as well as social structural analysis in feminist scholarship. Admittedly, there are problems in theorizing gender inequality at an abstract and general level. Nonetheless, in our recognition of differences, we should not lose sight of the fact that there are widely repeated patterns and enough historical and cross-cultural continuity to make generalizations and causal theorizing possible (see Walby, 1992:36). Arguing for universality, Tanzania's Gertrude Mongella, UN Secretary-General for the fourth UN World Conference on Women, makes the point this way: "Women in Europe might be looking for dishwashers while women in Africa are looking for water with which to wash dishes, but both groups of women are washing dishes" (in Morna 1995:59). I have tried to incorporate the reality of difference in my analysis by referring to numerous case studies of African cultures and classes. I argue that patriarchy and capitalism take different forms and affect women's (and men's) lives differently, but there are pervasive, if not universal, commonalties in how patriarchy and capitalism interrelate to affect African women's lives.

Walby's point is, I think, well taken—letting women speak for themselves without theorizing causal or structural realities that influence or impinge on their representations is of limited value. It overlooks the fact that the views of the women themselves may be limited. "It is not clear," Walby (1990:16–17) notes, "why women's everyday experiences should be less contaminated by patriarchal notions than are theories." While systematic inquiry and theoretical development may be socially constructed and shaped by patriarchal institutions, they are also the means for exposing such biases and working toward more-universalistic knowledge.

My analysis of patriarchy and capitalism, and that proposed by Walby, has been called a dual systems approach. It posits the relative autonomy of capitalism and patriarchy, yet recognizes that they are usually but not inevitably mutually supportive and interrelated systems. Marshall (1994:84) maintains that "a degree of consensus" has been reached by feminist scholars to abandon dual systems theory because there is "general agreement" that capitalism and patriarchy are so interwoven as to be one system of domination integrated through the sexual division of labor. I think such conclusions are premature and hope through my analysis to show the fruitfulness of a dual systems analysis. As I have argued, positing the relative autonomy of patriarchy and capitalism allows us to appreciate the diverse manifestations each can take and to avoid reductionism (i.e., of patriarchy to capitalism or vice versa), which postmodernists also caution against. It also allows us to examine how and where women can maneuver within capitalist and patriarchal structures to promote greater gender equality.

Feminist political agendas are likely to be a factor in how my analysis will be received. Walby (1990:22) perceptively observes that what theories we espouse affect what we see as progress for women. I add that our feminist politics can influence what theories we accept. Admittedly, my analysis is limited to how and where African women are finding or creating opportunities for greater equality within currently hegemonic global capitalism. This analysis may have limited utility outside sub-Saharan Africa, nor will it solve the ultimate problem of completely eliminating patriarchal or capitalist or racial domination or exploitation. This limitation will likely be unsatisfying to some socialist, radical, or postmodernist feminists who see such things as women's gradual but growing access to paid jobs, education, political participation, and more-egalitarian relationships with men in their households as superficial or minor improvements in structures that seem to perpetuate men's exploitation of women. It is easy to point out how much remains to be changed before full equality between men and women is attained. I recognize these limitations but maintain that feminism needs to theorize not only the ideal political or economic system to accommodate gender equality but also how women can best flourish in the political and economic systems they are in.

## ▲ African Patriarchy and Underdeveloped Capitalism

Patriarchy existed in Africa before capitalism, while capitalism first developed in Europe in a very different cultural context, including uniquely European patriarchal attitudes and institutional arrangements. With the expansion of capitalism to Africa during the colonial period, heterogeneous modes of production and patriarchies were brought together. The historically constructed articulation of these systems is the foundation for the kind of capitalism and patriarchy we see in Africa now. Therefore, we need to briefly and in very general terms outline the process of articulation and the changing nature of the relationship between capitalism and patriarchy. I discuss these issues in more depth in the following chapters.

Although societies and economies varied widely in precolonial Africa, most typically, Africans produced for their own subsistence rather than for exchange. Production and consumption were centered in the extended family where both men and women had vital productive roles in predominantly agricultural or pastoral societies. But elder males tended to have more political authority and control over productive assets than females. In most African land tenure systems, land was owned communally, but inheritance of land or cattle favored males. In patrilineal societies, for example, women typically could not own or inherit land, but were guaranteed usufruct (use) rights to land or access to other productive resources through their husbands or sons. In most societies there was a distinct sexual division of labor, with certain crops, handicrafts, animal husbandry activities, and other tasks assigned to women and others to men. Food preparation, child care, and fetching wood and water were among the tasks usually performed by women. Oftentimes women did most of the agricultural labor. Especially in West Africa, some of the surplus of women's production was marketed by women, and the proceeds of such sales belonged to them. Much of the surplus produced by women, however, was appropriated by male household heads and provided men with resources to support clients and achieve political influence and prestige in their communities. For this reason among others, wives were highly valued assets in extended family systems headed by men (see Robertson and Berger 1986).

Although both men and women were subject to clearly defined obligations and rights within their households and lineages, elder males tended to have more power over the labor and fruits of the labor of other household members. Women often had considerable autonomy, however, that helped dilute tendencies toward male dominance. In some societies women had parallel authority structures to those of men, which allowed women control over their own spheres of activity. Also, because in many societies husbands and wives did not routinely pool their property or other assets, women had a measure of economic independence and control over productive assets.

With the widespread introduction of colonial capitalism, such "precapitalist modes and relations of production"[4] underwent considerable modification. Africa's role in the capitalist system was to be a supplier of cheap raw materials and labor as well as a market for European mass-produced manufactured goods. To this end, cash crops and wage jobs in mines and elsewhere were assigned to men. Women for the most part retained their job as providers of food for the family. Stamp (1986:30) summarizes the process by which the articulation of precapitalist and capitalist modes of production occurred in colonized African societies.

> Precapitalist elements, located in the peasantry, are retained in a domi-
> nated and distorted form. These elements include kinship structures and
> relations of production, age-based organizations, gender relations, and
> traditional ideologies. The transformed elements serve to subsidize un-
> derdeveloped capital through production of cash crops by both small-
> holders and plantation wage laborers. Surplus is not appropriated from
> landless "free" labor . . . but from peasants who either own the produc-
> tive land or who depend upon family-owned land for subsistence while
> earning a wage. . . . The key to underdeveloped capitalism is that subsis-
> tence activities are more important than wages or the returns from cash
> crops in the reproduction of labor power.

It was women who provided the subsidy through their food crops, child rearing, and other productive activities that ensured the reproduction of the labor force in the face of low wages and prices.

There are some important points in Stamp's remarks that need to be emphasized. One is that African economies are a mixture of two modes of production—the precapitalist and capitalist. The result is underdeveloped capitalism, not capitalism as found in more-mature capitalist industrial economies. As socialist feminists point out, the labor of women is the key to underdeveloped capitalism because it is women's labor that undergirds capital accumulation and the reproduction of labor. That is, women's un-paid or underpaid labor allows capitalists to pay lower wages and lower prices for commodities; it also maintains and reproduces labor (men, chil-dren, and the women themselves). Women's labor in underdeveloped cap-italism has been largely shaped by precapitalist, kinship-based gender re-lations, including the sexual division of labor, that have been transformed by their articulation with capitalism. These transformed gender relations have remained patriarchal, providing men with even greater control over family (especially women's) labor, decisionmaking, and productive re-sources (e.g., land and income). Dominance by males in kinship systems, households, and property ownership is echoed in wider behavior and in-teractions within society, including the state. Pervasive patriarchal domi-nance of the state, business enterprises, and other social institutions rein-forces discrimination against women that serves to maintain unequal and exploitative gender relations (see Stichter 1987; Parpart 1988).

It is clear that patriarchal relations originating in precapitalist modes of production benefited to the construction of underdeveloped capitalism, but how did they benefit men? Underdeveloped capitalism exploits both men and women in Africa through the family-based production system.

Men have been compelled to produce cash crops or seek wages in mines or on plantations to pay exploitative taxes, to provide goods or services for their families, or because they lost their land. Pressures introduced by colonial capitalism encouraged many forms of domination including male domination of women, if not always exploitation. As Langley (1983:91) points out, elders dominated the young, elder brothers dominated younger brothers, notables dominated ordinary people, and men dominated women. Women in food and other low-cost survival activities are "the last link in a chain of exploitation. They are the most alienated strata of an exploited society in which both men and women receive very low returns on labor." In other words, most men have attempted to assert their traditional prerogatives to control women in an effort to maximize their own opportunities for survival or advancement within the context of poverty and inequality generated by underdeveloped capitalism. To quote Langley (1983:91), "It is not the elder brothers, the husbands, the uncles and fathers who exploit women, but those social forces which dominate the economic system, which encourage pre-existing inequalities and domination and use them to ensure reproduction of the labour force at the lowest possible cost." An important implication of Langley's analysis is that African patriarchy was not so much an effort to preserve "backward customs" from the past but a creative and, in some ways, new form of patriarchy designed to preserve male privilege within the new, underdeveloped capitalist system.

Ideology and state policy typically aid men in their effort to maintain control over women and preserve male dominance, although, as will be discussed in later chapters, women have always resisted their subordination. Obbo (1980:9) remarks that the African male's ideal woman is "an educated woman who will blindly obey their [men's] wishes and who will stay in the rural areas cultivating food." Appeals to African custom are frequently used to justify African patriarchy and limit women's rights and opportunities or justify their status within the family production system. But as Guyer (1986:399) observes, "There is nothing 'natural' about the marginalization of women into low-status, poor return occupations. It is a question of resource control, itself a legal and policy issue which in the past has been rendered unapproachable by the association of local practices with the idea of 'custom.'"

Keeping most women in subsistence farming or low-paying jobs has additional benefits for men. Minimizing competition from women for scarce resources or better-paying wage jobs ensures that the benefits of economic development in underdeveloped capitalism will go mostly to men. Male economic power, in turn, promotes the continuation of male dominance over women by reinforcing women's dependency on men. Men who depend on African patriarchy for their privileged position in society are threatened by the economic or emotional independence of women or by women who are in other ways "uncontrollable" (Obbo 1980:4, 9).

African patriarchy has benefited Africa's ruling classes as well. Africa's elites in both the state and private sector are the product of underdeveloped capitalism; therefore, they depend heavily on the patriarchal family production system to generate the surplus they expropriate for their own power and enrichment (e.g., through taxes on producers or profits generated by cheap African labor and cheap commodities in agricultural or business enterprises). The ruling classes have used the state to provide the legal and policy supports for African patriarchy and thus for underdeveloped capitalism.

My argument at this point may suggest a unified capitalist patriarchy, contrary to what I claimed earlier. This is not true for several reasons. For one, even underdeveloped capitalism has created economic, political, and cultural (including ideological) changes in many African societies that undermine its foundations. Among these changes are the weakening of ethnic and extended family kinship bonds as a result of urban migration and class formation. Other factors are education and Westernization, which promote individualism and liberal ideologies of equality and rights that threaten both patriarchy and underdeveloped capitalism by exposing their roots in oppression and inequality. The biggest problem, however, is that underdeveloped capitalism has failed to bring development and prosperity to Africa—and African patriarchy, with which it is so closely linked, is a significant factor in that failure.

## ▲  African Patriarchy and Capitalist Transformation

As I will argue more fully in Chapter 2, underdeveloped capitalism is self-limiting. As discussed by many scholars (e.g., Hyden 1983, 1987; Nyang'oro 1989; Taylor 1979; Delphy 1979; Caldwell 1982) and under many labels (e.g., the economy of affection, the domestic mode of production, the familial mode of production), African economies are in many respects not capitalist. As we have already discussed, transformed precapitalist and capitalist elements have for some time existed side by side, but this hybrid economy is less and less able to generate capital accumulation or promote growth in production and living standards.[5] Although the trappings of capitalism exist (some industry, commercial and financial institutions, business people, and commercial farmers), these are not enough in themselves to indicate that a capitalist mode of production is dominant in society. As Caldwell (1982:173) explains, "the real productive divide lies between modes of production based largely on networks of relatives and those in which individuals may sell their labor to complete strangers." This depends on a change in land tenure from communal to private holdings,

urban wage labor, a breakdown of the power of elders over the young—
and the breakdown of patriarchal authority over women (Caldwell
1982:177), a process only partially under way in Africa. Hyden (1987:135)
adds that only if capitalism or socialism become hegemonic (i.e., dominant) will new relations of production and power replace the "economy of
affection."[6]

One implication of Caldwell's analysis is that capitalism and African
patriarchy (in its underdeveloped capitalist–linked form) have conflicting
interests in the labor and reproduction of women. Mature capitalism depends on mobilization of the forces of production—land, labor, capital—
to maximize profit, efficiency, and capital accumulation. This is predicated
upon a market economy where supply and demand, competition between
buyers and sellers, and incentives for productive effort and risk taking are
institutionalized. Most of women's disadvantaged position can be attributed to African (and to some extent Western) patriarchal institutions that
function to maximize the advantages of men at the expense of women and
the economy. To some extent, the unpaid or underpaid and exploited labor
of women in the economy (especially in agriculture) and in the household
benefits capitalism by allowing low returns to producers (mostly male
workers and peasants). However, there are diminishing returns to capitalism in this. As long as African patriarchy and the familial mode of production in which it is embedded prevail, capitalism will remain weak; and
a capitalist transformation of Africa will be postponed or undermined altogether. If groups supporting capitalism—for example, Western development agencies and lenders, donors, multinational corporations, the indigenous private business sector, and small-scale entrepreneurs—are to achieve
sustainable developmental results, African patriarchy will have to be
weakened, along with other social structures tied to the familial mode of
production.

Although capitalist development has well-known disadvantages for
men and women (which will be further discussed in the following chapters), two options—capitalism or underdeveloped capitalism—appear to
me to be the only ones available to Africa in the near future. Alternative
development strategies, such as populist socialist and African Marxist development paths,[7] have been largely discredited, undermined, and abandoned. Socialism is in "disarray," as Amin (1990b:183) concedes, and
there are no serious challengers to some form of market economy on most
of the continent (see Sklar and Whitaker 1991; Sandbrook 1993).

The apparent triumph of capitalism raises three questions about the
capitalism patriarchy relationship in Africa. What changes in patriarchy
and women's status would be most supportive of capitalism? What kind of
capitalism would be in the interests of women? And what accommodation
between patriarchy and capitalism is likely?

As already mentioned, scholars like Mies (1988:6–10) and von Werl-hof (1988a) have argued that the "housewifization" of women is the major outcome to be expected from capitalist penetration and disruption of fa-milial modes of production. Women's (and men's) ownership of or au-tonomous relation to their own land is destroyed, and mostly men become "free" labor. Most women are relegated to the home or to subsistence pro-duction where their unpaid labor sustains the male breadwinner and their children. Some women undertake low-paying factory jobs, especially where men control and farm the land, leaving women's labor available for work in "the global assembly line." Also, women as housewives become a convenient reserve army to be called into the wage labor force when needed. Even when women work for cash, however, such as in develop-ment projects, factory jobs, home or piece work, they are treated as house-wives. That is, they remain largely dependent on a male breadwinner (women's earnings are considered supplemental and may not be under women's control), they are not protected by unions, and they receive low pay and few if any benefits.

For middle-class Third World women especially, the housewife role is a "false symbol of progress," cautions Mies (1986:207–209). Commercial interests in growing capitalist economies mobilize the housewife to pursue a new role—that of consumer. The increasingly dependent housewife, hooked on consumption made possible by her husband's wages, sacrifices her "self-reliance, courage, and independence of thought and action." She is trained for the role of wife-mother, isolated in the home (of increasingly nuclear families), and has few social support networks. The idea of ro-mantic love becomes a new dominant ideology of patriarchal domination of women. It portrays men as protectors of women (often falsely) and urges women to become emotionally (as well as financially) dependent on patriarchal and sexist man-woman relations.

This "feminine mystique" scenario so far fits Africa only to a limited extent and seems to be waning significantly all over the world, as the trend in most countries is the growing labor force participation of women (see Bloom and Brender 1993). Although privatization of land is growing, com-munal land tenure allows most Africans to control their own land and or-ganize production under the familial mode of production; thus women re-tain their vital roles in agricultural production. Also, global restructuring has not resulted in the transporting of many manufacturing jobs to Africa to employ either men or women. Wage jobs in general are few and mostly low-paying. Although this varies from country to country, most women as well as men work either in farming or the informal sector, or in both. They are a self-employed, "uncaptured peasantry," to use Goran Hyden's (1983) expression. In fact, according to Bujra (1986:129–130), women often have more options and make more money in the informal than in the formal wage economy. And because farming is so dependent on women, and women can often earn more in informal sector enterprises, capitalism has a lesser market of cheap female labor to exploit in Africa than in other Third World regions where men dominate farming and other employment, leaving women few options besides factory work. Instead, as we have seen, where wage jobs are available in Africa, it is usually men who migrate to get these jobs, while women subsidize men's employment through their farming and informal sector activities.

The typical depiction of women's work in agriculture and the informal sector as "reproduction" rather than production tends to overlook these as well as some other essential realities in Africa. For instance, often the surplus of women's food crops are marketed (thus becoming cash crops), and women often sell their labor at least part-time; therefore, women are important in market exchange, not just subsistence activities.[8] Additionally, women are becoming increasingly important to the export crop economy, the economic lifeblood of many African countries. In some cases, they are helping their husbands with his cash crops; in others, women grow cash crops themselves. One reason women are becoming more involved in cash cropping is that women in many parts of Africa head their households—there is no male breadwinner; women often must manage both food and cash-crop farming. Or, where the husband has migrated to leave his wife in charge of his land, women are running the entire farming operation (see Davison 1988b).

Another difference in Africa is that the dependent housewife ideology, while influential and growing, is compromised by African traditions of male-female economic independence. Even among the bourgeois classes, most women strive to assure their control over some economic resources independent of their husbands. Some of this is a response by women to the overall precariousness of African economies, but it is also a rational response to African patriarchy, since many women do not have any secure access to the resources of their husbands or to marital assets. In many cases, widowhood or divorce can leave wives with nothing. Even within marriage, men's responsibilities in providing support for wives and children are poorly defined and not institutionalized—a legacy of the precapitalist gender relations of the familial mode of production. Illustrating the effects of these contradictory norms, Schuster (1982) writes that in Zambia the cultural ideal remains one of a woman who can provide (food) for her children, but in urban areas the dependent housewife, whose husband generously provides for her and her children, is becoming the norm. The problem is that men get respect, not by supporting their wives and children, but by buying drinks for friends at a bar, keeping many women, and supporting lineage relatives.

The bottom line is that the familial mode of production remains stronger in Africa than in most other regions of the world. While this mode is linked to capitalism, the two are in many ways incompatible. The articulation of the two modes of production has been a marriage of convenience, allowing a limited amount of capital accumulation, class formation, and societal transformation to occur. African patriarchal relations have been a vital ingredient in this process, benefiting both capitalism and men. But the familial mode of production and the patriarchal relations that undergird it are an obstacle to the deepening of capitalism in Africa.

In the past, the underlying incompatibility of capitalism and African patriarchy has been obscured by patriarchal forces and assumptions. Caldwell (1982:368) writes, for example, that the free labor characteristic of the (capitalist) "labor force mode of production" breaks down at the household level where women and children remain. Women (and children) remain outside the labor market because they can produce certain goods and services (e.g., presumably, such things as housework, child care, food preparation) more cheaply than the market, or the return on the labor of wives is not worth their being in the labor market. In other words, the sexual division of labor that creates the housewife is rational from the family's and economy's standpoint. Superficially, this scenario reflects a gender-neutral, rational decisionmaking process that maximizes efficiency. Caldwell's analysis, however, ignores the role patriarchy plays in making housewifization seem rational. It neglects the fact that males' comparative advantage over women in the labor market is based on existing gender relations and the patriarchal subordination of women, not on free competition. Because in patriarchy women are typically viewed as wives and mothers first and subordinate to men, women are not allowed to compete on an equal basis with men as laborers. Instead, patriarchy ensures that women acquire neither the resources nor the will to do so. In addition, insofar as it denies property ownership or control to women, patriarchy also guarantees that most entrepreneurial, risk-taking capitalists will be men. In reality, the free market picks the winners only after the game has already been rigged in favor of men.

By rigging the system, patriarchy has guaranteed male dominance in African economies and states. This has produced a largely male ruling class composed of a bureaucratic and business bourgeoisie (often overlapping groups) who have been characterized as a comprador class serving the interests of international capital within Africa. They have been the primary beneficiaries of underdeveloped, neocolonial capitalism (see Markovitz 1977; Nafziger 1988; Lubeck 1987). Robertson and Berger (1986:10) correctly conclude that changes associated with colonialism and capitalism, which have used domination of women as an important element in the peasant subsidy of capital accumulation in Africa, "have been beneficial to local ruling classes and often to male household members, as well as to the capitalist world economy."

Stamp (1991b:227) shows how the domination of women in Africa operates through the collusion of the state and subnational structures like ethnic groups ("tribes"), clans, and lineages. Patriarchal elements from within these groups evoke African custom and tradition in order to preserve male dominance over women. It is also these groups and the social structures they reinforce that are indicated as impediments to a deepening of the capitalist mode of production and class formation in Africa. The familial mode of production allows family heads to control family labor to serve male or group interests, thus preventing individuation and a more economically rational use of land, labor, and capital. The state, because it must have the support of these same groups, often caters to them in order to maintain political stability. The results are often cronyism, corruption, and misallocation of resources that, by undermining market forces, reduce the ability of and incentives for peasants and others to produce or invest in entrepreneurial activities (see Blomstrom and Hettne 1988; Caldwell 1982; Hyden 1983).

Many scholars contend that the strengthening of class identity and interests is a necessary component of a developed capitalist economy. It is generally agreed that class formation is still rudimentary in most African countries; instead, ethnic and kinship identities and loyalties cutting across class lines are primary for most Africans. This reliance on kinship and ethnicity is not a symptom of backwardness or traditionalism but a rational response to the economic and political structures of underdeveloped capitalism, which frequently exploit and perpetuate such ties. Familistic identities and ties provide the major access for most people to social security or to productive or political resources; therefore, people often have little alternative but to maintain kinship and ethnic bonds. An apparent impasse is created, however, because the pressures of kinship limit capital accumulation by compromising the ability of capitalists to make economically rational decisions. Similar pressures prevent the state from effectively mobilizing the forces of production for economic growth and development (see Fatton 1988; Bates 1989; Nyang'oro 1989).[9]

This does not mean that capitalism and capitalist classes are entirely absent in Africa. But, as Kennedy (1988:87–88) observes, the capitalist mode of production is nascent rather than dominant, and, although there is a growing African bourgeoisie, the bourgeoisie's strength is largely dependent on the state rather than having an independent base in the economy. Indeed, there is often considerable overlap between those who rule and those who own business enterprises. Moreover, because Africa's bourgeoisie have been largely a comprador class, modern sector manufacturing and other productive enterprises are dominated by foreigners and parastatals. Without the ability to command the forces of production through extensive private ownership of manufacturing enterprises or land, Africa's bourgeoisie remains weak and unable to transform the economy.

Expanding the basis for capital accumulation in Africa would benefit both foreign and local capital. The lack of hegemony of the African capitalist class and the related incapacity of the state to provide an environment favorable for local or foreign productive investment are partly responsible for the decline of foreign investment in Africa in recent years. A strong indigenous capitalist class is now perceived as a necessary partner rather than rival to foreign capitalist interests. "It is becoming increasingly evident to Western capitalist interests," claims Kennedy (1988:191), "that their ability to anticipate significant and expanding opportunities in African countries in the years ahead depends on the attainment of political stability and competent government but also on the existence of strong domestic bourgeoisies capable of consolidating the conditions for further capitalist advance." The African bourgeoisie's share of the spoils of underdeveloped capitalism have enabled them to accumulate considerable private wealth and business investments on a largely mercantile or rentier basis (see Boone 1990). However, with most land and labor still controlled by peasant households and communal groups or the state, profitable ventures and entrepreneurship are limited.

According to Hyden (1983, 1987), the only way to strengthen or create a productive rather than comprador or rentier bourgeoisie is to weaken the familial mode of production through privatization of land and proletarianization of the working population, which will draw them into the market economy so they can be captured by the capitalist mode of production. As a market economy expands, ethnic-kinship identities will weaken in favor of class identity. This in turn provides the necessary impetus for further economic growth. To quote Kennedy (1988:146–147),

> unless and until the wider society undergoes substantial socioeconomic differentiation—so that each emergent class, or incipient class, possesses its own sub-culture and the means of providing viable, intra-class support for fellow members—then the possibilities for corporate business endeavour and intensive capital accumulation over many areas of economic life will be held severely in check. Indeed, the ability of capitalist entrepreneurs to distance themselves socially from the pressures of community life is simply an aspect of a far wider, more complex process whereby much larger, impersonal, national markets gradually evolve along with a system for mobilizing loanable funds and a supply of free wage labourers . . . [who] are also separated from their community of origin.

A capitalist transformation in Africa cannot proceed by a process of radical, brutal "primitive accumulation," by which the peasants are dispossessed of their means of production and forced to sell their labor to the ownership class. Such massive impoverishment under African conditions of bare subsistence and few employment alternatives would be both politically and economically suicidal. Instead, concentration of wealth, especially in land, is likely to be gradual. This partly reflects what some scholars see as a changing corporate capitalist culture in the mature capitalist countries and its influence on the process of capitalist development in Africa. In mature capitalist economies, ruthless exploitation of workers and disregard of community interests are no longer the prevailing modus operandi (not that such behavior does not still occur; see Sklar 1987). While not claiming that capitalism has become humanitarian at the expense of profit seeking, Becker (1987:210–211), for one, suggests that "corporate liberalism" is the prevailing ideology of today's international bourgeoisie. Undoubtedly because of pressure from democratic and grassroots organizations, international capital accepts some deviation from the market in the interests of such humanistic aims as some redistribution of wealth and assistance for the world's poor. International capital wants to be perceived as humane; this is politically and economically justified because it helps "stabilize the system of class domination." Also, capitalists realize that workers of the world represent a vast potential market. Limited redistribution of wealth can spread consumerism and help capital accumulation. In other words, being perceived as a good citizen can be profitable.

This evolving "capitalist humanism" is evident in recent World Bank[10] publications on Africa. The needs of the poor and their potential contributions to development have been given more emphasis than in the past. Africa's peasant producers in both agriculture and the informal sectors are seen as potential, if small-scale, entrepreneurs. Given the unlikelihood of "proletarianization" in economics with little industry, the Bank advocates giving peasants more incentives to produce for the market rather than eliminating them from the agricultural economy. To achieve these results, however, the poor need economic resources like credit, training, access to "appropriate" technology, and individual ownership or assured access to land. Development agencies like USAID devise various development projects and income-generating activities to promote these goals (see Chapter 5).

What does all of this mean for African women? As already discussed, the centrality of African women's productive as well as reproductive roles is gaining more recognition. Capital accumulation tied to ever-increasing exploitation of women's labor within the familial mode of production is proving to be, like the familial mode of production itself, self-limiting. If structural adjustment and other market-oriented reforms designed to promote private enterprise, entrepreneurship, and greater productivity are to succeed, women's exploitation and subordination under African patriarchy must be changed. As Afonja (1986:134), writing about the Yoruba, remarks, while capitalism has expanded women's occupational opportunities, it has also exploited built-in gender inequalities rooted in "women's tasks of reproducing and nurturing the family, which were established in the subsistence economy," to its own advantage. The price of women's exploitation is, however, a growing threat to women's ability to perform their productive and reproductive tasks. This threat is already being manifested in lower overall production, especially lower agricultural production, greater poverty and debt, environmental degradation, high infant mortality, and declining health and nutrition.[11]

The World Bank (1990b:32), in its report on women in development, tacitly acknowledges the counterproductive consequences of exploiting and neglecting women. "No country can afford to underequip and underutilize more than half of its human resources. Alleviating poverty, ensuring food security, reducing population growth, and properly using the natural resource base all depend substantially on women."

Writing for USAID, Sandra Russo and her coauthors (1989) argue that "the use and expansion of women's productive capacities is a necessary condition for social and economic progress." In a 1984 publication, AID cites dependency on imported food as a particular threat to Africa, in human terms as well as a contributing factor to the debt crisis. This can only be addressed by increasing women's productivity, since in some areas 90 percent of the food is produced by women. In addition to their productive activities in food production, women play important roles in the informal sector, service and farm labor force, and export-manufacturing labor force (AID 1984). Lastly, educating women is critical to lowering fertility, protecting family health, reducing infant/child mortality, increasing women's labor force participation, and achieving greater economic growth (Russo et al. 1989:A3). Women may in fact be more-productive assets for their countries' economies than men. As Guyer (1986:401) points out, women work harder and are less inclined to spend money on economically wasteful social and ceremonial expenses, and they are more inclined than men to save, invest, and innovate when they have access to resources. In terms of investing in human capital, women spend most of their income on maintaining the health, nutrition, and education of their children, in contrast to many men who are likely to spend more on luxury goods for themselves. Women's productive potential is indicated also in the World Bank's (1989a) study of women farmers in Kenya. Women farmers with the same access as men to inputs, extension services, credit, and education produced about 7 percent more per acre than the men. Currently, the average woman farmer produces 4–15 percent less than the average man (World Bank 1990b:5). These studies show the economic cost of denying women the same resources (including land) that men have.

Indeed, current economic liberalization policies may be undermined unless patriarchal biases are recognized and rectified. Studies by Joekes and associates and Palmer of current economic reform efforts reveal that gender differences in productive activities, resources, access to markets, and family responsibilities have typically not been taken into account by market advocates. But it is becoming apparent that the cultural pressures placed on women to help their husbands with export crops while at the same time maintaining their own food crops despite lack of access to extension services, land, credit, or inputs is no longer sustainable. Gender biases frequently result in growing exploitation of women's labor but declining economic security and rewards to women for their efforts. Without control over their own labor or productive resources, however, women may be unable or unwilling to respond to market incentives to increase agricultural production (Joekes et al. 1988:9; Palmer 1991:v–ix). Another problem is that supposedly gender-neutral structural adjustment policies designed to promote efficiency, such as cutting expenditures by government, often simply shift costs and work to the unpaid economy—and largely to women. More specifically, government spending cuts have resulted in decreased expenditures for clean water, schooling, sewerage, and health services. This has caused women to spend more time and money to maintain these services for their families or to forgo such services altogether. As more time and money is required for these additional tasks, women have less time for their farming or other productive activities, thus lessening overall productivity and economic growth (see Palmer 1991: 104–105; also Elson 1989:57 58).

In essence, the continuing disadvantages African women face are not logical or beneficial to capitalist development; they actually are undermining capitalism while perpetuating a distorted version of it that is a result of its articulation with African precapitalist, familial modes of production (i.e., underdeveloped capitalism). It is patriarchy and the advantages it gives men in access to property, education, training, and the labor and services of women that allows men to dominate the capitalist economy and limit women's access. It is also patriarchal ideologies that disguise gender-based restrictions on free competition and equality of opportunity while portraying them as natural, divinely ordained, freely chosen, or customary. Gender-biased economic and development theories can also obscure the fact that gender discrimination is a crucial variable undermining capitalist principles of the efficient allocation of productive resources and rational decisionmaking so crucial to capitalist free markets.

A major reason the negative effects of patriarchy on capitalism have not been better recognized is that capitalism all over the world has from the beginning developed and coexisted with patriarchal cultures and ideologies. Its resulting masculinist character has been taken for granted as natural. Therefore, gender discrimination has been ignored in capitalist economic theory and practice rather than being factored in and its true costs measured. The prevalence of unexamined patriarchal assumptions is apparent in capitalist development planning in such places as Africa as well and continues to undermine capitalist development efforts. As Stamp (1989:26) concludes, formal commitment to WID has not had much impact on development practices as a result of the "continued adherence of many scholars and practitioners to a conservative framework of thought regarding women and gender issues." The prevailing view is that gender inequality and the sexual division of labor are natural rather than socially constructed.[12] In a report for USAID, Ernst and Young (1988:1–7) write, "The role of gender is the least explored in the area of private enterprise development." Program directors and planners have tended not to view gender issues as crucial to their work and, without such recognition, gender issues cannot be effectively incorporated in AID's development efforts.

The relationship between women's roles and status and class formation is another element in the patriarchy-capitalism equation. As radical feminists have argued, patriarchy is found in precapitalist, not just in capitalist, societies. In Africa, patriarchal relationships, as we have seen, were rooted in the familial mode of production. Within the familial mode of production, the means of production (mainly land and cattle) were usually held communally, and their use and distribution governed by redistributive norms that assured all adults access to the means of subsistence; the goal was not capital accumulation, economic growth, or profit maximization. Concentration of wealth was mitigated by norms that encouraged "big men" (or women) to gain prestige and power by dispersing wealth through patron-client relationships and communal feasts on such ceremonial occasions as weddings and funerals. Families were obligated to make bridewealth payments, usufruct rights assured women access to land, and inheritance laws provided all sons (and sometimes daughters) a share of lineage and family land. Therefore, while definite economic and political inequality existed, classes—in the modern sense of owners of the means of production; intermediate middle classes of petty bourgeois business owners, professionals, and clerical workers; and a proletariat—did not. Since access to the means of production and other resources typically depended on kinship and ethnicity, individual welfare was maximized through observing norms of reciprocity to members of these groups. The conjugal relationship was less valued than the family of origin, and marriage was essentially a means for extended family groups to gain access to the labor and children provided by wives. Husbands and wives typically inhabited very different social and economic worlds, and the husband-wife relationship was often not emotionally close. In the event of the death of the husband, there was little concept of marital property. Instead, such assets as land and children belonged to the lineage. In patrilineal societies, wives could not inherit land, but even in matrilineal societies, land was more often inherited by lineage men than women, and nonlineage wives often found themselves entirely dispossessed. With divorce, as with death, women could lose everything they had worked for.

The relationship between family form, class formation, and capitalism is clear. In the early stages of capitalist development, extended families often provide mutual assistance, social security, and even support for entrepreneurial activities to their members. In every mature capitalist society, the monogamous nuclear family has become the norm and is even considered to be, if not a prerequisite, a concomitant of capitalist development. One reason is that as a market economy grows, nuclear families are better able to pursue private gain and accumulate capital because they are less pressured to share their assets with a seemingly endless array of extended family claimants. With more control over their assets, nuclear families can invest productively in business or in their children's education and advancement. When the wife and children are favored in property and inheritance laws, they have more incentive to work and promote the family's economic fortunes. Death of a spouse leaves the family fortune and investments intact, thus allowing continuing transgenerational capital accumulation rather than fragmentation. The monogamous nuclear family system promotes lower fertility for similar reasons. Fewer children allow for greater parental investment in each child and less fragmentation of family assets. Initially, the upper- and middle-class elites have the most to gain from the monogamous nuclear family since they have the most assets to protect and the least need for the social support system provided by the extended family. The conjugal bond is also strengthened as husbands and wives reside apart from kin and rely more on each other for companionship, economic cooperation, and child rearing.

The expansion of the middle class is thus beneficial to further capitalist development but also to a reduction of many forms of gender inequality. It is largely educated, middle-class women (including workers, intellectuals, commercial farmers, and business and professional people)—as demonstrated in women's movements all over the world—who have the resources and influence to articulate women's issues and perspectives and to organize in support of gender equality, women's rights, and other political issues important to women. Their relationship to elite men also gives them more leverage and access to male-dominated institutions and policymakers.

For all of the above reasons, the relationship between capitalism and patriarchy needs to be viewed as a complex, variable, and changing one. Capitalism does not necessarily benefit from the exploitation and subordination of women or their relegation to child rearing and domestic chores. On the contrary, capitalist expansion can be hindered by patriarchy and, by the same token, capitalism's expansion can create conditions favorable to women's emancipation and more-egalitarian gender relationships. Although capitalism and patriarchy have worked together to exploit women in Africa, we need to avoid both economic and patriarchal reductionism as well as the pitfalls of denying the realities of structures of power altogether.

## ▲  Notes

1. Essentially the same points have been argued by Hartmann (1981:18), who sees men's control over women's labor in patriarchy as the basis of gender hierarchy in capitalism.

2. See also the preface.

3. Abu-Lughod's (1993) portrait of Bedouin women in Egypt is a good example of this essentially narrative approach.

4. Cliffe (1982) distinguishes five distinct precapitalist social formations in Africa: feudal; tributary; lineage; slave; and pastoral, which were modified under colonialism.

5. Scott (1995:15–16, 103–104) criticizes mode-of-production analyses, especially Hyden's "economy of affection," for dichotomizing and essentializing two societies: the precapitalist vs. the capitalist. Such conceptualizing is similar to modernization theories that dichotomize traditional and modern societies, with the former being backward and inferior to the latter and thus needing to be changed. Such concepts also treat precapitalist modes as lacking agency, as being acted upon by capitalism, which is the dynamic, determining force. In my analysis, I use the concept of familial mode of production to indicate an economic system in which the household is the unit of production, usually under male control; the primary goal is subsistence rather than exchange. I also emphasize that, in the context of underdeveloped capitalism, the familial mode of production is no longer exclusively precapitalist, existing apart from capitalism. It is a hybrid resulting from the introduction of capitalist elements and pressures on the household economy. As my analysis shows, the familial mode of production affects capitalism as much as capitalism affects it.

6. Hyden gives little attention to gender in his analysis, but he is rightly criticized by Scott (1995) for some of the gender-biased assumptions and omissions in his arguments.

7. As discussed by Young (1982).

8. Although African women contribute a great deal to production, their contributions remain largely uncounted and unacknowledged in official gross national product and labor force statistics, as is true all over the world.

9. For example, a businessman's ethnic ties may lead him to hire unqualified kinsmen or spend hard-earned business profits back in his village in compliance with "customary" family obligations rather than investing those profits into his business, thus undermining the enterprise's success (see, e.g., Himbara 1994; Gordon 1994). At the government level, politicians dispense scarce financial resources or jobs to ethnic leaders and cronies (many from their own family and ethnic group). Moreover, political organization and parties are often ethnically and regionally based rather than being a reflection of transethnic occupational and class interests. Both economic and political elites find themselves in the sometimes

difficult position of serving two masters: the patronage demands of kinship vs. a rational allocation of resources that promotes economic growth and development.

10. See bibliography for post-1989 World Bank publications, all of which espouse growth with equity as the model of capitalist development.

11. In Tanzania, for instance, malnutrition and maternal and infant mortality are on the rise in some areas after previous decades of progress (Vuorela 1992:109, 118; see also Jacobson 1993).

12. Scott (1995) does an excellent job of deconstructing the gendered basis of much development theory and practice.

# ▲ 2
# Underdeveloped Capitalism and the Status of African Women

To understand women's roles and status in African societies necessitates that we first situate these societies within the broader context of the expansion of the global capitalist economy. Amin's analysis, with its focus on the articulation of precapitalist and capitalist modes of production, reveals the variable and often conflicting relationship between precapitalist and capitalist societies and modes of production. Amin (1974) argues that the world capitalist system is not the same as a world capitalist mode of production; that is, the world capitalist system is actually a conglomeration of capitalist and precapitalist systems. Integration of the periphery into the global economy beginning with the colonial period did not necessarily mean imposition of the capitalist mode of production on colonized societies. Rather, precapitalist modes of production could exist along with capitalism to be modified and used to promote capitalist accumulation. The specific nature of the articulation of the precapitalist and capitalist modes can vary, but articulation has the effect of creating a distorted quasi capitalism rather than transforming the precapitalist mode of production into genuine capitalism. This distorted development is sometimes referred to as "dependent capitalist development" or (the term I prefer) *underdeveloped capitalism* (see Stamp 1989).

The failure of capitalism to fully transform the precapitalist mode of production in Africa has resulted in the survival of what Hyden (1983, 1987) calls the "economy of affection." Similar concepts are the "domestic mode of production" (Meillassoux 1981) and the "familial mode of production" (Caldwell 1982). Each concept refers to the widespread reality in Africa that proletarianization is limited because most people are still tied to the land within extended family units, and the major means of production (i.e., land) is largely owned communally and by smallholders rather than by an ownership class. At the same time, the state in league with foreign and local elites, who dominate the process of capital accumulation, have helped to perpetuate the familial mode of production to further

47

their own political and economic interests. The results are that the forces of production (i.e., land, labor, and capital), while certainly influenced by market forces, are often allocated on the basis of nonmarket criteria such as kinship obligations or custom whether real, invented, or politically motivated.

More specifically, colonialism typically incorporated African societies into the capitalist system by force. Africans were not free labor, able to sell their services on the basis of supply and demand. Instead, they were, as Berman (1992:136) describes, "servile and dependent subjects of state control." Other factors of production, such as land, were also either expropriated or their use dictated by the colonial powers; therefore, the cheap labor and cheap prices for raw materials that so enriched the colonial economy were in no way the reflection of a free market economy.

A defining feature of the colonial economy was that, in most cases, precapitalist family-based production systems remained largely intact, although what they produced changed. In some cases farmers began growing cash crops such as cotton, coffee, and cocoa. Some proletarianization also occurred, as some villagers (mostly men) migrated to cities to sell their labor to mines, factories, or other employers. Most women remained in the rural areas growing food, helping their husbands with cash crops, and performing most of the domestic and child care responsibilities. This articulation of capitalism with the precapitalist familial mode of production allowed capitalism to pay low wages and prices to workers and cash-crop farmers because part of family subsistence was being provided at no cost (to the capitalist) from the labor of other family members in the precapitalist subsistence sector. Thus the extraction of surplus and the accumulation of capital were made possible not by the rational, competitive allocation of the forces of production but by the colonial state, which made profits possible through expropriating both the labor and the fruits of the labor of peasants—both men and women.

The underdeveloped capitalism of the postindependence period in Africa has its roots in the same phenomenon. Although it is part of the periphery in the global capitalist economy, Africa remains neither capitalist nor precapitalist; it is an unfortunate mix of both. Unfortunate in the sense that the system is inherently exploitative and inequitable, it ties Africans into a disadvantageous dependency relationship with the global capitalist economy, and it is unsustainable, as Africa's current economic crisis clearly demonstrates.

Africa has become the most marginalized economic region of the world as a result of its underdeveloped capitalist economies. As Callaghy (1994:32) writes, "Even a neocolonial Africa is not of much interest anymore." Africa's share of world output has fallen while its share of international development assistance has grown from 17 percent in 1970 to 38 percent in 1991. From 1982 to 1992, average gross domestic product (GDP) growth was 2 percent for Africa (less than its average population growth), over 5 percent for South Asia, and 8 percent for East Asia. Africa's share of developing country agricultural exports fell from 17 to 8 percent between 1970 and 1990, while South and East Asia's climbed rapidly. Disinvestment of foreign business capital is also occurring, and debt has risen from $14.8 billion in 1974 to $183.4 billion in 1992 (Callaghy 1994:32–33; see also World Bank 1981:19; 1989b:19–20).

As Berman (1992:135) discusses, the "contradictions of articulation" that created underdeveloped capitalism are the major source of its weaknesses. These contradictions include:

1. Cheap labor and cheap prices, subsidized by the familial mode of production, do not reflect free market forces but the unpaid labor of family members. This process degrades and destroys the original culture of production and self-sufficiency of farmers, with resulting declines in productivity and widespread impoverishment (Berman 1992:135).

2. The purchasing power of workers and peasants is undermined, thereby limiting the development of a domestic market for consumer goods; at the same time, parasitic elites demand imported and luxury goods from abroad or from import substitution industries, thus promoting such economic problems as dependence on imports, foreign exchange shortages, and lack of linkages between rural and manufacturing producers (see Blomstrom and Hettne 1988:142–144).

3. There are contradictory tendencies to both stimulate and repress development of the forces of production and the full development of capitalism, such as creating an accumulating capitalist class and markets alongside ethnic communitarian redistributive elements that undermine capital accumulation and market forces (see Berman 1992:134–135).

4. The familial mode of production that preserves ethnic-clan solidarities not only undermines class formation, it also compromises the ability of the state to promote economic development—whether capitalist or socialist (see Hyden 1987:119–121; Fatton 1992:34–37). Instead we witness, as Hyden (1983:193) observes, "the battle between forces defending these [precapitalist] forces and those [capitalist—] still much weaker—trying to conquer them." This battle is occurring in the economic, political, and cultural arenas. *Precapitalist* is perhaps an unfortunate and misleading term for what are in reality elements of the precapitalist familial mode of production that have become a structured part of a new system of production—that of underdeveloped capitalism (see Blomstrom and Hettne 1988:82–84).

Currently there are two basic viewpoints on the economic crises and contradictions that I have mentioned. One is that these problems are inherent to capitalist development; therefore, further integration into the capitalist system must be rejected if Africa is to develop. The second is that Africa's problems are due to the distorted and exploitative way Africa has been integrated into the capitalist system. What Africa needs is more capitalism, real capitalism, not less. I will discuss each of these basic positions in general terms. Informed readers will no doubt recognize that my remarks do not reflect all of the variations in viewpoints that exist in the literature. My objective is to outline the basic issues and to point to their implications for Africa's development and to provide a general perspective on the problems and prospects for African women.

## ▲ Alternatives to Capitalism: Delinking

Essentially, the only realistic current alternative to capitalism in Africa is some version of "delinking," as espoused by such scholars as Amin (1990a, b). As advocates of delinking argue, the global capitalist system is expanding worldwide, and the tendency is toward the "complete freedom of movement of the factors of production" and "the commoditization of the world" (Mahjoub 1990:160–161). Integration into the global capitalist economy results in a division of labor disadvantageous to Third World countries such as Africa's, because the main niche they can occupy on the basis of comparative advantage is as producers of raw materials. This is a dead end because it locks countries into the dependent (on external markets), weak position that has already brought many to ruin; that is, hobbled by undiversified economies, with little industry and dependent on the export of a few raw or semiprocessed products whose prices have mostly fallen in recent years. Amin (1990c:xi) contends that Third World efforts to develop under the aegis of capitalism are futile because the global capitalist economy no longer will support the growth of new industrial centers. Even such seeming Third World industrial success stories as South Korea and Taiwan will not be able to escape dependency or achieve center status (i.e., become relatively self-sustaining industrial economies rather than dependent on foreign capital and exports).

Another problem with integration into the global economy is the domination over the national economy that foreign corporate and financial capital will exercise. Openness to transnational capital leads to a loss of self-determination over economic development, that is, to "recolonization sweetened by charity" (Amin 1990c:xi). It also promotes dependence on imported technology that does not favor employment, provides for few linkages in terms of inputs from domestic producers, and results in little or no improvement in the living standards of the masses. Delinking, by contrast, means the subordination of the external relations of the global economy to the logic of desired internal development of the national economy. This "autocentric" development reflects the need of societies to promote self-reliance and minimize dependency. Delinking differs markedly from capitalist development in its goal to ensure that political and economic power and the benefits of economic development are distributed in favor of the masses. Capitalist development, by contrast, assumes a particular class structure and control of the means of production and political power by a dominant class (i.e., the bourgeoisie) (Mahjoub 1990:164, 167).

There is certainly ample evidence that dependent, capitalist development has left Third World economies vulnerable and dependent on exports, foreign investment, and loans; moreover, only a minority of the population may see any benefits. Hellenger and coauthors (1988:4) summarize the issues well, quoting Mexican economist Gustavo Esteva:

> Northern advocated development strategies have irresponsibly left Third World economies increasingly and precariously vulnerable to any changes that can, and do, occur in the international arena. If this were not bad enough, the policy advice that Third World governments receive today from the World Bank and other lenders remains fundamentally unchanged, encouraging them as it does to export their way out of their economic difficulties.

As for the often devastating impact on the poor,

> development means the sacrifice of environments, solidarities, traditional interpretations and customs to ever-changing expert advice. Development . . . for the overwhelming majority has always meant the progressive modernization of their poverty: growing dependence on guidance and management. . . . Most peasants are aware that development has undermined their subsistence on century-old diversified crops. Slum dwellers know that it has made their jobs redundant and their education inadequate. . . . Finally, the truly marginal groups know how it feels to be pushed, inch by inch, into the cash economy [Hellenger et al. 1988:14].

Recent neoliberal structural adjustment programs (SAPs) in Africa are designed to "resurrect the primary product export economies that existed at independence"—but make them work better (Callaghy 1994:33). But critics such as Onimode (1989:33) complain that SAPs mainly benefit the rich and powerful—import-exporters, bankers, some businesspeople, technocrats, politicians, military leaders and their multinational allies. The burdens fall mainly on workers, peasants, women, children, old people, students, and the middle class. This is consistent with Amin's (1990b) claim that adjustment and integration into the global economy results in further compradorization of the indigenous bourgeoisie rather than self-reliance or equitable development. And even where improved returns to farmers have occurred, as in Ghana, taxes and other prices have gone up, and most wages and farm incomes are still near the poverty line. Moreover, slack demand for African exports, protectionism in industrial nations, and competition from imports continue to threaten the success of economic reform efforts (see Ninsin 1990; also "Ghana . . ." 1991; Adams 1995). Although the World Bank (see, e.g., 1994a) maintains that African countries under SAPs have done better than those not under SAPs, it also acknowledges that changes are needed to protect the poor and other vulnerable groups suffering the greatest hardships resulting from economic reform efforts. The Bank also claims that many of the problems attributed to SAPs would have been worse without them. The World Bank (see, e.g., 1990a) also admits, however, that of the thirty-seven African recipients of adjustment loans, only Ghana and Tanzania could be termed successful.

Africa's long-term prospects for sustainable, not just self-reliant, development look ominous. As Amin (1990c:xi) points out, the world system has confined Africa to specializing in agriculture and mining while exploiting soils to near exhaustion. At the same time, technological change is making African raw materials unnecessary, leading to the conclusion that Africa's peril is worse than dependency; it may be gradual irrelevance and virtual exclusion from the world division of labor. Added to economic problems mentioned earlier, poor infrastructure, costly transport, and an "unskilled, poorly disciplined, and expensive labor force" cloud the picture and are compounded by political and economic uncertainties (Chazan et al. 1988:287). Moreover, as Chazan and her coauthors (1988:286) point out, Africa's economic crisis makes it difficult to bargain with foreign capital, and Africa's debt dependence on donor assistance will further limit its ability to pursue a self-reliant development strategy ("Closing . . ." 1991).

The bottom line is that, despite the problems with SAPs, there may be no alternative to some form of market-oriented economy in Africa in the near future. As Callaghy (1994:33) observes, such counterproposals as the Economic Commission for Africa's (ECA) "alternative framework," amount to a warmed-over version of earlier statist and "self-reliant policies" that have already failed. Such policies are also "vague, often contradictory," and not implementable. For one thing, they require a huge infusion of aid—an unlikely prospect.

As appealing in the abstract as delinking may be, for the near future the question is no longer whether African economies will become integrated into the global economy, but what kind of integration will take place, and whether integration can enhance the welfare of more of Africa's people—especially, from our perspective, the status of women.

## ▲ The Argument for Capitalism

As most scholars recognize, the dominant class in African countries is the "bureaucratic bourgeoisie," or "managerial bourgeoisie," whose control of the economy and politics is derived from their access to resources from the state (see Markovitz 1977; Fatton 1988; Sandbrook 1985; Chazan et al. 1988). What has also become clear since independence is that the bureaucratic bourgeoisie or their equivalent have dominated both underdeveloped capitalist and avowedly socialist regimes. The major difference is that in more-capitalist African countries many of the bourgeoisie are developing business enterprises of their own (see Swainson 1987; Nafziger 1988). Sklar (1991b:301–304) argues persuasively that socialism in Africa is in effect a class action by the socialist bourgeoisie whereby they control and administer state property for their own advantage rather than having outright ownership. In the Third World in general as well as in Africa, socialist ideologies of equality and so on too often justify dictatorship and unpopular, repressive economic and political policies without any commensurate improvement in people's living standards (see also Young 1982; Becker 1987).

Some defenders of socialism in Africa contend that external opposition, such as that mounted against Angola and Mozambique, and the withdrawal of support from previous socialist allies in the now defunct Soviet bloc are to blame for the failure of socialist experiments in Africa (see Schatz 1987). But this underscores the reality that African governments do not have the economic or political capacity to delink or implement any radical development strategy as an alternative to the greater penetration of capitalism. Indeed, as Cheru (1989:89–90) observes in Tanzania, government failures in creating socialism have so weakened the economy that efforts at delinking (e.g., by reducing agricultural exports) have actually increased dependency rather than self-reliance or industrialization. Capacity underutilization in industry has also become a serious problem because of cuts in essential imports. In Zimbabwe's socialist-oriented economy, Tandon (1990:89–90) demonstrates that, while the government appears to have considerable economic autonomy, its power is limited by parameters set by the international capitalist system in which Zimbabwe's economy is firmly entrenched. One obvious limitation is the inability to undertake serious land reform in Zimbabwe because of the economy's dependence on exports produced by white commercial farms (see Herbst 1990).

Another problem with socialist development strategies, according to Sklar (1991a:301), is that African farmers themselves prefer market incentive systems and dislike state-managed agriculture. This is understandable given the sorry record of state marketing boards, price controls, and collectivization experiments in Africa. Also, Africa's many small entrepreneurs and workers resent dictatorship and "ideological fetters on their freedom of action." Most men and women, Sklar (1991b:304) concludes, favor an environment "conducive to economic achievement by industrious persons, particularly entrepreneurs"; most do not want "equality." As an illustration, in the recent elections in Mozambique, 40 percent of the population voted for Renamo and against the previously Marxist ruling party FRELIMO. Among the reasons given by some villagers for their antigovernment vote were resentment against the collective villages forced on people by the FRELIMO government. Many villagers also resented government efforts to stifle their entrepreneurial activities. As Albino Rafaele, chief of the village of Zero, expressed it, "The road is open now and we want to open shops by the road to sell to passing motorists. But only one man is allowed to have a shop, and he comes from the city. It seems we are not allowed to own anything here except our chickens" (in Isaacs 1995:15).

Perhaps the most compelling argument in favor of more capitalism in Africa, one that socialists and other critics of capitalism tend to ignore, is capitalism's ability to renew and extend itself on a world scale. This cannot be understood if we see only its exploitative side. Although, admittedly, capitalism has not yet produced economic development in much of the Third World, and capitalist development is often accompanied by maldistribution of income (see Schatz 1987:196–197), such results are not inexorable. In fact, as experience has shown in the developed capitalist economies in the West and in at least some of the newly industrializing countries (NICs), political liberalization and redistributive economic policies are associated with successful capitalist development, especially once the capitalist economy matures and economic growth becomes more self-sustaining (see Becker 1987:210–211).

In the developing world, such previously autocratic countries as Brazil, Chile, Taiwan, and South Korea are allowing multiparty elections and other liberal political reforms. There are also indications that "primitive accumulation," the often brutal process by which the capitalist class gains control of the means of production and subsistence producers are forced into the market economy as proletariats, is being rejected as a flawed model of capitalist economic development, especially for areas like sub-Saharan Africa, in favor of growth with equity models. Moreover, underdeveloped capitalism, based on the familial mode of production and the patrimonial state, is recognized as unsatisfactory as well (see World Bank 1989b). If Africa is to be integrated as a productive part of the global economy, rather than as a perennial economic and political albatross, reforms are necessary that will force the African state and the elites to act more like capitalists and enable the masses to produce for the marketplace and benefit from economic development. Otherwise, efforts to promote economic rationality, capital accumulation, and the hegemony of capitalism on the continent will continue to be frustrated.

The evidence for the evolution of capitalist development thinking is noticeable in numerous World Bank reports on sub-Saharan Africa over the years. In 1981, for example, the Bank argued that capitalist development and accumulation in Africa was blocked by the dominance of subsistence production and the absence of a landowning class such as Asia or Latin America had. Farmers, the Bank (1981:12, 114) lamented, had to be induced to produce for the market, adopt new crops, or undertake risks. In 1984 the Bank's emphasis shifted to poor economic management that resulted in low returns on investment as the major cause of the deterioration of African economies. Declining production and a falling share of exports were among the signs of mismanagement of the economy. Only by expanding exports and increasing their share of global markets could African economies begin growing again (World Bank 1984:1–25). Partly in response to criticism that International Monetary Fund (IMF)–World Bank structural adjustment reforms were hurting the poor, by 1989 the emphasis was on growth with equity and helping the grassroots poor. The Bank now asserted that African governments and donors had neglected peasant agriculture, a distinct departure from 1981 when the very existence of peasant agriculture had been depicted as a major problem. Another area of focus on the poor was that the informal sector, with its micro-small enterprises, was positively reappraised as a "seedbed for entrepreneurs," if only support services and credit were made more available. Large-scale enterprises were to be encouraged as well, however, through a partnership between indigenous and foreign investors. The role of the state was no longer to be one of entrepreneur in the absence of an indigenous capitalist class but of promoter of private producers of every scale (World Bank 1989b:1–29).

During the 1990s even more startling pronouncements have come from the World Bank. In a departure from liberal economic orthodoxy, the Bank's 1991 *World Development Report* rejects the argument that greater equality of income is antithetical to economic growth, or that savings for capital accumulation requires concentration of income in the hands of the rich. There is no evidence for this, the report concludes. If anything, gross inequalities of wealth promote slower growth. The countries that consistently perform the best—Costa Rica, Indonesia, Japan, South Korea, Malaysia, and the Scandinavian countries—are those with less inequality. At the same time, the report points out, greater equality is not achieved through income transfers—except as a safety net for vulnerable groups— but through eliminating policies and practices that distort the market. For instance, the report criticizes some policies that are disguised as procapitalist: industrial protection, discriminatory taxes on farmers, or subsidies for capital. These policies actually distort market forces and mainly promote urban bias and capital-intensive modes of production (World Bank 1991:137). The Bank (1991:137–139) is also emphasizing that discrimination by such factors as gender and ethnicity create labor fragmentation and inequities and undermine allocative efficiency and growth.

The Bank concedes that the state has a role to play in promoting growth with equity capitalism. For instance, land reform and other agricultural policies that favor the smallholder farmer are strongly encouraged because they promote political stability, economic growth, and equity—all positive factors for capitalist development (World Bank 1991:138–139). There are numerous studies that lend support to growth with equity and capitalism. For example, agricultural output and employment improve when farmers have secure access to land; and farmers are more likely to undertake improvements, adopt technological innovations, and use more labor (Nafziger 1988:169). Small farms have even been shown to be more productive than large farms, as in Kenya (Bradshaw 1990:8–9). There are other economic benefits of helping the poor. As Langdon (1987:377–378) writes, redistributive policies that help urban workers, small-scale entrepreneurs, peasants, and the landless and unemployed to be more productive promote capital accumulation and capitalist transformation by stimulating demand for domestically produced goods and services, while land reform can improve both food and export crop production.

Even foreign capitalist enterprises stand to benefit from growth with equity capitalism, as a recent collaborative project between the government of Cameroon, Pioneer Seed, and the U.S. Agency for International Development (USAID) demonstrates. The three are working together on a commercial seed production program that is developing hybrid seeds for such food crops as peanuts, corn, cowpeas, and sorghum. They hope to sell the seeds throughout Central Africa. Pioneer's logic is that development for farmers will be profitable. If people become more productive and their standard of living improves, they will have more demand for products and thus there will be more profits. As Robert Hans, chief of the Development Assistance Corporation working with AID, admits, this program is designed to promote U.S. business and the free enterprise system in Africa, but "this can best be done by involving private sector businesses in activities that are aimed at achieving development" (in Novicki 1991:32).

These new positions coming from the World Bank suggest a dawning awareness that capitalism can no longer thrive in Africa without transforming the structures that perpetuate underdeveloped capitalism. This means, among other things, uplifting the poor who make up the vast majority of Africa's people—and a rapidly growing majority at that. Shivji (1992:48–49) summarizes the problem well: "There is a technical limit on the expansion of acreage based on the hoe, just as there is a social limit to the extent of the exploitation of the peasant." Africa's economy, based on superexploitation of the peasantry during the 1960s and 1970s, allowed for growth of the state and the elites connected with it. But this has now reached a breaking point. The oil crisis, declining prices, corruption, and inequality have brought the continent to its knees. The peasants are no longer willing to cooperate; they are resisting the state and further exploitation through such means as shifting from cash to subsistence production, black markets, and the informal sector and parallel economy. Falling export prices and crop production lead to shortages of foreign exchange, which in turn lead to declining imports of raw materials and parts for import-dependent industries, which lead to declining industrial production, which results in a shortage of manufactured goods, and so on (Shivji 1992:48–49).

At the heart of Shivji's critique of underdeveloped capitalism is that the peasant is the key to capitalist development or capitalism's failure in Africa. Africa's integration into the global capitalist economy cannot be achieved through more of the same failed policies from the past or from economic reforms that further impoverish the masses, deny them the resources they need to be productive, or subsidize unproductive political and economic elites who undermine their own and the general populace's ability to use the nation's resources in a way that improves people's lives.

## ▲ African Women in the Global Economy

Our analysis of the evolution and present impasse of underdeveloped capitalism in Africa provides the context for understanding the status of women in Africa and the relative significance of capitalism and patriarchy as explanatory variables. As discussed in Chapter 1, capitalism and patriarchy are interrelated, but they do not comprise one system, a "capitalist patriarchy," as some claim. Both capitalism and patriarchy are dynamic and changing and their interests do not always coincide. In Africa, as I will discuss, capitalism has used but also modified patriarchal institutions, just as patriarchy has sought to preserve or extend those institutions under the political, economic, and cultural changes introduced by capitalism. The results for women and gender relations are complex and variable, and they reveal significant elements of conflicting interests between capitalism and patriarchy. Moreover, while underdeveloped capitalism has benefited from certain aspects of African patriarchy, current efforts to reform Africa's failing economies will not succeed without reforming African patriarchy as well.

Mies's analysis of the relationship between capitalism and patriarchy provides a compelling argument for the importance of gender inequality to the process of capital accumulation, relevant to Africa as well as other Third World areas. Mies (1988:6–10) argues that in the articulation of capitalism with precapitalist modes of production, the destruction of people's autonomous relationship to their own land and to subsistence production is necessary in order to produce "free labor." This free labor is mostly male.

Capital accumulation necessitates that males be paid below subsistence wages and requires such low prices for commodities (i.e., below their true labor costs) that social reproduction (i.e., maintenance of the worker himself and his family) would be threatened. Therefore, social reproduction necessitates the "housewifization" of women. That is, women's work, defined as private housework for her family, is unpaid, benefiting both men (who get women's services for free) and capitalism (which can pay men less for their work). What results is a new sexual division of labor, with men given greater access to and control over the monetized and industrial sector, and greater access to education, jobs, organizations, and other resources; and women generally excluded from political power as well as being incorporated into the economy as either cheap labor for agribusiness and industry or left in precapitalist forms of production (Ward 1984:20–21; Mies 1986:48).

In her writing on African women, Robertson (1988:185) generally concurs with the above analysis and adds that male dominance in the household is a tool to perpetuate this exploitation. The implication is that capitalism requires a sexual division of labor in which women are seen as primarily housewives (even if working for money), and benefits from male dominance over women that limits women's free access to the marketplace.

Caldwell (1982:368) sees this sexual division of labor as mainly a result of economic efficiency. He writes that, as capitalist relations penetrate society, the familial mode of production breaks down except at the household level where women (and children) remain because they can produce domestic goods and services cheaper than the market can, or the return on the labor of wives is not worth their being in the labor market. This overlooks several important possibilities, however. One is that capitalism does not require the housewifization of women as much as patriarchy promotes this in order to protect men's privileged access to the monetized economy and the public arena in general. Another is that it neglects to mention the role of imperialism in promoting the form of capitalist exploitation and the sexual division of labor that developed in Africa. The sexual division of labor in which African men produced cash crops and worked for wages, and women produced food and took care of children and housework reflects the patriarchal prejudices and political priorities of Africa's colonizers, in conjunction with Africa's own patriarchal structures, rather than any requirement of capitalism per se. As Safa (1986:59) points out, it is because of the preexisting, often inferior position of women due to patriarchy that capitalism can exploit women as it does. Similarly, Pearson (1988:455) concludes that capitalism's exploitation of female labor is determined by the parameters set by patriarchal cultures. Also, as Joekes (1987:80–89) and Walby (1990:184) demonstrate, preexisting patriarchy gives men more power to monopolize new and prime economic activities for themselves.

In precapitalist African patriarchal societies, women already were assigned the primary tasks of food production for the family and child rearer under male authority. For this reason, maintaining that system as the basis for the sexual division of labor under colonial capitalism was the cheapest and most expedient means of reproducing labor. The resulting oppression of African women that occurred under colonialism, as Barrett (1988:249) also concludes, was not a "functional prerequisite" of capitalism.

Indeed, as long as the familial mode of production and patriarchy dictate the sexual division of labor, it may matter little whether the political economy is capitalist or socialist—another reason we need to avoid the reductionism of seeing patriarchy and capitalism as one system. As Mies (1986:184) points out, even in socialist China, with its ideological emphasis on women's political and economic involvement,

> the maintenance or reconstitution of a patriarchal sexual division of labour with women responsible for household and subsistence production still provides the cheapest means not only for the reproduction of labour power, but also for lowering the production costs of marketable consumer commodities. Thus, a policy of rapid modernization will, of necessity, lead to the reconstitution of the housewife model.

## ▲ The Articulation of Capitalism with African Patriarchy

The previous discussion suggests that as capitalism articulates with precapitalist familial modes of production, it also articulates with the sexual division of labor and gender relations embedded within the familial mode of production. How this articulation with capitalism takes place is affected not only by patriarchal relations within the familial mode of production but by those existing in capitalism at the time. For instance, colonial authorities working to establish the colonial capitalist economy superimpose their own patriarchal notions of appropriate roles or work for men and women. The patriarchy of the colonizers may or may not fit with that of the society colonized, but the resulting gender relations will have a profound effect on the articulation that occurs between capitalism and the familial mode of production. Another important point is that the sexual division of labor attributed to capitalist development is not an inherent result of capitalism; it reflects more the extent to which patriarchal practices and attitudes make child rearing and housework women's work, and give men control over women and productive resources. Patriarchy can transcend changes in the mode of production and appear to be economically rational since, as we have seen, it occurs in both capitalist and socialist economies (see Caldwell 1982:368; Croll 1986:243–249; Mies 1986:184).

However, the articulation of patriarchy and capitalism may be actually dysfunctional in some respects rather than beneficial, producing diminishing returns in the long run. Among these dysfunctions: (1) patriarchy limits capitalism's access to the labor of women and forces capitalism to hire or favor men who may be less productive or profitable; (2) where women do much of the productive work but resources and rewards are monopolized by men, women's productivity is negatively affected because they lack access to the resources they need; (3) although women's unpaid and underpaid work in the home or in the labor force subsidizes capitalist development by allowing capitalism to pay men low wages and prices for commodities, because both men's and women's compensation is not being determined by market forces but by patriarchal gender relations, the system is inherently inefficient and unsustainable. Diminishing returns reflect this unsustainability. For one, because women are to varying degrees "free goods" for men, the temptation is to overexploit them through excessive demands on their labor and reproduction. Women's health, productivity, and ability to fulfill their role of social reproduction (i.e., meeting the subsistence needs of men and children) begins to suffer as a result. If children's health, nutritional status, and education decline as women are unable to meet their children's needs, society's human capital resources for development are undercut as well. Lastly, the exploitation of women and the limitations on their opportunities is a major factor in rapid population growth, a significant obstacle to capital accumulation and economic development, as was emphasized at the 1994 United Nations Population Conference in Cairo (see Chapter 6).

Previous generalizations on the articulation of capitalism and patriarchy in colonized areas of the world fit sub-Saharan Africa to some extent, but the relationship between capitalism and patriarchy in Africa is, as I have already mentioned, complex and variable. During the colonial period in Africa, capitalist penetration meant for the most part exploiting the familial mode of production to produce cheap commodities or extract minerals for export. Mostly men migrated to cities to seek wage work or produced cash crops, while women typically remained in rural areas producing food. Rather than women's being privatized in the domestic sphere, however, the African "housewife" was often compelled by a combination of economic hardship and women's customary productive roles to supplement household income through petty commodity production, trade, or occasional paid work in addition to her work on her own fields and often on her husband's cash crop fields as well (see Robertson and Berger 1986:15). Although women's economic, political, and social status is said to have declined as a result of colonial capitalism, in Africa this was not always the case; insofar as women's status declined relative to men, it was often patriarchy, not capitalism, that was the determining factor. In other words, it is necessary to separate the poverty and exploitation of women due to their colonized status from the poverty and exploitation of women because they were women.

First of all, the alleged high status of women in precolonial Africa was variable and still limited by patriarchy. As Courville (1994:34; see also Guyer 1984:55) points out, in precapitalist Africa patriarchy and simple commodity production combined to control the productive and reproductive labor of women. While not all women were oppressed or exploited to the same degree, gender shaped the exploitation and oppression when it did occur. That women's status declined even more than men's under colonialism is due to the fact that, in an already sexually inegalitarian system, African men exploited their positions as guardians of family and lineage values, status, and resources to protect or improve their position in the colonial system. Patriarchy allowed men to gain control over new technology and capital, dominate cash crop agriculture, and maintain their control over women's labor and reproduction in the subsistence economy. Afonja (1986a:128–132) claims, for instance, that it was Africans, not the colonial administration, who organized cash crop production in ways that limited the participation of women to mainly the subsistence economy.

Eldridge's study of the nineteenth-century BaSotho provides insight into how patriarchy in the familial mode of production worked and the interests men were trying to protect. Among the BaSotho, and many other African cultures, status is derived from wealth and the ability to gain clients through the distribution of wealth. It is because women's productive activities are the source of that wealth that men have an incentive to subordinate women. In other words, control over women was a key element in the creation of "big men" in many African systems of stratification. Among the BaSotho, women could gain power mainly from their contributions to the overall wealth of the household. Men prevented women from having access to material resources or made them dependent on men to get them. Women's economic dependency on men was necessary to prevent women's building their own networks. "Only by limiting women's power could men ensure their own control over reproduction and production, from which their own wealth and power derived" (Eldridge 1991:728).

Davison agrees with Afonja that capitalism's impact on women's production and land use has been variable depending on preexisting and changing forms of production and exchange. Kinship systems of inheritance and land use, region, and ethnic group are factors as well. These combined with attitudes toward sex and gender relations to create gender inequality in relations of production. For example, in largely patrilineal East Africa, both men and women harvest tea and coffee, but mostly men own land and they often control the profits. But in West Africa, among more-matrilineal or bilateral kinship groups such as the Yoruba, Akan, Ibo, and Ga, cash cropping and the commercialization of land often benefited women because they were able to control both land and capital, hire labor, and become traders. Also among the Yoruba, women were compensated by their husbands with gifts and cash for work on his cash-crop farm (Davison 1988b:13–14; Afonja 1986b:90).

There is no necessary or consistent relationship between patriarchy and capitalism that favored male versus female labor migration either. In some cases, capitalism benefited from male migration; in some cases it did not. In fact, male labor migration and restrictions on women's movements sometimes resulted from patriarchal pressures and attitudes or even conflicts of interests between factions of the capitalist economy. For instance, in Kenya until World War II, colonial authorities lamented the negative economic and social consequences of both male and female labor migration from Western Kenya because of the depressive impact it had on agricultural production. This opposition eventually changed when men migrated but left their wives and children back on the farm to grow food, thus allowing the capitalist sector to extract a greater surplus from paying males low wages while assuring agricultural production (Hay 1982:119). Although a similar situation prevailed in Southern Rhodesia, as Schmidt (1991:732–733) observes, both colonial and African patriarchal ideologies, more than economic rationality, were at work in discrimination against female migration. African men opposed all proposals to give women property rights or more independence because it offended their notions of proper female behavior and male roles of authority over women. The resulting male migrant labor system may not have been optimal for capitalism; it reflected the struggle between Africans, especially male elders and women. In South Africa, capitalism was divided over female labor migration because of conflicts of interests involving international capital, national industrial capital, and commercial agriculture. Until the early 1920s international capital promoted male-only urban migration; women were to remain behind to grow food. By 1948 secondary industries owned by local capital worked in favor of urban migration for women because these businesses wanted a permanent, stable black working class and needed female labor (which could be paid less than men). The interests of local industry, however, conflicted with commercial agriculture, which needed cheap female farm labor. Agricultural interests won out and were instrumental in bringing an end to women's freedom of movement by 1960 with the imposition of new pass laws on women (Wells 1982:127–129).

In many areas, the urban expansion capitalism created resulted in new opportunities for women traders and farmers, but discriminatory patriarchal practices and ideologies kept women from benefiting equally with men. For many women, the economic independence gained from urban employment allowed them to loosen the control of kinsmen (Henn 1988: 48–49; Merry 1982:87–89). In Zambia, for example, Mambwe girls who visited the Copper Belt developed new and independent attitudes that conflicted with patriarchal norms of their villages. They refused to marry the men their families chose for them; instead, they insisted on marrying their lovers. Married women put pressure on their husbands to take them to the Copper Belt because women's lot was perceived to be easier there. For both women and men, wage labor was seen as a means to escape intolerable economic and social conditions at home (Watson 1958:47). In Senegambia and Upper Guinea coastal regions in the eighteenth and nineteenth centuries there were many influential trading women. Signareship in Senegal, especially involving Wolof and Lebou women in Gorée and St. Louis, was the result of expanding opportunities for women traders due to European contact. Successful signares had a great deal of independence, and many owned their own slaves. *Nharas* in Cacheu and Bissau in Portuguese Guinea were similarly successful African urban women (Brooks 1976). In Lagos in the 1850s European capitalism also opened new opportunities for women in agriculture as well as trade, but patriarchy created obstacles for women in the form of new land tenure and property laws justified on the basis of African custom. These laws gave most land and houses to men. Women's lack of property in turn limited their access to credit and their ability to trade. Without land or houses, women were less able to control their own labor, to call on the labor of their dependents, or to hire labor. Most women had to depend on men for access to aid or property. This gave men the means to control and punish women and keep them subordinate (Mann 1991:703–705).

Male privilege originating in the precolonial period has also allowed men to dominate in the area of large-scale trade and business activities. Afonja writes that West African women traded mostly subsistence items such as pots, cloth, and food. Men controlled the most valuable items from the farm and had exclusive control of long-distance trade until the nineteenth century. Women's trade generated little individualism or profit motive and added little to a woman's status or economic power. This changed in the nineteenth century with the expansion of trade due to European capitalist penetration. Women came to dominate retail trade and the open market, where foodstuffs and imported consumables were sold, and many small retail shops were owned by women. However, men took over from the European commercial houses after independence and now control large-scale wholesale trade and more capital-intensive shops. They also have the advantage when it comes to accumulating capital, getting credit, and acquiring managerial experience (Afonja 1986a:133).

Ethnicity is another variable affecting the impact of capitalism on women. In Kenya, for instance, Kikuyu women in Nairobi have faced few customary constraints on their independence and economic enterprise.

Consequently, most Kikuyu women are involved in trading and other enterprises and are active in community affairs. On the other hand, Luo and Luhya women are much more under the control of their husbands economically and socially (Clark 1984). It is the nature and strength of patriarchy found in the two groups, not capitalism, that accounts for the differences in these women's economic fortunes and status (see also Gordon 1995).

Another important variable is the legal system. Certainly, colonialism and capitalism have generated legal changes reflecting both class and patriarchal interests. In many cases, customary law, used to legitimate patriarchal control of women, was codified during the colonial period and still coexists with common law based on European precedents. While common law in many ways supports capitalism, in many ways it conflicts with African patriarchy (see Cotran 1989). Indeed, the European legal systems introduced under colonial capitalism provided women with some new opportunities for redress from African patriarchy. As Chanock (1982:56–57) points out, men, women, and elders all tried to use the colonial state and courts to promote their own interests. Although men were more successful than women, law under colonial capitalism provided some means of escape for women from nineteenth-century patriarchal controls; for example, from slavery and restricted economic roles and mobility. Killing widows, child marriage, and using women and children as collateral for loans were also outlawed (Courville 1994:37). Indeed, men often complained of the court's leniency toward "misbehaving women." The courts were also not always favorable to men in cases of abuse, child labor, or custody (Wright 1982:38–43).

In many respects, customary law must be understood within the context of the political economy of colonial capitalism and the struggle of African patriarchy to preserve itself against threatening economic and social change. As Chanock (1982:56) writes, law is not just codifying customs; it is a means of "gaining, defining, and perpetuating positions of power and advantage for some over others." In Africa the ideology of traditional law has been used by males to entrench patriarchal institutions that allow male dominance over women. Under the colonial system, women's previous rights and sources of status and political power were often undermined by the patriarchal prejudices of the colonizers and by Africans under the banner of customary law (see Okonjo 1976; Wright 1982). The result was that women were subjected to new forms of subordination and economic dependency on men (see Merry 1982). Perhaps most destructive for women were the perpetuation of laws from precapitalist Africa that assured male ownership, control, and inheritance of property.

As Wright (1982:37, 45) discusses, the colonial administration had to work with chiefs and other local male leaders and be on good terms with them in order to get food, labor, and cooperation from the local populace. African male leaders used this as leverage to demand customary law and other forms of control over women (and young men) who they feared were getting out of their control. A good example is Zambia, where male migrant labor to mines was essential to the economy. Shortly after 1900, male migrants had to go farther from home to get jobs. They demanded more control over women both in their absence and when they returned home; male elders especially feared "female volition and action." In another example, among the Luo in Kenya, women farmers before 1945 were becoming central to the agricultural economy because so many men had migrated to the city to get jobs. Women were in a position to gain greater influence, access to property, and rights. Indeed, women were beginning to avoid arranged marriages and gain greater control over their sexuality. But these things provoked a conservative backlash from Luo men, especially male elders, who sought to tighten their control over women. These efforts to control women influenced the codification of customary law in Kenya in the 1950s. To protect the property rights of migrant males, Luo elders even opposed efforts to consolidate and register land—a legal change designed to promote capitalist commercial farming (Hay 1982:117).

Sometimes colonial laws designed to promote capitalism reflected Western rather than African patriarchal ideology but inadvertently strengthened African patriarchy. In Transkei, for instance, the hut tax was instituted to force "lazy" African men to be more productive by entering the labor market. Colonial authorities saw African women and children as the productive workers in African society (albeit under patriarchal control), while men were often idle or at beer drinks. This offended European views of the appropriate sexual division of labor in which men do monetarily productive work while women do domestic work. The tax laws had the effect, however, of increasing male status at female expense. By subjecting only men to taxation, the authorities conferred adult status and the status of landholder exclusively on men. Women were further reduced to being "economically productive but completely subordinate within African patriarchal families" (Redding 1993:57).

The above discussion suggests that although capitalism and African patriarchy benefited from and cooperated in controlling women and creating a sexual division of labor that subsidized men and the capitalist economy, this is not the whole story. Capitalism also modifies, perhaps gradually and unevenly, gender relations as it promotes capitalist economic interests or Western patriarchal conceptions. Moreover, capitalism generates social changes that can provide new opportunities and rights for women, allowing at least some women to escape the limitations placed upon them by precapitalist family structures and gender relations. However, capitalism is more likely to serve the interests of African men than women because African males have historically had more power than women and had authority over women. And because of males' positions of authority and control over human and productive resources, placating men was more central to the success or failure of the capitalist project in Africa. The resulting gender relations may not necessarily be the most economically rational for capitalism, and they certainly are not a result of free markets. Rather, they more often reflect political expediency and both European and African patriarchal practices and prejudices.

In examining the relationship between patriarchy and capitalism, it should also be mentioned that the penetration of capitalism in Africa by means of exploitative imperialism and colonialism is another factor influencing subsequent gender relations. That is, the patriarchal response to capitalism might have been different if capitalism had not been associated with military and political domination, forced labor, land seizures, and so on. It was often duress, not choice, that led men to seek wage work while women farmed and raised children. It was also growing inequality, land scarcity, and fear of landlessness that led men to seek to maintain their traditional claims to land and family solidarity against the encroachment of white and later African capitalist agricultural interests. Eldridge (1991: 729) notes that "by depriving Africans in general of their productive resources [colonialism] intensified the struggle over remaining resources, which heightened the struggle between rich and poor and between men and women. Because the colonial system favored rich over poor and men over women, women were losers on two counts."

It should also be noted that the struggle to preserve African patriarchal relations and other customary practices can be viewed as a form of struggle against the inexorable expansion of capitalism itself by some of society's most vulnerable members. Customary practices represent to many Africans alternative modes of survival that do not entail total subordination to capital, as Bujra has observed. Even women may act to defend these institutions, for, although women may be subordinate, customs allow women to retain at least some control over the conditions of their production and reproduction in the face of an advancing impersonal capitalism that seems to threaten all petty production, be it peasant farming or artisanal and other informal sector activity (Bujra 1986:120, 138). Moreover, as Courville (1994:36) writes, custom did not serve men alone; it provided women with recognized ways of voicing their grievances against men. With age, women's status often improved as they had more control over their children, daughters-in-law, grandchildren, and household labor. In many societies women could also accumulate wealth and social rank through their community service, spiritual leadership, or rights as mothers, wives, or daughters. "Women's responsibilities in the familial household were not only the site of their oppression and exploitation, but also the source of their social standing and their limited protection within the society, and the site and foundation for collective action to express their dissatisfaction and bring about change." For many, both male and female, the family and the familial mode of production in all its imperfections is a preferable option to the insecurities and vagaries of capitalism.

## ▲ Capitalism Versus African Patriarchy

Despite the relationship that has existed between patriarchy and underdeveloped capitalism and the struggle of patriarchy to maintain male dominance and control over women, capitalism is a threat to African patriarchy. This was first noticeable in a limited way in the colonial period, as we have seen, with some women gaining new opportunities and freedoms from male dominance and patriarchal kinship structures. Since independence, and despite the obstacles and hardships women face, the expansion of women's education, economic activity, political participation, and urbanization; the penetration of Western cultural values; and the growth of the nuclear family and the conjugal relationship in the family are among the many social changes capitalism has promoted that are gradually eroding the familial mode of production and its patriarchal base.

A major source of the erosion of patriarchy comes from the liberal, individualistic ethos of capitalism. As society becomes more commercialized and labor becomes a commodity, women as well as men develop a new awareness of the value of their productive activities and seek more autonomy. As Bujra (1986:139) observes, gender struggle combines with class struggle as a result. And, Eisenstein (1981:23–25) adds, capitalism exposes the patriarchal, unequal base of the family. In Africa this results in women's growing discontent with farming within such constraints of the familial mode of production as little access to ownership or control over the means of production, subordination to their husbands, and limited rewards for their labor. Increasingly, husbands and male elders function as the exploiting capitalist, and women become the immiserated proletariat in African political economies.

Despite the hardships they impose on women, current economic reforms imposed under structural adjustment are in some cases undermining the economic base of patriarchy in Africa, because many men are no longer able to claim to be the breadwinners supporting their dependent wives and children. In many households the labor power of women has become primary, as Vuorela (1992:118–121) demonstrates in Tanzania. Male salaries have been sharply reduced, often well below what is necessary to support a family. In addition, as unemployment grows and jobs become harder to find, family members are forced to commute between rural and urban areas. This breaks down the family as a stable unit with a clearly identifiable head and promotes a family of individuals. Women are assuming even greater responsibility for economic survival, and there are a growing number of female-headed families. Lastly, daughters are becoming more valued as they assume more responsibility for the care of the elderly.

There are other changes capitalism is introducing that are providing benefits for women, which may have long-term if not immediate impacts on patriarchy. In contrast to the assertion that women's status was higher in precapitalist Africa, Guyer (1984:30) reports that Beti women farmers in Cameroon who are marketing their own food feel better off and are better off in many ways. Eventually the effects of political, economic, and cultural change may be the narrowing of the status gap between men and women, Guyer claims. She adds, however, that this may be due in part to the decline in most men's status and authority as most become manual laborers, rather than to a rise in women's status.

The commercialization of agriculture can raise household incomes, with benefits for women as well. In the early 1980s, studies of The Gambia, Kenya, and Rwanda by the International Food Policy Research Institute found that households participating in cash-crop schemes had significantly increased incomes compared to noncash households. In Kenya, for example, where sugarcane was grown, the absolute income of women was higher, whether the household was headed by a man or woman, because the higher income allowed women to diversify their productive activities. It is interesting to note that households headed by women earned more income from sugarcane than households headed by men. As a caveat, however, the Kenya study also revealed that, when men control the income from sugarcane, women may not always benefit from increased household income. Moreover, malnutrition among children is higher in male- than in female-headed households. The lesson from these studies is that cash-crop schemes can benefit women if women are incorporated into the planning and implementation of these schemes to ensure their access to income and benefits (Gittinger et al. 1990:19–20).

Ironically, capitalism's long-term impact on farming may be to displace men more than women, with mixed results. This has already been occurring as men have long been the major migrants and holders of wage jobs. In 1985 in sub-Saharan Africa, over 80 percent of economically active women were in agriculture, and they were 47 percent of the total agricultural labor force. On the other hand, women were only 27 percent of the nonagricultural labor force (Bloom and Brender 1993:8). According to Palmer (1991:141–142), as large-scale commercial farming increases, it competes mostly with small-scale male "tradables," while female farming mostly escapes such competition. Large farms also use more paid labor and create jobs, often for women. Palmer concludes that the agricultural transformation of Africa will mean the demise of small-scale male farming and an expanding rural wage-labor market largely benefiting women (given the prevailing sexual division of labor). She also foresees some interesting developments in female own-account farming, such as selling high-value food crops for export as well as in local markets. All in all, women's prospects in agriculture may be as good or better than men's.

Gladwin and McMillan (1989:346–349, 357–361) disagree somewhat with Palmer. They believe that over time women are likely to continue to lose access to the means of production as a result of privatization, technological change, and intensification, although they may not necessarily work less in agriculture. The degree of displacement of women in agriculture will depend on such variables as population density, male migration, and gender-neutral incentives to produce. Where food is easy to produce with little labor, as in most of Africa, men will work less in agriculture. On the other hand, population pressure and use of the plow result in more male farming, and women shift to other work. Also where there is still much arable land and low population density, there is little pressure for intensification, and female farming is likely to persist.

All of these different trends in agriculture have divergent implications for gender relations and the familial mode of production. Migration to cities can erode the patriarchal extended kinship system and promote individualism. Privatization of land and land consolidation that results in fewer farmers undermines the familial mode of production and patriarchal power rooted in male and lineage control of the allocation of land. Patriarchal norms that specify exclusive male ownership of land and control of income conflict with the reality of de facto female farming systems in many parts of Africa. But regardless of whether men and women both farm, women farm and men work for wages, or men farm and women do not, unequal access to resources, land, and income often produces gender conflict and may have other negative effects as well. Among these effects are lower production, rapid population growth, environmental problems, and poorer maternal and child nutrition and health. Finally, if more women lose their status as farmers, their role in the family and in relation to men will change as well. Depending on whether or not women assume new productive roles or become dependent housewives and what their class position is will be major determinants of how patriarchy and capitalism combine to affect the status of nonagricultural women.

Although all of these issues will be discussed in subsequent chapters, some preliminary observations about women in the wage-labor force, in the informal sector, and as housewives are needed to complete this chapter's examination of the relationship between patriarchy and capitalism in Africa.

The informal sector in Africa is a response to the growing rural exodus and not enough wage jobs. Estimates are that the informal sector employs over 50 percent of urban workers. While men are the majority of informal sector workers, the informal sector is the major source of employment for women in urban areas where wage jobs usually go to men. Although often marginal in terms of the income they generate, some informal sector jobs are quite lucrative. Women have been especially successful in trade, men in small-scale manufacturing, repairs, and construction. Women have more-restricted opportunities as a result of less education and fewer marketable skills than men and less access to credit. Most women rely on activities transferred from their domestic roles as food or beer producers, child care providers, or prostitutes (see MacGaffey and Windsperger 1990:81–83).

The informal sector is likely to grow in importance as employment opportunities continue to lag behind population growth in most African countries. The informal sector has been praised as the seedbed of entrepreneurship in Africa (see World Bank 1989b) and could be even more so if conditions become more favorable to private business activity. Structural adjustment programs in the 1980s were designed to favor the private sector, and more development aid is being targeted to informal sector businesses. Palmer (1991:127–128) believes women's enterprises may benefit from such initiatives while men may be more negatively affected. For one thing, since women are more likely to be self-employed than to work for wages, adjustment-induced declining wages hurt men most. Palmer also points out that the formal sector will be given priority in access to import licenses and foreign exchange, before mostly male informal sector businesses that need such resources to operate or expand. In addition, male informal sector enterprises as suppliers of intermediate materials are more linked to the fortunes of the formal sector. Since the formal sector is in serious trouble in most countries, male informal sector enterprises suffer as well. Women's enterprises are less linked to the formal sector; for example, women are more likely to be selling food. Such enterprises may benefit from the declining demand for formal sector restaurants as a result of structural adjustment programs' negative effects on urban wages. In rural areas, informal enterprises are smaller and involve more manufacturing than services. Such activities as blacksmithing, repairs, and processing of produce will gain the most from SAPs. The major problems for women entrepreneurs remain access to credit and raw materials.

MacGaffey, in her study of women in the informal sector in Zaire, shows both the economic potential for women in the informal economy as well as the constraints on women's entrepreneurship arising from patriarchy. By the 1960s there already were wealthy women traders in urban Zaire, although for most women the informal sector was a survival strategy in response to capitalist penetration. In Kinshasa women owned land and rental housing, often acquired with earnings from trading or prostitution. Women also invested in shops and agricultural land. By the late 1970s, in both Kinshasa and Kisangani, many rich women had diversified into the formal sector, for example, in importing and other commerce. Women comprised 28 percent of the private business owners in Kisangani, and 25 percent of those with fixed shops in the central areas of the city. Unfortunately, discrimination in access to education (both level and content) made it difficult for women to compete in the modern formal sector. There were also legal constraints on women with regard to contracts, banking, or even working. For one thing, husbands had the right to take over women's business property or profits "in the interests of the household." Women had to develop numerous strategies to evade male control and gain economic independence in the face of such obstacles. Perhaps not surprisingly, many of the more successful businesswomen were unmarried (MacGaffey 1986, 1988).

Similarly, in her study of women traders in Nairobi, Robertson (1995: 77, 79–86) characterizes urban trade as both a survival strategy and a bid for independence for women. While some women have been able to build successful businesses, most women struggle against multiple forms of patriarchal dominance and discrimination. Women have been forced into trade through landlessness; have assumed the major dependency burden when men do not support their families; have suffered reduced business profits due to lack of credit or other resources and due to the unequal sexual division of labor; and have been denied legal urban selling space or licenses and been persecuted by police. Many women traders, especially younger ones are rejecting marriage in order to maintain control over their profits (and children). As one woman said, "I can make it on my own. A husband is good for what?"

I have already mentioned that African women comprise only about 27 percent of the nonagricultural labor force. Here, as well as in the informal sector, unequal educational opportunities make it difficult for women to compete with men for jobs. Among West African women, Peil (1981:92–93) has observed that those with only Koranic or primary school education are the least likely to be active in the labor force. Nonetheless, even these women may pursue income-generating activities from their homes (see Schildkrout 1982). Illiterate women go into trading. Those with primary education who are active cannot compete with their better-educated sisters for clerical jobs; instead some become traders or seamstresses. The small majority of well-educated women have far more job opportunities and continue to work after marriage. Most such women expect to work and find it rewarding, and their economic independence gives them some autonomy.

For several reasons, the Western housewife role with its dichotomous male breadwinner–female dependent roles has only limited application to

Africa, especially West Africa. Not only does this conflict with African norms on women's economic independence, but many women have learned from experience to reject Western marriage as well. Mann, (1982: 156–160) studying Nigerian women in the nineteenth century, found that educated Christian women were initially attracted to the Western marriage model because it promoted monogamy and husbands supporting their families. Unfortunately, such marriages often did not work. Husbands deserted their wives or coerced them into accepting outside women. In the twentieth century women began abandoning economic dependency and taking jobs. Because the housewife role often failed women, concludes Mann (p. 171), "the independent, resourceful and calculating woman of the present may be reacting to the disappointment and vulnerability of her forebearers, as well as adapting customary norms to modern urban realities."

The opportunity for wage employment for women afforded by capitalism can be an important first step in loosening the bonds of patriarchy rooted in precapitalist and underdeveloped capitalist societies. Indeed, if Blumberg (1995:1–3) is correct, women's control of income is the most important predictor of gender equality and women's empowerment. Despite the fact that, globally, women are often paid less than men and relegated mostly to lesser "women's jobs," wage jobs can provide some financial independence from men, promote independence and self-esteem, give women more decisionmaking power in the home, promote more sharing of household chores, and prepare the way for "class consciousness" and collective organizing among women.[1]

These effects can be observed in many diverse capitalist-oriented developing countries, as several recent studies show. One example is Taiwan. Although gender bias and patriarchy are strong and have been used in the process of industrial development (such as limiting women's options while expanding men's), as women are being incorporated into the labor force, change is beginning to occur even at the village level. Money in the hands of women results in modifications in gender relations in the family. It lessens their financial dependence on husbands, which women find oppressive, and increases their self-respect and autonomy in financial matters. It has the potential to erode patriarchal ideology and norms (Gallin 1995:126–128). In Puerto Rico and the Dominican Republic women have become major contributors to their household economy. They claim to have more authority and decisionmaking power as a result. As dependence on men erodes, so does male authority over women (Safa 1995:106–108). In Mexico power arrangements, especially in middle-class households, are shifting as more women go to work. Women report their relationships with their husbands are more egalitarian, including attitudes about the sexual division of labor. Middle-class women who work often see their marriages as a team relationship and see their incomes as essential to their households.

These changes are beginning to affect all social classes. Young working women are in growing support of husbands and sons sharing housework and of more-equitable decisionmaking in the family (García and Oliveira 1995). Lastly, in Latin America women report they are better off today in terms of living standards, literacy, life expectancy, health, and economic, social, and political participation. "Gender bias at every level of institutional arrangement" is now provoking a surge in women's movements and demands for more equality, and there is more media attention and public awareness of women's issues. "Each wave of feminist struggle . . . has pushed the agenda of social justice in new directions. We are now in the midst of the most broadly based struggle for women's rights and gender change that has ever occurred in Latin America. . . . The distance traveled is extraordinary" (Monteon 1995:54–56).

The effects of capitalism and wage work for women on gender relations is also affected by the way women are incorporated into the economy. The global economy has been "restructuring" and moving new employment opportunities to developing countries. Rakowski (1995:287–288) suggests that, if industrial and agricultural change is incorporated into existing gender relations at the household level, capitalism may net little improvement in gender equality (as is true for much of Africa). On the other hand, capitalism can undermine male dominance at the household level (private patriarchy) if, as in the studies cited above, women's productive roles and incomes increase relative to men's.

The current global trend is toward the "feminization of employment." Increasingly, industrialization, capital accumulation, and the expansion of the service sector are based heavily on female labor (Moghadam 1995:20–22). There is a distinct movement away from previous import substitution industry, which mostly employed men, to export-oriented industrialization where workers are predominantly female, drawn from the subsistence economy (Blumberg 1995:4–5). So far, only a few African economies (a notable example is Mauritius) have been major beneficiaries of this process. But a major focus of current SAPs in Africa is to encourage African governments to abandon their frequently uncompetitive import substitution, parastatal industries and encourage both indigenous and foreign-owned export-oriented industries. If this strategy succeeds, the impact on African gender relations is likely to be profound.

We must acknowledge, however, that capitalism alone will not produce gender equality regardless of the work women do. Even if labor markets are free of gender discrimination, the benefits to women will continue to be limited if patriarchal gender expectations remain elsewhere in society, especially those that require women to bear the burden of reproduction and maintenance of human resources with little help from men. Such expectations prevent women from competing with men on equal terms. This is a major reason for the housewifization of women often attributed to capitalist development (see Mies 1986; Bennholdt-Thomsen 1988; von Werlhof 1988a, b; Elson 1992).[2] The patriarchal idea that the production of goods is separate from the production of people and that women's primary role is the latter while men's role is producer, creates, as Marshall (1994: 91) observes, "a fundamental relational asymmetry between women and men—actually between women and fully individuated, autonomous human beings."

The inequality of housework and child care can be changed by societal provisions of child care services for women who need them or by men's sharing housework responsibilities equally with women. Unfortunately, this will be difficult to achieve in Africa, just as it is in other regions of the world. In fact, in much of Africa, especially eastern and southern Africa, men often contribute little to household maintenance at all. Most men do not see daily household expenses, much less housework, as their obligation, and many men contribute little cash. This is another reason most African women see little applicability of the housewife role, with its idealization of a male breadwinner who financially supports his wife and children.

Capitalism and gender-neutral markets also cannot undo decades of patriarchal oppression and its effects on both men's and women's devaluation of women. This especially applies to uneducated peasant women who suffer the dual burdens of class as well as gender inequality. Oboler's (1985:320–321) study of the Nandi provides a good example of this from East Africa. Nandi women perceive that men have always owned everything and held all the power, so there is no break between the past and present. Nandi women also do not realize how their situation relative to men is deteriorating. They tend to focus instead on positive changes they see, such as the general improvement in material well-being, lower infant mortality, and some positive cultural changes (e.g., young men having more contact with children). In West Africa, Koon's (1988:13) study of a development project in West Cameroon revealed the prevalence of negative attitudes toward women and the need for education to change them.

> Both men and women regarded women, and the crops they grew, as low status and inferior to the social and economic position and activities of men. Women were thus regarded as ignorant, unwilling to change, and unable to learn unless forced. In addition, women are trained to be deferential to men. They are taught not to speak out, not to ask questions which may challenge or offend men, and not to request solutions to their problems. This training is particularly apparent among older women and often far less so with younger women who have had more education and experience outside the villages.

Capitalism is also limited in its ability to benefit women because— even if it does promote economic growth, break down the familial mode of production and patriarchal family, and create new economic opportunities for women, and so on—capitalism also promotes new forms of inequality based on class as well as gender. As Shivji (1992:49) observes, in Africa current liberal capitalist reforms mainly offer opportunities for those who have gotten rich through corruption, government positions and favors, speculation, and exploitation of workers and peasants. Only a radical change in governance and state policies and organized popular movements for equitable development can ensure that capitalism benefits more than just a few—women or men. After all, gender equality is not about an equal sharing of poverty and powerlessness but about empowering all people and improving their lives.

Finally, it may be necessary to acknowledge that efforts to promote gender equality and alter the sexual division of labor may be limited by the lack of economic development itself as well as by patriarchal resistance to change. Socialism, capitalism, delinking, or whatever economic system or strategy is pursued will have to face this structural reality. Croll (1986: 243–249) discusses this problem in the context of socialist societies ranging from the USSR and China to Cuba and Tanzania. In socialist societies, just as in capitalist societies, there is little change in the sexual division of labor. Attracting women into waged labor (or collective labor) occurs without enough concern for redefining or socializing women's reproductive and domestic roles. Instead, women's labor is intensified and subsidizes rural development programs. Part of the problem is that economies are too poor to provide social services to replace the unremunerated domestic work of women. Only in Cuba was the ideology of sharing stressed, with a family code that specified that men and women share domestic chores when both are employed. More typically, the sharing of domestic responsibilities in peasant households is shared by women of the household, the kin group, or the village. Nonetheless, it is still difficult to combine productive and reproductive tasks. Too often, because of patriarchal power and custom, most of the responsibility for household labor and reproduction continues to fall on women.

Perhaps the lesson here is that only when an economy is productive and rich enough, and women's labor outside the home more valuable than their role in social reproduction, are more of the costs of social reproduction likely to be assumed by the market or through public expenditures, thus freeing women from these tasks. If, as capitalism expands, the economy grows, women's education and training and jobs are likely to increase too. Women become more of a productive resource to their families and societies, and they become more marketable. To acquire the use of women's labor or for women to sell their labor, however, provisions for child care and housework must be made by families and/or societies. Since an expanding economy also leads to less agricultural employment for women initially, this can promote housewifization and more economic dependency among women, especially if alternative urban employment is unavailable; but in the long run female employment grows, as is evident all over the world. In research reported by Bloom and Brender (1993:9), for instance, female nonagricultural employment globally is growing, although rates vary from region to region because of both cultural and economic factors. Developed industrial nations lead the way with an average of 41 percent of females economically active in 1990, and the percentage working is likely to continue to grow. In developing countries women are only about 24 percent of the nonagricultural work force, but their share of industrial and service jobs is also expected to increase in response to both gains in education and lower fertility. Muslim countries report the lowest rates of female employment. One important finding is that growth in job opportunities for both sexes is the crucial element in whether or not the education of women increases their employment opportunities—or the commitment of society and the government in promoting more-equal opportunities for women.

## ▲  Notes

1. See Skolnick 1991:110–111; Safa 1986; Joekes 1987:136–137; Ward 1990: 14. Ironically perhaps, while capitalism plays a role in the creation of the housewife and male breadwinner dichotomy, evidence from industrial societies suggests that these dichotomous roles occur mainly in the early stages of development. Later stages of industrial development tend to reverse it as more wives find jobs in the growing service sector. The work force also becomes increasingly feminized as women work to meet rising costs of living and inadequate male wages. Declining birth rates and higher levels of female education are important as well (Skolnick 1991:11–12, 109).

2. Housewifization, as discussed in Chapter 1, refers to the sexual division of labor in which women do unpaid or poorly paid work. Men work for money and derive higher status for what they do. Men gain power over women because of their access to money, while women lose autonomy. Because child care and domestic work are assigned to women, their economic opportunities are limited. The best jobs are built around men's supporting women or women as secondary earners (see Bennholdt-Thomsen 1988).

# ▲ 3
# Women's Responses to Capitalist Development and Patriarchy

One contribution of feminist theory has been to expand our understanding of the common forms of oppression women are subject to all over the world regardless of their class, race, or region. As Jaggar (1983:77–78) writes,

> all women are subject to rape, to physical abuse from men in the home, and to sexual objectification and sexual harassment; all women are primarily responsible for housework, while all women who have children are responsible for the care of those children; and virtually all women who work in the market work in sex-segregated jobs. In all classes, women have less money, power, and leisure time than men.

We must not overlook, however, that there are also marked differences in women's experience of oppression. The reason is that such variables as race, class, or ethnicity frequently result in women's subjection to other forms of oppression besides sexism or may mitigate the extent of patriarchal oppression women encounter. Because women are situated differently within social structures, their responses to patriarchy and other forms of oppression are often as variable as their experiences are (see J. Smith 1994:28). For this reason we find that, despite the existence of patriarchy as a system of oppression, women may sometimes actually feel greater solidarity with their menfolk than with other women.

Moreover, since men share many common concerns with women, it is as much a mistake to assume that all men share a common interest in oppressing women as it is to assume that all women, because they are women, are similarly oppressed and experience a common sisterhood. The empirical reality of patriarchy is too complex to support such a simplistic view of women's oppression by patriarchy. This is not to deny the universality of women's second-class status and subordination to men or that feminism provides the ideological basis for consciousness raising and political activism on behalf of improving the status of women. I am suggesting, however, that some women are more oppressed than others and that some men are more oppressed than some women because of the other sources of inequality and exploitation to which they are subject. I am also suggesting that men can have their consciousness raised by feminism and oppose at least some patriarchal practices and attitudes. By the same token, there are women who uphold patriarchy. Unraveling such complexities and explaining them is one of the greatest challenges confronting feminist theory and research, as postmodernist feminists have made us more aware.

These issues are crucial in understanding Third World women, including African women, who are confronted with an array of oppressive structures, besides patriarchy, against which they must struggle. Goetz (1991: 152) observes that,

> while certain issues of sexist oppression may unite women cross-culturally, women of different nations within these broad alliances may be involved in struggles for racial justice or national liberation in which they will have to confront women from oppressor nations. Or third world women may struggle for freedom from personal oppression within the family while at the same time engaging in a common project with their menfolk to protect the integrity of their traditional economies.

Because the dominant feminist perspectives have been shaped largely by white, middle-class, First World women, who see gender inequality and the sexual division of labor as the source of their oppression, Western feminism is seen by some as having limited relevance to Third World women and their struggles. Liberal feminism, with its stress on equal rights and opportunities for women, has been castigated for focusing on gender discrimination while ignoring Third World women's main struggles with their communities and men against racism, poverty, and economic exploitation through imperialism (A. Russo 1991:308–309; Johnson-Odim 1991:315–318). Liberal feminism's emphasis on gender as the cause of women's inequality is seen by critics as part of a political agenda that reflects the interests of women who are already advantageously placed to benefit from new rights and opportunities. As some Third World feminists see it, liberal feminism would result in a few women entering the ranks of privileged (mostly white) males. This would better the lives of some women but basically would only "change the sex of the master" (Johnson-Odim 1991: 319; see also hooks 1993).

Some Third World women question the relevance to their own experience of feminism's focus on the conjugal relationship and women's dependency on men as the source of women's oppression. For many Third World women, the conjugal relationship is not the central one, and they are psychologically as well as economically often much less dependent on men than their Western, middle-class counterparts. Third World women also feel that feminism's emphasis on the sexual division of labor creates an artificial competition between men and women that underestimates their common interests in structuring the household to ensure survival (Goetz 1991:141).

The upshot of all of this is that feminist theory and social action to help women improve their lives must take into account not only the diverse forms of patriarchal oppression women face but the other sources of oppression women must contend with both from within their societies and from their society's place within the world system. For this reason there is a need for a diversity of feminisms responding to different women's needs (Johnson-Odim 1991; Cagatay et al. 1986). We must also realize that feminist struggle may not be best served by pitting women's interests against men's. That men sometimes oppress women is certainly true, but in many cases this is a response by men to their own struggles within oppressive social structures; achieving gender equality is impossible without the support of men and without changing these other oppressive structures.

For many African women, gender alone does not describe their oppression, nor is gender equality enough to end such oppression. As Pala Okeyo (1981) discusses, women need justice not only at the household level but also in the local, national, and world economic orders. Johnson-Odim (1991:316) adds that feminism for Third World women involves not only women's equal participation in society but a movement for social justice that is "inclusive of their entire communities" and addresses "the racism, economic exploitation, and imperialism against which they continue to struggle."

One reason liberal feminism in the West fails to address such oppressions as imperialism, classism, and racism is that this would require feminists to acknowledge that their own privileges are tied to the oppression of poor, nonwhite, and Third World women (A. Russo 1991:299–307). Indeed, liberal feminism is compatible with liberal capitalism and what some view as the paternalistic, women in development (WID) economic strategy in the Third World, which will be discussed in Chapter 4. Liberal feminism's emphasis on legal reforms and equal rights is not only the most acceptable version of feminism to the First World, it has also gained the most support among Third World feminist politicians, jurists, and academics. It was liberal feminism that inspired the UN Decade for Women, which won support from male-dominated governments all over the world. The reasons for this support are obvious. Liberal feminism's reformism is more politically acceptable because it leaves unchallenged the underlying structural causes of gender inequality and its relationship to other systems of oppression such as the inequitable world economic order and internal systems of social and political inequality (see Stamp 1989; Cagatay et al. 1986; Barrow 1985; Steady 1985).

Apfel-Marglin and Simon (1994:35–36) criticize the entire ideological underpinnings of the development of women feminist project, which, they claim, descends from Victorian colonial feminism. WID posits the white Western independent woman integrated into a commodified world as the norm. Rather than questioning the development process, WID identifies the barriers (i.e., tradition and social constraints) to women's access to the market. WID sees women as oppressed victims of societies in need of transformation to liberate women. If Third World women's self-perception is not one of an autonomous, independent self, but one embedded in kinship and other social bonds, such perceptions are invalidated. "Cognitive authority" belongs to the experts who know what women need to be "developed." Not surprisingly, the modern, developed individual/self with rights (to its own labor with the rights to sell it), equality, and autonomy is a reality created by and functional for industrial capitalism.

I agree with Apfel-Marglin and Simon that the feminist perspective is transformative and asserts that women should be treated as autonomous individuals. And indeed, the individual is a creation of Western capitalist society. This is not inherently dismissive of Third World women's self-perceptions of being embedded in relational structures as well. I maintain, however, that a feminism that does not assert women's fundamental right to dignity and personhood independent of traditional relational structures that allow men to control, abuse, or exploit women—even if women are socially conditioned to accept such structures—is not the answer. Moreover, we must deal realistically with the fact that global capitalism is hegemonic and that Third World men are largely the beneficiaries of the social, political, and economic changes under way. Third World women risk marginality, and feminists risk irrelevance, if they do not fight to assure women's rights and access to resources under the prevailing social conditions. In fact, empowering women to compete and become "integrated in development" will give women access to the institutional positions and authority that is arguably the only way women can challenge, modify, or transform capitalism and patriarchy.

## ▲ African Women's Issues

The criticisms of Western feminism caution us of the need to understand African women's problems and issues from their own perspective rather than superimposing ethnocentric biases drawn from the experiences of First World women and their cultures. We also need to recognize the diverse ways African women perceive and deal with women's issues and incorporate these into development programs and other reforms designed to help African women, rather than imposing Western strategies and solutions that are insensitive to deeply held cultural beliefs and practices. Too often, as Stamp (1991a:844–845) observes, African women have been treated as passive targets of oppressive practices and discrimination. This coincides with sexist ideologies that view women as inferior, passive, apolitical, privatized beings. In reality, women do react to and struggle against oppression, albeit from within the constraints imposed upon them.

It is important to realize that women's present status in African patriarchy is a product of precapitalist gender relations that were modified and distorted as African societies were incorporated into the world economy. Both gender ideology and gender relations that have subordinated women and relegated them to specific roles in the sexual division of labor reflect patriarchal power and the dynamics of underdeveloped capitalism, and they have been maintained through state policy and law. Women's resistance to oppression must be seen within this context. That is, as Stamp (1989:83) observes, women are resisting the appropriation of their labor and its products by the international commodity market through the agency of their husbands. Women thus confront a dual system of exploitation: the sex-gender system and underdeveloped capitalism.

How women perceive their interests and their ability to meet their needs varies by class, ethnicity, race, and religion. Therefore, in discussing women's interests, we need to be aware that, while women may share some gender interests in common because of their status as women, we must avoid false notions of homogeneity among women—or men for that matter (Molyneux 1985:232). At the same time, I agree with Goetz (1991: 146), who argues that feminism needs to remain critical (even at the risk of being accused of ethnocentrism) "by refusing to grant undue authority to cultural traditions that sustain sexist oppression. . . . Feminist ideology has always argued that the fact that women may accept oppression does not make oppression acceptable if women have little choice of roles in a male universe."[1] So, while respecting African women's perceptions of their needs and interests and examining how women cope with patriarchal and other sources of oppression linked to underdeveloped capitalism, we cannot abandon a critical scrutiny of the social factors shaping those perceptions and responses or of their consequences for gender relations and women's lives.

Women's constructions of women's interests develop out of their social positioning, including such attributes as caste, class, age, and race. One way to conceptualize how women attempt to meet their needs is to differentiate between "practical gender needs" and "strategic gender needs" (see Moser 1991). Practical gender needs are for resources to meet women's immediate and pressing needs for their families and are directly related to their struggle to survive (Elson 1992:36; Kettel 1995:251). Molyneux (1985:90) adds that practical gender needs are based on the conditions experienced by women within the sexual division of labor and specific social organization of their societies. The goal is not usually gender equality, nor do women challenge the prevailing forms of subordination they face, even though their practical needs arise from them. Strategic gender needs are oriented to lessening women's subordination to men, promoting gender equality, and changing the patriarchal organization of society. These may include the abolition of the sexual division of labor, alleviation of women's burden of child care and housework, the elimination of institutional sexism (e.g., discriminatory property rights and access to resources), political equality, reproductive freedom, and measures to end male violence against women (Molyneux 1985:232–233; Elson 1992:36). Strategic gender needs, in contrast to practical gender needs, require a feminist consciousness in order to struggle for them. They also require women's organizations and political activism. State intervention alone cannot achieve women's strategic gender needs (Molyneux 1985: 89–90).

There are numerous studies that provide us with good indications of what African women perceive their needs to be. In general, African women do not identify with the private versus public dichotomy so characteristic of some Western feminist thinking. Most African women see themselves as active in both production and reproduction, which are interwoven in their lives. In reality, because of the labor intensity of African agriculture, women's activities in the reproduction of labor are as vital to production as are their roles in actual cultivation (Davison 1988b:7–8). Obbo (1986:193) claims that most African women share at least two specific goals: (1) to establish their own economic and social position, eroded by colonialism; and (2) to protect themselves against material and status vulnerability from divorce, widowhood, or singlehood. This, of course, leads to different strategies among women on how best to meet their needs in the context of the often diverse circumstances of their lives.

One of the factors conditioning women's responses to and perceptions of patriarchy are sexist ideologies and negative views of women that are held by men and women alike. Such ideas rationalize female inferiority and gender inequality and thus impede the development of the feminist consciousness necessary for women to develop effective ways to meet their strategic gender needs. These ideologies have their material basis in the familial mode of production and are institutionalized in customary or traditional law. Referring to Kenya (but this is true elsewhere in Africa), House-Midambo (1990:108) remarks that "the ideology of African traditional law has provided the cornerstone for the entrenchment of patriarchal institutions . . . which have led to relations of dominance based on gender." Notions of tradition and family values are readily appealed to in Africa (as well as other places in the world) to sanctify patriarchal gender relations and the sexual division of labor that guarantees male control and superiority over women. We must understand, however, that the appeal to tradition is not an effort to preserve a distant past but modern forms of relationships that were transformed by the world economy, often originating during the colonial period (see Smith 1994; Stamp 1991a, b).

African women often see the necessity of struggling for their rights and opportunities within the constraints imposed by such traditions. This is partly explained by women's internalization of the ideology of patriarchal tradition as "timeless and absolute" (Stamp 1991a:842). For instance, in her study of women traders in Lusaka, Zambia, Schuster (1982: 122–123) found that women accepted the view that wives must subordinate themselves to their husbands, and all wanted their daughters to have wifely virtues and responsibilities. Yet at the same time, they believed marriage needs drastic reform and traditional customs produce great suffering for women. Women's attitudes also reflect their lack of education about their legal rights or lack of resources to use the law to protect them. Moreover, in many cases, the state does little to enforce the laws that do exist (Parpart 1988:218–219; Stamp 1991a:841–842).

While legal gender equality remains a major strategic gender issue in much of Africa, women also confront inequality in the household. Here, too, tradition becomes a means of perpetuating male privilege and a highly inequitable sexual division of labor. In Nkwi's (1987) study of married women in Yaounde, Cameroon, for example, he found only three of 152 families that were egalitarian. Few men shared housework with their wives, and most women said their husbands would not even discuss the issue of equality. Women accepted their double work load as wife-mother and as workers outside the home. Farming, marketing, and unpaid work in family artisanal enterprises were seen as extensions of their basic female roles.

Africa's worsening economic crisis is in some cases provoking a conservative backlash against even minor efforts to promote greater gender equality. Molokomme (1991) writes about the negative reactions from some politically powerful men to recent efforts in Botswana to create a women's research group. The female group participants were branded as "unattractive, frustrated women," and propaganda about "the crisis of social disintegration" taking place in society and women's being "the backbone of society" were used to counter any real efforts on behalf of women. Many people, including women, accept women's subordination and are hostile to the idea of equality of men and women.

Middle-class educated women are affected as well as poor women by efforts to preserve men's privileges at women's expense during economic hard times. In her highly publicized case of blatant gender discrimination in Tanzania, Mukarasi (1991) discusses how she lost her job as Manpower Development and Administrative Manager of a parastatal where she had worked for ten years. She was the only woman manager at the firm and the only manager to lose her job as a result of World Bank–International Monetary Fund (IMF) austerity measures. Among the reasons she cited for her job loss were stereotypes about women as weak and less capable than men of managerial or other high-status positions, and notions of "the good woman–good wife" as docile and passive; Mukarasi was faulted also for having the temerity to leave her husband.

Negative views of women are also reflected in scapegoating and violence toward women and in the treatment of women as legal minors under male control, especially in eastern and southern Africa. Ampofo (1993: 108) reports that in Ghana, for instance, scapegoating market women for economic problems is common and accepted even by many women, as is rape, wife beating, and sexual exploitation. Such treatment reflects a view of women as the "property of men, to be coerced, dominated, and brutalized." In Tanzania, a Women's Crisis Centre opened in 1991 in Dar es Salaam to deal with violence against women, often accepted and justified under customary law. In such countries as Namibia, Zimbabwe, and South Africa, the treatment of women as minors and discrimination against them are routine despite constitutional ideals about the equality of all citizens (see Gawanas 1993; COSATU 1992; Batezat and Mwalo 1989; Dorsey 1993).

Women's reluctance to challenge patriarchal institutions directly is a result mainly of their political and economic vulnerability, and understandable reluctance to incite male anger and retaliation. Also, as discussed earlier, women often see males, especially kin, as their main source of security under the conditions created by underdeveloped capitalism. For these reasons, Western feminism often has little appeal, especially to poorer classes of women. As Joan Harris (1985:30–31) notes in her study of Kenyan women's groups, women must struggle against men's views of women as only wives, mothers, or food gatherers. Moreover, many rural and urban women are "totally dependent economically and psychologically on their husbands." For these reasons, women, when they do organize, are more likely to be women's rights activists than feminists and to see their activities as community work. Lack of education compounds women's inability to work for their interests outside of socially acceptable parameters or to develop the feminist consciousness necessary to struggle for women's strategic gender needs rather than just practical gender needs, as discussed earlier.

Stamp (1989:84) characterizes women's responses to patriarchy as consistent with their precapitalist role in the village. Women use the discourse of family solidarity and welfare to struggle for their rights and to defuse male fears of losing their position as head of the family. She adds that by appealing to women's rights and responsibilities as wives and mothers, women attempt to overcome patriarchal interpretations of tradition that deny women their rights and limit their access to resources. Raising strategic gender issues (such as legal rights and property rights) often provokes a sexist backlash. Anything perceived as feminist is associated with imperialism, and anti-imperialism becomes associated with right-wing, antidemocratic, and sexist political positions. Feminism is also labeled as elitist and appealing only to the minority of educated women (Stamp 1991a:827–833, 842). Such negative ideological propaganda obviously makes it difficult for formal feminist organizations to gain strength or have much political impact.

Despite the ideological and practical constraints women face, they do have a keen sense of their interests and the patriarchal system that oppresses them. They also have definite ideas of how their needs can be met within the parameters set by the familial mode of production and underdeveloped capitalism. In her study of poor rural women's groups in Mali and Senegal, for instance, Cloud (1986) found that practical gender needs related to women's food-producing activities were primary. That is, women wanted relief from their enormous work load. Specifically, technological aids such as power mills for grinding millet, water pumps, and animal traction for plows were mentioned. They also wanted help with their gardens in the form of better seeds and drip irrigation, help with food preservation (e.g., smoking fish, drying fruit), and help with small animal husbandry (e.g., disease control, nutrition). Women also requested access to training, more opportunities to earn money, and improved literacy and health information. Palmer (1991:25–26) adds that women do not want to be restricted to food crop production; most want to grow export and industrial crops in their own right (i.e., not under male control). Where they appear to want to grow only food crops, this is due to women's fear of losing control of resources to men if they change (i.e., men may take over the crop or the income from it). In Dunbar's (1983:1) study of rural women in Niger, women were asked what their most important needs were. Here, too, help with agriculture and health improvement was important, but the Niger women also indirectly criticized the sexual division of labor and male control over women. For instance, the women expressed a desire for more help from men with maintenance of the household and acceptance from their husbands of women's need to be away from home for training as community development specialists and midwives. Dunbar's findings demonstrate how women tend to strive primarily to meet practical gender needs necessary for them to help their communities and families without challenging the patriarchal system directly. Some women are willing to express more-radical views, however. In Zimbabwe's 1982 Report on the Situation of Women, 99 percent of women wanted an end to the prevailing land tenure system and control over their own land (Batezat and Mwalo 1989:10).

While most poor rural women do not challenge their place within patriarchy, many women are not afraid to criticize men. Staudt (1987:206–207) reports, for example, that there are some common complaints that African women have about men: (1) women work while men sit around telling them what to do; (2) women carry heavy loads (e.g., tools, water, wood, children) while men carry nothing; (3) men do not support their families—they drink and take other women and take women's money for themselves. Staudt adds that most women seek to deal with these problems individually rather than collectively, that is, through organized women's groups or political movements.

A major individualist strategy for women is to acquire property and income of their own independent of husbands. Through systems originating in precapitalist lineage systems, many women—though with little access to the income or property of their husbands—do, especially in West Africa, have rights to income from their own crops and enterprises, such as trade. Avoiding economic dependency by participating in the labor force is "deep-rooted and central to [a woman's] well-being" (Lewis 1982:273). Patriarchy and underdeveloped capitalism have both created conditions that limit women's abilities to acquire skills or other resources necessary to compete on equal terms with men. The results are that women usually sell in the marketplace the skills or products they normally provide in the home (e.g., sex, nursing, teaching, food, clothing, knitting, vegetables, beer) while men have more options and access to more-lucrative jobs such as electrician, auto mechanic, plumber, delivery man. Moreover, men are not limited by the child care and domestic responsibilities of women (Nelson 1988:197–198). There are many examples of women's entrepreneurial pursuits that the pressures of patriarchy and underdeveloped capitalism have generated. While some African women have bought or been given land, most women are losing secure rights to land. Davison (1988b:5–6) discusses how many women are trying to maintain some measure of control in agriculture by moving into food processing and beer brewing. Discrimination against women and lack of opportunity in the formal economy compel many others to pursue self-employment, often through trade and various "income-generating projects."

Most of this self-employment is in micro-small enterprises and results in only marginal incomes for women, but a minority of women have prospered and even moved into large-scale business enterprises. Peil (1981: 132) writes that women traders in urban West Africa are investing in the lucrative housing market, often selling or renting to local elites or expatriates. Trading is also a route to economic independence and wealth for Ghanaian women, as described by Robertson (1984), among others. In East Africa, Kenya's Kikuyu women traders are especially successful in running businesses of their own independent of men. To ensure that their husbands will not appropriate their assets, as many do, many of these business women are choosing to avoid formal marriage (Parkin 1978:128–131, 255). In his study of Mathare, a large slum settlement in Nairobi, Nelson (1988:186–190) found that most women were earning money by brewing and selling beer (*buzaa*) and produce, but as much as 50 percent of the housing in Mathare (often rental) was owned by women as well. In Kisangani, Zaire, some women are becoming very successful in commerce. Many of Kisangani's wealthier women traders are diversifying their business holdings and avoiding marriage or using other strategies to keep their holdings and profits out of the reach of their husbands who, as "heads of households," can seize women's assets (MacGaffey 1986, 1988).

Structural adjustment reforms are another source of economic pressure to which women are responding through self-employment. In this instance, male advantages in the wage economy have worked against them since wage cuts, layoffs, and inflation have greatly lessened the earning power of many employed men. In Tanzania, urban women's informal sector businesses (*miradi*) are the main source of income in many households, often as much as 90 percent. An estimated two-thirds of women in Dar es Salaam are now self-employed, often in farming for family consumption and sale or in trading activities. Their husbands sometimes provide the start-up capital, but this is usually their only contribution to their wives' businesses. Although most of the miradi are small-scale enterprises, some women are moving for the first time into such large-scale, formal enterprises as shipping companies, textile mills, bakeries, and export-import businesses (Tripp 1991:16–24, 170–171).

Pursuing advantageous relationships with men is another individualist strategy of women. These can range from selling or using sex, marriage, or some kind of business partnership. In Nelson's (1988:188) study of women in Mathare, sex and beer selling were major sources of income for poor women—either casual sex or with lovers ("town *bwanas*"). MacGaffey (1986, 1988) and Dinan (1983) find that many women become "sugar girls" or mistresses as a means of acquiring capital to invest in business. Obbo (1986:189) discusses the sometimes fierce competition among women for husbands, lovers, and protectors. Even elite women's success often depends on their relationship to men (e.g., for access to credit, labor, income, or business opportunities). Although most elite women have jobs or pursue their own business ventures, marriage to rich men is the only means most women have of pursuing the dependent housewife role extolled in the West.

Islam creates some exceptions to the above generalizations. Because in so many African ethnic groups women have to provide much if not all of their own support, some women prefer to marry Muslims because Islam requires men to support their wives (Boserup 1986:42–43). Hausa women in West Africa find benefits in the practice of purdah, which secludes women at home. Purdah is practiced by the wealthy; therefore it becomes a status symbol for women and reduces the heavy work load assumed by most women. Moreover, some Hausa women manage to run businesses from their homes, using their children to run errands and carry on trade for them outside the home. Such enterprises have produced significant income for women and their families (Schildkrout 1982).

In some respects, economic independence or dependence is chosen by women based on a rational assessment of their options. Under some circumstances women find that economic dependence is in fact preferable to independence. As Roberts (1988) convincingly argues, if men's resources and income are much greater than women's, economic dependency may benefit women more than earning on their own (especially if there is pervasive discrimination against women). This suggests that the more capitalism and patriarchy are skewed in favor of men (i.e., wealth and income are a male monopoly), the more African women may opt for dependence and subordination to men as the price for access to male-controlled resources.

There is already some evidence for this. As mentioned, the dependent housewife role is mainly found in marriages where women have wealthy husbands. Even in Ghana, where female independence through trade is a long-established practice, capitalism and patriarchy are eroding the economic independence of many women. As capitalism expands, well-capitalized formal sector businesses begin undercutting small, less efficient businesses (e.g., chain stores vs. Mom and Pop stores). These bigger businesses are usually owned by men, and many women traders are beginning to abandon their "business ghettos" (forced upon them by patriarchal stereotypes and the sexual division of labor) and "the uncertainties of material independence" for economic dependence on a man (Robertson 1984: 224). Women are also more willing to accept economic dependence and subordination to men if, as among some tea-growing families in Kericho, Kenya, wives feel they and their families are benefiting from such arrangements, that is, women feel they are fairly compensated for their labor and men provide for their family's needs (von Bulow and Sorenson 1993: 48–49).

Women's effort to improve their status or meet their needs individually has mixed consequences. First, it does encourage female enterprise as women seek to own their own property, businesses, and income safe from expropriation by their husbands or other male relatives (see Obbo 1986:

179). Second, because most resources are owned or controlled by men, women's access to resources often depends on their relationship to men. This leads to a competition among women for men or resources controlled by men—for example, wives versus girlfriends, sisters versus wives, clans-women versus nonclanswomen, rich women versus poor women. Obbo (1986:187–188) describes the relationship between many men and women as a form of patron-client relationship through marriage. Competition for elite men is so intense that women see other women as rivals rather than allies. Third, because powerful men are often the best way for women to gain resources, hypergamy and willing subordination to men is encouraged (see Bujra 1986; Pankhurst and Jacobs 1988:212). Marriage to a success-ful man is often the key to many a woman's own entrepreneurial success. Obbo (1986:187) points out, for instance, that elite women often manage their husband's businesses and have their own businesses as well. They also have more access to credit and loans, a point Tripp (1991:19) makes as well.

Mukurasi's battle for her job in Tanzania is instructive on the vulner-ability of women working as individuals to advance themselves in the face of institutionalized patriarchy. Although she eventually got her job back, Mukurasi (1991:112–113) discovered how difficult it is for women to fight institutionalized patriarchy alone.

> When a woman decides to break the chains of her oppression, victimiza-tion and degradation, . . . she discovers that she is not fighting against the actions of the individual husband or employer. She discovers that she is fighting against a significant portion of the patriarchal superstructure in which men gang up together and use their positions against her as a sin-gle women in order to destroy her.

## ▲ Women's Organizations

While many African women are attempting to improve their lives through individual action, African women have joined in a multitude of national as well as grassroots organizations. In fact, according to Staudt (1988:203), Africa has the most female solidarity organizations in the world. The vast majority of these, as mentioned above, are designed to deal with issues of community or family welfare—that is, practical gender needs. While some women's organizations seek genuine political and economic empowerment for women, most do not.

There are several major reasons for women's political weakness. Iron-ically, women played an active role in the independence struggle in many countries, but after independence, "the woman question" and women them-selves were for the most part relegated to the periphery of public concern

and to the "private sphere" (Staudt 1988:202–203). Women hold few decisionmaking positions in African states, and "their gains from pressuring
states have been minimal," concludes Parpart and Staudt (1989:8).[2] National women's organizations are typically subordinated to male-dominated states and political parties, and their agendas largely reflect the concerns of elite women rather than the poor, especially the rural poor.
Another problem is the heavy work and domestic demands on women's
time along with male hostility and resistance to women voting for women,
holding leadership positions, or running for office (see Nzomo and Kibwana 1993; Tripp 1991). Lastly, the obvious male bias in legal rights, office holding, and distribution of resources show that the state is typically
more responsive to male concerns than to those of women.

These factors plus the corruption and lack of accountability of African
governance in general have resulted in many women's alienation from formal politics. Consequently, many women are bypassing the state (and formal politics) and seeking to avoid "the rapacious, badly-run African bureaucracies" (Parpart 1988:220–221). They are concentrating instead on
economic survival, and in Africa that increasingly means reliance on individual effort (often in alliance with men or in the parallel economy), one's
children, or grassroots self-help organizations. In many cases, women
avoid collective action with women for political or economic ends, relying
instead on the indirect influence they have in their families, often through
their fathers, sons, brothers, or husbands. An example is in Sudan, where
most women are illiterate and have very limited roles in public life. "Even
educated and employed women are satisfied with a low profile of participation in the development of the country," reports Badri (1990:112).
Wealthy women are absorbed in creating a "false model of luxurious life"
and show little interest in formal public life; they participate in few organizations. Most middle-class women do not participate in the national
women's organization because of its association with the ruling regime to
which they are opposed; moreover, the major cultural pressures on such
women are to submit to male "protection," please men, and help the family's prestige while minimizing contact with nonkin women (Badri
1990:110–112).

Increasingly, however, women are banding together to promote common interests and meet their needs. Despite their limitations to date,
women's groups have been instrumental in promoting many advances
African women have made since independence (see J. Harris 1985:30).
And as most African economies have stagnated and the state has been
forced to cut back on providing many basic services and resources,
women's groups are the key not only to women's advancement and empowerment but to the survival of their families and communities as well.

There are two main types of women's groups in Africa. One is national women's organizations and the other is grassroots, often local, women's groups. Typically, national organizations are dominated by educated, elite women from urban areas, and their agendas. While on the surface class-neutral and focused on promoting women's rights, the activities of national women's organizations center largely on issues important to more-elite women, such as reform of marriage and divorce laws or maternity leave. They have also focused primarily on community welfare activities and women's practical gender needs, although some strategic gender needs are sometimes addressed as well. Most attempt to avoid association with feminism, which is often branded as imperialist and elitist. National women's organizations often have limited autonomy and invite cynicism because of their close ties to the ruling party and the state.[3]

Nigeria is a good example of the origins and limited agendas of many African women's organizations. Many of Nigeria's women's groups have their roots in the colonial period and were modeled on Western ladies' associations. They supported charitable efforts and held classes for women, often to teach them gender-appropriate homemaking skills. After independence, they were used by the government to promote nation building and "good citizenship" and promote such welfare activities as inoculation and health campaigns, environmental cleanups, female education, day care for working mothers, and assistance for orphans and the handicapped (Enabulele 1985).

Kenya's national women's organizations, Maendeleo ya Wanawake (MYWO) and (to a lesser extent) the National Council of Women of Kenya (NCWK), have been the subjects of considerable critical scrutiny. They provide a useful case study of both the possibilities and limitations of such groups as agents for empowerment of African women. MYWO and other women's clubs were formed during the colonial period with the encouragement of the colonialists, some say to work against Mau Mau and the nationalist movement in general. After independence MYWO and other women's groups became "tools of male politicians"—providing entertainment, dancing, cooking, votes, and praise for the ruling party, all roles subordinate to the men. Any direct effort to be involved in politics was frowned upon (Kabira and Nzioki 1993:41, 72–73). MYWO is still considered to be largely an elite women's organization despite the fact that it has many branches in the rural areas and does publicly speak to issues such as women's access to land and women's rights. Its main emphasis remains on social welfare issues and a stereotypic notion of women as homemakers (Nzomo 1989:10–11). Obbo (1980:159–160) contends that MYWO is in fact an obstacle to equality, because its elite leaders and members are mainly interested in preserving their own status and marriages to elite men. It has even opposed policies that would help many women. For instance, MYWO opposed the 1976 Marriage Bill that would require men to support their children, allow women to own and sell property, punish anyone forcing a man or woman to marry, and punish adulterers with up to six months in jail. In 1971 MYWO also advocated limiting the purchase of contraceptives by married women (apparently to counter extramarital sex).

More recently, MYWO has taken a stronger public stand on women's rights and rural development issues, but even this has been criticized as largely window dressing. Bujra (1986:136) charges that the true class purpose of MYWO is not development for women, but "to press women to work harder and longer in order that they, the petty bourgeoisie, might live better." Similarly, Staudt (1987:204–205) maintains that MYWO's support for equitable laws and such reforms as equal pay, maternity leave, child care, or marriage and divorce laws would mainly benefit elite women. Truly transformative positions that challenge male privilege and female oppression or that would result in redistribution of societal wealth and power from the elites to the poor are not strongly pursued. MYWO "expresses public concern" over issues like male authority and rural women's labor burden, but group political activities deal with issues that reflect class and gender ideological issues that stress the primacy of female domesticity and would "neither transform gender realities nor affect the mass of ordinary women." Moreover, "should the wealthier women take up this redistributive issue in Kenya's zero-sum politics, more for other women would mean less for themselves. Their economic stakes lie more in their households than in solidarity with other women" (Staudt 1987:203–204).

Stamp (1991a) and Kabira and Nzioki (1993:72–73) agree that MYWO has done little to empower women, especially rural women, or to improve their status in society. It has been further compromised by a leadership scandal in 1986 that resulted in a government takeover of the organization. In 1987 MYWO was placed under the Kenya African National Union (KANU), the ruling party, and in 1989 male politicians took over its elections, "ensuring that their relatives and allies were nominated to leadership positions" (Stamp 1991a:831). Although this arrangement did not work out, MYWO's autonomy and willingness to press for women's strategic gender interests is still in doubt (Kabira and Nzioki 1993:72–73). As Stamp (1991a:832) observes, MYWO has received government support because "it espoused Kenya's conservative development ideology and eschewed feminist rhetoric."

The NCWK has also been labeled by some as elitist, but it appears to be more willing to champion significant gender issues that would benefit ordinary Kenyan women. NCWK's leadership comprises Kenya's more-educated and professional elite women who take what the Kenyan media term a "women's lib" position on issues (Stamp 1991a:830–831). NCWK is weaker and has less government support as a result of its stand on issues. As Nzomo (1989:11) remarks, NCWK is "the only local NGO [nongovernmental organization] that has attempted to take a position on national issues and make demands for legislative changes on issues where women's rights are adversely affected."

It is not just elitism or class interest alone that compromises the effectiveness or dictates the agendas of women's organizations in Africa. As Nzomo (1989:11) notes, groups that attempt to go beyond what male-dominated governments view as reasonable demands on policies or laws will find themselves deliberately weakened by a lack of government support or influence over decisionmakers. Until women have more power, as officeholders and ministers in the political system, it will be difficult for women's groups not to be the "focus of other people's agendas" rather than started by and controlled by women to meet their own needs (Kabira and Nzioki 1993:44). Or when they do have the temerity to address significant gender issues, too often they are defeated. As Nzomo (1989:15) observes, the Kenyan government, like governments elsewhere in Africa, does not perceive the women's movement to be important for the regime's survival; therefore, there is little to be lost by ignoring women's demands.

Despite these problems, some national women's organizations are becoming more political and feminist, and achieving some successes. In 1991 in Lusaka, Zambia, the National Women's Lobby, composed mainly of lawyers and other well-educated, middle-class women, was formed. It has a very feminist agenda, according to Liatto-Katundo (1993:79–81). The Lobby calls for equal access for women to education in all subjects, male paternity leave and child care involvement, more participation of women in politics, equal access for women to land and loans in their own right, equal access to employment on the basis of merit and the same perks as men, repeal of all discriminatory laws, and a Woman's Bureau in the president's office. In 1992 in Kenya, a record six women were elected to Parliament, many of them members of MYWO and/or NCWK and backed by another women's group, the National Committee on the Status of Women (NCSW). NCSW's agenda is to increase women's political participation and officeholding, eliminate all discriminatory laws that perpetuate women's subordinate status, mainstream gender issues in political party documents (e.g., constitutions and manifestos), and sensitize both men and women to issues of gender equity (see Nzomo and Kibwana 1993).

House-Midamba (1990:120–121) points to some of the successes and failures of women's activism in Kenya. Women have been able to influence elite politicians to enact laws beneficial to at least some women—for example, maternity leave, equal rights provisions in the Constitution, the right to vote, and the Law of Succession. The Law of Succession was passed in Kenya in 1972 and gives women the right to inherit property that previously would have automatically gone to male relatives. Failures seem to be greater than successes, however. The government did not put the Law of Succession into effect until 1981 and even now only weakly enforces it. The Law of Marriage and Divorce bill has been defeated twice. Women failed to overturn the discriminatory Housing Allowance Law (that denies housing allowances to married women in public service) or the Employment of Women, Young Persons, and Children's Act.

National women's organizations, despite the limitations discussed above, can be beneficial to women and their communities. And by encouraging women to voice their concerns and get involved in community affairs, women long subordinated and silenced can empower themselves, as the following account of Ghana's women's movement shows. Nana Konadu Agyeman Rawlings, wife of Ghana's president Jerry Rawlings, was interviewed about Ghana's 31st December Women's Movement. The organization was started by elite women, including university women, in 1981–1982. In the beginning it very much reflected an elite, "intellectual perspective," Rawlings admits. The group realized eventually that it needed to go to ordinary women to find out "what they wanted." They found that women wanted a serious group that could stand up and get things done. Most women were primarily interested in meeting their practical gender needs; they wanted things like access to water and the means to improve life for their children. Their main objective was to earn money through income-generating projects to help their families and communities, but some strategic gender needs were addressed as well. The organization wanted to promote the "total development of women"—economically, socially, politically, and culturally. To meet their objectives, the women learned they had to be political, but politics took on a new meaning. As Rawlings discussed, the women were encouraged to view politics as how you run your everyday life rather than as the domain of men sitting in an office, wearing beards and suits. Regarding politics as a male domain is a "patriarchal myth" that keeps many women from participating. When politics was constructed as an activity relevant to women's everyday lives, they realized they could participate and even confront male politicians with their concerns. Women were encouraged to be the first to be involved in local community activities so they could be part of the decisionmaking and be identified as people who cared about their community. Government policies were explained to the women so they could see how they affected them and their children. Such efforts "emboldened" the women and gave them self-esteem and the confidence to speak in public. In the beginning, says Rawlings, you could not even get women to come to rallies, much less to speak. "Now we can't stop them from talking." Women are now running for and winning elections to village and district assemblies. They won on their own merit "because their communities knew who they were" and how they had helped their communities. Some of the women are even running in parliamentary elections, although there are still relatively few women elected (nineteen in 1992) (Novicki 1995).

## ▲ Grassroots Women's Groups

The typical weakness and elitism of national women's organizations and their failure to effectively address the needs of poor women is one reason that a multitude of women's grassroots organizations have been spawned throughout Africa. The major reason for these groups, however, is economic necessity. As underdeveloped capitalism slips into greater crisis, the private economy, the state, and the aid and development community have all failed to meet the needs of the poor. Many Africans are no better off or even worse off than they were at independence. While many men are also suffering from Africa's economic and political malaise and from structural adjustment reform efforts, women are the most vulnerable group, the poorest of the poor, and the most neglected by those in control of economic resources. As Kabira and Nzioki (1993:93) observe, increasingly "women see themselves as the only source of power for their own advancement."

Many grassroots women's groups are self-help groups oriented toward income-generating activities. In Kenya, ideologies of *harambee* (community self-help) or traditional family values (women's economic activities are for the benefit of their homes and children) are used by women to legitimate their efforts on their own behalf. In some self-help groups women pool resources to reduce their work load, invest in savings societies, or invest in cooperative business ventures. Their goal is to accumulate capital for themselves and a measure of economic independence from husbands who would otherwise appropriate their wives' labor and product (Stamp 1986:41–42). Davison (1988c:172) discusses agricultural cooperatives and other self-help groups in Kenya that are raising capital to purchase or lease land for food production in light of the difficulty women have in securing title or access to land as individuals. Kabira and Nzioki (1993:62–64) point out that groups are the only way for most women to get power because husbands have no power over the group as they have over women as wives. Realizing this, many men oppose women's groups because male control over land is the main avenue men have for controlling their wives. Group solidarity also builds women's self-confidence, another threat to male dominance.

In some cases, women's group pressure is a way for women to change government development policies that discriminate against them. In one instance in Kenya, women farmers banded together to get the Kenya Tea Development Authority to change its policies to ensure that women got part of the tea bonus previously given only to men. Although women were doing much of the work, the money was being spent by the men on themselves (Davison 1988c:168). In Zimbabwe, women married to Master Farmers in land resettlement areas are beginning to demand money from the sale of cash crops, previously going only to their husbands (Batezat and Mwalo 1989:15). Professional groups, such as African women's business groups, are pressuring governments to safeguard their interests and to fight against the tendency to stereotype and relegate women entrepreneurs to income-generating projects and dependence on donor aid ("Fallacy . . ." 1993).

On the economic front, women's cooperatives have launched notable successful farming and business enterprises. In Cameroon, for example, corn mill societies have been highly successful. The co-op movement began in the 1950s with fifteen mills loaned to village women. Societies formed with members paying a monthly fee to use the mill. As more villages participated, more mills were purchased. Eventually there were over two hundred societies with eighteen thousand members. The societies expanded their activities—women held classes in cooking, soap making, child care, and nutrition. They then branched out into brick making and bamboo used to make a meeting hall. Fencing was bought to protect members' gardens. The Department of Agriculture provided improved corn seed for better harvests. The women began contour farming, poultry schemes, reforestation, and water storage projects. A co-op store was established and stocked with imported items; this led to several additional stores with women raising the capital on their own (Stamp 1989:73). In Burkina Faso, the Six S Association is similar. There are over five thousand affiliate groups in Burkina alone; 60 percent are headed by women. Six S Associations have now spread to five neighboring countries and are the fastest growing organizations on the continent ("People Power . . ." 1992). Even in war-torn, poverty-stricken Mozambique, women's co-ops have launched successful enterprises. The almost all-female, eleven thousand–member General Union of Cooperatives (UGC) has built 210 farm cooperatives that supply most of Maputo's fruit and vegetables. Recent privatization reforms have given the UGC new opportunities for economic advancement of its members. The UGC assisted 95 percent of its members to secure land titles. With partial World Bank financing, the co-ops have now diversified and invested in poultry farming. They have become the leading supplier of day-old chicks to nearly all co-ops and private poultry farmers in Maputo. Women of the co-ops were also among the first poor women farmers to open their own bank accounts, a major advance for women unused to having economic assets of their own. Co-op women are also breaking gender stereotypes by training for such nontraditional jobs as electrician and mason. In another first, the UGC has built over one hundred houses for its members. Because of the empowering nature of these activities for women, the number and status of UGC women leaders in Mozambique is growing (Lima 1994).

In Tanzania, mostly informal rotating savings associations are making it possible for women to invest in businesses, projects, school and health costs, and home improvements (Tripp 1991:26–27). The susu-credit system in Ghana helps mostly informal sector women get credit (Gabianu 1990), and in Zimbabwe there are over ten thousand savings clubs with more than fifty thousand members, 97 percent of them women (Safilios-Rothschild 1990:104). Many women's savings associations provide credit for women farmers, as in Cameroon (Guyer 1984:123) and in The Gambia. The Gambia's women's credit scheme WISDOM (Women in Service Development Organization Management) has sixty thousand members. Its focus is on women in farming and in the informal sector. Along with credit, it provides political education and training so members can influence official policy. Among the enterprises the credit system has helped fund are the selling of crops and processed food, soap and shoe making, running large canteens, and handicrafts. WISDOM has also provided women with labor-saving devices for seeding, milling, and weeding and with implements such as ox carts. Women's rights materials are used to teach literacy, and marketing skills are being taught to help women link their new enterprises with larger commercial agricultural and horticultural outlets (Senghore and Bojang-Sissoho 1994).

Women's realization of the need to economically empower themselves has also produced some exciting entrepreneurial results in Kenya among both urban and rural women. As Kabira and Nzioki (1993:86) put it, women are moving from buying utensils to buying and controlling resources. In Nairobi, women in the Mukuru-Kaiyaba Women's Group began growing vegetables on a ten-acre wasteland owned by Kenya Railways; soon they expanded. Each member got food for her family, while the surplus was sold. Next, they cleared land next to the Ngong River for irrigation. They dammed and fenced off an area of the river and stocked it with fish, and plan to charge entrance fees and open the area to fishermen (Stamp 1989:73). Also in Nairobi, urban farming is an important source of food, income, and investment capital for women. While much of the crop is used to feed their families, some women open restaurants or market stalls, while others have even managed by working together to start lucrative businesses and eventually move into formal sector enterprises (Freeman 1993:9–15). Buying land is a high priority for many rural groups such as the Nyakinyua Women's Groups, and in Thika Township women formed a company with over one thousand members and bought a coffee farm. The business is prospering and all the directors are women. In Turkana District, four women, with help from a Danish development agency,

formed a women's group that started a bakery; they made their own bricks
and ovens. The business has expanded into selling sun-dried fish and
handicrafts. The group has also used its profits to buy land on which they
built a women's center, a bakery-duka, an office, and a butchery. They
have also started a block-making factory, a catering business, a water-sell-
ing kiosk, an educational program, and a training center. The center is
breaking stereotypes about the sexual division of labor by teaching women
carpentry, masonry, plumbing, and accounting—traditional male activities
(Kabira and Nzioki 1993:57–58).

Dei's study in Ghana reveals how women's initial efforts to meet their
practical gender needs can lead to women's empowerment, which, in turn,
can be the impetus for more-fundamental reforms in gender relations. In
the early 1980s, in response to Ghana's growing economic crisis, a group
of village women in Ayirebi went to the local chief to get "stool land" for
a rice farm. The farm's success gave the women the resources to contribute
to community projects. This gave the women more community respect and
political power, and organization leaders were increasingly consulted by
the chief on other development projects. The economic success of the
women and their newfound respect has become a model for other women
in launching their own economic ventures. By 1989 there were over
ninety-five women in the group. They were so successful that they have
become more self-confident and bolder in pursuing their interests as
women. Women began addressing their strategic gender needs by bringing pressure on local leaders to end the traditional male bias in the allocation of stool land. Other women are now getting land as individuals or
groups; women are also demanding more access to other resources, such as
extension services and credit and an end to government gender bias in
agricultural aid. They are also successfully fighting against land degradation and deforestation. The success and respect women have earned in the
public arena has improved their position at home as well. Many women report that their husbands have greater respect and appreciation for them because of their contributions to the household and the community, and they
have gained more input into household decisionmaking as a result (Dei
1994:126–129). Dei's study also reveals that women's income-generating
projects can evolve into profitable ventures if an enabling environment
supportive of individual initiative exists. While most of the women Dei
studied with access to land continue to grow food, many others are ab-
sorbing capitalist development ideologies promoting individualism and entrepreneurship. They are going into trading and other commercial ventures
as new opportunities open up; some are becoming wealthy and influential
members of their communities, and gaining new power and responsibilities
in their households. Legal changes strengthening the conjugal nuclear family and women's rights to property are also adding to the status of many
Ghanaian women (Dei 1994:137–138).

These are just a few examples of what grassroots women's groups can accomplish. Obviously, not all are as successful as the examples given here. Moreover, while some women's group activities are entrepreneurial, most are still limited or largely devoted to welfare activities that benefit women's families and communities, for example, producing and selling handicrafts; laying water pipes; building dams, schools, or roads; providing child care; working on conservation projects; or caring for the sick or elderly. Some groups, however, are also confronting such serious women's issues as sexual harassment, domestic violence, female circumcision, and abortion rights[4] (see Tripp 1991:28–29; TAMWA 1993; Ampofo 1993).

Despite the promise and successes of some women's groups, many researchers see them largely as failures. Many fail because they are too small, have too little access to capital, and too many women. Lack of education, inadequate business and technical skills, and legal constraints are also problems (Kabira and Nzioki 1993:64–65). While women often feel their efforts have made improvements in their lives, most women's groups are, as Kabira and Nzioki (1993:73) conclude, "only modestly addressing the issues relating to structures that perpetuate inequality and subordination of women." Welfare activities are "the lowest form of empowerment" while control of resources beyond the household is the highest (Kabira and Nzioki 1993:77–78).

A major reason welfare activities provide such limited benefits for women is that they often place major demands on women's time but do not significantly improve women's skills or earn them tangible rewards, such as greater participation in community decisionmaking or income. In her study of women's social welfare organizations in Kitui, Kenya, for instance, Safilios-Rothschild (1990:103–104) found that women were doing most of the work on the soil and water conservation and afforestation projects but were given fewer project resources in the way of training, cash, or decisionmaking power. Most of these benefits were going to the small minority of participating men. Male dominance of decisionmaking is, in fact, an important reason why women do most of the work on community projects, according to Thomas-Slaytor (1992). Because men are in authority positions over women, the women do as they are told. Women's labor on projects is also expected because it is seen as an extension of women's family roles. Moreover, women do most of the welfare work because it is unpaid, volunteer work that men do not want to do unless they are paid for it.

Such gender stereotypes work to women's obvious economic disadvantage. Women's work in general is often undervalued, unpaid, and regarded as unproductive (i.e., for family subsistence). But also many of the hard, labor-intensive jobs women are doing as volunteers are considered men's jobs when they are paid jobs, and often such jobs are rewarded more highly than the jobs women are allowed to do in the paid economy. As Thomas-Slaytor (1992:820) wryly observes, women will not shovel dirt for a job, but they will do it for free! These restrictions on what women can do for money and the belief that women should volunteer their labor while men should be paid for theirs further privileges men by allowing them more freedom to move into various occupations and life options.

Women's community self-help groups have without a doubt provided valuable services and benefits to their families and communities, but they are largely a survival strategy that reinforces patriarchy, not a transformative strategy. While helping women meet their basic gender needs, they perpetuate the sexist idea that unpaid work to benefit others is women's work and that women's roles in the community should be only extensions of their domestic roles. Men's role in the community, by contrast, is to control the decisionmaking process. The results are that women run soup kitchens while men control local political organizations (Elson 1992:41). Tripp (1991:4–5) adds that women's welfare groups promote "passive solidarity" rather than "active solidarity" among women. In passive solidarity women get together to carry out tasks associated with biological and social reproduction. Such groups and activities are based on women's exclusion from male society and help to perpetuate the patriarchal system. They are largely defensive and a response to adversity or a crisis. Active solidarity occurs when women act to effect political and economic change, to create new horizons for women, and to lessen their subordination as women. Active solidarity depends on raising women's consciousness "to challenge the sexual division of labour which subjects [women's] labour to men" (Stamp 1989:91).

## ▲  Grounds for Male-Female Solidarity

Kenyan women's activist Wangari Maathai has said that the oppression and misery of most African women's lives is closely linked to the oppression and misery of most men because of the systemic inequalities and conflicts both face in underdeveloped capitalism (in Hultman 1992). These include imperialism, economic dependency, political oppression and corruption, and ethnic strife. Current patriarchy, although rooted in the precapitalist familial mode of production, is a modern adaptation to these conditions that allows men to control women's labor and reproduction to their advantage. As Stamp (1991a:844) has observed, women are the linchpins of a patriarchal system that defines women as wives and mothers and is based on a particular sexual division of labor. This system is necessary to the maintenance of underdeveloped capitalism. But underdeveloped capitalism benefits only a minority of Africans while exploiting the majority of men and women. Nonetheless, in the struggle to survive, patriarchy becomes a major means by which men, by expropriating the labor and product of women, can acquire a surplus for their own advancement. Men preserve patriarchy, Henn (1988:40) argues, because no matter where they are located in other oppressive hierarchies, all men eventually become patriarchs, the dominant class in the sex-gender system. Therefore, they have little incentive to support women's struggles for equality; gains by women can only threaten men's "class" interests.

It is not hard to find evidence for this position. As already discussed, men are often highly resistant to women's participation in politics or women's organizations, especially if they have feminist agendas. Men resist equality in the household, steadfastly asserting their position as head of the household and decisionmaker. Women's access to economic resources, especially to the means of production, is carefully circumscribed, although women's labor is essential to men and to the well-being of their families and communities. What men fear is women's independence, because it is "seen as a threat to men's dominant position in the household and to his control over family labour" (von Bulow and Sorenson 1993:41).

While patriarchal structures oppress women, we have also seen that many African women do not see male dominance as their biggest problem, and feminism appeals mainly to an educated minority. Most women do not want to engage in conflict with their menfolk but to work with them for their mutual benefit and for that of their families and societies. To paraphrase Caulfield (1993:446), most women are not interested so much in combating the domestic dominance of their husbands (though this may indeed be a problem for them) as in ensuring the inclusion of men in domestic networks of mutual support. The direction of female strategies under the exploitation of underdeveloped capitalism is toward strengthening kin bonds with both women and men and resisting the dichotomization of roles that underdeveloped capitalism fosters.

The question remains whether and to what extent men can be expected to work with women to overcome specifically patriarchal oppression. In Africa and many other colonized areas of the world, men readily work with women in anti-imperialist or other liberation struggles. But once these struggles are won, men expect to and do monopolize the formal positions of economic and political power. They typically create agendas for development that ensure that men will be the major beneficiaries, and use patriarchal ideologies and policies to relegate women to subordinate roles in the domestic and public arenas.

Nonetheless, there are grounds for and examples of solidarity between African men and women in support of greater gender equality. The basis for male support of women's rights is in some instances a matter of support for general principles of equity that may be the results of the internalization of Western liberalism among the educated middle class. As discussed in Chapter 1, while capitalism creates and legitimates material inequality, it also espouses liberal notions of equal opportunity and rights that can be used to challenge traditional gender stereotypes and patriarchal gender relations. Research does suggest that, although not widespread in Africa, Western ideals of gender egalitarianism in roles and relations between the sexes are beginning to influence some middle-class men (see Stamp 1991a; Gordon 1995) as well as public policy (see, e.g., COSATU 1992).[5] A good example of male support for women's rights is the case of Laeticia Mukarasi in Tanzania, discussed earlier. Tanzania had passed statutory legal rights for women, but, as is so often the case, the laws were weakly enforced. Mukarasi decided to demand her rights and fight for her job. Although many men and many of her male colleagues castigated her, Mukarasi points out that men were also instrumental in her ultimate success in being reinstated in her job. She reports that the male-dominated media was largely on her side, as were some of her male colleagues. She concludes (1991:12), "The fact that I could get justice in the end through male-dominated structures showed me that *there are some men* with consciences who are committed to the principles of equality, fairness and justice and who see people as individuals and not as members of a particular gender."

For most men (as well perhaps as for many women) the acceptance of patriarchy is more likely to break down when men no longer get the same benefits from it. Or, to put it somewhat differently, where greater gender equality benefits men, they are more likely to support it. It has been my contention that underdeveloped capitalism rests in part on a particular kind of patriarchy (i.e., African patriarchy) that originated in the familial mode of production but has been modified to serve the process of capital accumulation in underdeveloped capitalism. Underdeveloped capitalism is in crisis, however; and capitalist expansion is blocked in part by African patriarchy. This hurts men as well as women and could provide some basis for changing gender relations.

The research literature provides some tantalizing evidence that greater gender equality can benefit men and thus gain men's support. In his study in rural Kenya, Orvis (1993:31) found that more-cooperative and equitable gender relations within the household were crucial to economic success in the face of an expanding market economy. The typical sexual division of labor whereby women farm and men earn cash is often the most successful economic mobility strategy for most families if men invest adequate capital in their wives' farming and the well-being of their families. Women's farming is the key to the family's accumulation of capital because it allows men to take off-farm work. If husbands fail to provide enough of their earnings for their households and wives, however, women reduce their labor input and shift it to their own nonagricultural businesses in order to care for the family and themselves. Those households in which gender relations are more equitable result in stabler marriages and greater economic success. Their farms are more productive, benefiting household consumption as well as income. The husband's income is used to educate the children so they can compete for good jobs (and help their families) or hire labor on the farm, thus improving farm productivity. Such families are more likely to be able to keep their land, whereas households that only farm cannot afford to have a man employed off the farm, are unable to invest in their farms or education, are being forced to sell their land, and must join the growing ranks of the impoverished and landless. What Orvis demonstrates is that the men may not benefit in the long run from exploiting their wives' labor and failing to invest in them and their households. While squandering money on beer, women, or consumer goods may be a patriarchal prerogative, it is those men who cooperate with and care for their wives and children and invest in education and the land who are more likely to prosper.

Freeman's (1993:18–19) research on women's urban food crop farming makes similar observations. Women's food crops allow scarce cash earned by other household members to go for children's education or reinvestment in small businesses or craft activities. These in turn provide job opportunities for others in women's enterprises. Both Orvis's and Freeman's research clearly indicate another important point: the relegation of women's work to the category of social reproduction obscures the fact that women's work may be the foundation for wage employment, the development of human capital, business investment, and capital accumulation in many African families. As such, the importance of women's labor goes far beyond its usual depiction as social reproduction (i.e., as work that provides goods and services for consumption that help to reproduce or maintain the labor force) rather than production.

Clearly, women's production activities are important to the welfare and even advancement of men. For this reason, as we have seen, many men want to control and exploit women. But this subordination is counterproductive if it hampers women's productivity or willingness to cooperate with their menfolk. Many studies show this. Examples include von Bulow and Sorenson's (1993:49) study of tea growers in Kenya. Men own the land and the crop, but women's labor is crucial to the crop's success. Women withhold their labor if men do not meet their family responsibilities. Withholding their labor from rice production schemes is reported among women in Cameroon (Gittinger et al. 1990:11) and Kenya as well. In the Kenya case, men controlled household labor and could claim all the income. Women were paid in rice by their husbands but it was not enough to cover household expenses; moreover, the women found their work load was increasing. Some women even left their husbands (Stamp 1989:64–66). In Tanzania, Grosz (1988:10) found that women were withholding their labor from men's cash crops in favor of doing other activities that benefited the women themselves, such as producing cooking oils, brick making, or biogas production. In other words, men's control over household labor is often contingent upon women's consent to help them. This consent is largely determined by the degree of equity in intrahousehold gender relations.

By contrast, among the Kofyar of Nigeria, men have found that women's labor is too valuable to risk alienating the women, and gender relations have a high degree of equity. Women have a great deal of autonomy in how they allocate their labor, and they divorce their husbands at a high rate, "an effective check on compulsory appropriation of their time and work" (Stone et al. 1990:29). In Kofyar households, most labor goes to household fields under the direction of the male household head, but women have their own fields and retain the income from them. Household income is controlled by the male head, but a significant portion goes to benefit household members, for example, for school, medical care, food, taxes, and bridewealth. Women's income is actually more disposable than that of the male household head, and some women have become quite prosperous, owning motorcycles and livestock. Men's and women's labor burdens are similar and there are few gender-specific tasks in household fields. Unlike most of Africa, Kofyar men help with wood gathering, crop processing, clothes washing, and hut construction; they even occasionally fetch water (Stone et al. 1990:9–10, 17–18).

The existence of a sexual division of labor does not necessarily imply inequitable gender relations, as the above studies suggest. Women may farm while men work for wages. Men may be heads of households but women have considerable control over their own labor and product. Too often, however, the sexual division of labor is not balanced, and women's work load becomes a major source of gender inequality that negatively affects their productivity and ability to participate fully in political or economic development. Labor studies in Africa consistently show that, on the average, women do much more work than men. In Zaire, for instance, men do only 30 percent as much work as women; and in Burkina Faso women's average work day is 27 percent longer than men's. Men rarely do domestic or child-rearing tasks, even when women have wage jobs (Tiano 1987:223). Liatto-Katundo (1993:83) views women's labor burdens at home—"they are tied to the hoe, to the pot, to the laundry basket and to the nappies"—as a major cause of women's relative absence from the public sphere.

More men and women are recognizing the need to change the sexual division of labor. Here too, where men benefit as well as women from changes in gender relations, men will change. In Iringa District of Tanzania women were spending about two thousand hours per year walking to fetch wood, water, and perform other chores. There was growing concern that malnutrition might increase because women were cooking less often in order to conserve wood for their cook fires. This led to community leaders asking men to help gather firewood. At first the men strongly resisted, but then they were shown a film called "Sharing the Responsibility," and women talked to them about the problem. The men over time began to help and even provided wheelbarrows to make the task easier and more efficient (Gittinger 1990:32). In urban areas of Tanzania women are becoming the de facto main providers for their families. Structural adjustment reforms have compelled most women to start their own informal sector businesses as their husbands have lost wage jobs, and the purchasing power of their incomes has drastically eroded. Many husbands feel threatened by this role reversal in which they are economically dependent on their wives. Some fear that women will become too independent or will leave them; others refuse to let their wives go into business or restrict the kind of business they can have. Most men, however, according to Tripp (1992:170–171), are encouraging their wives, and gender relationships in the household are changing to become more egalitarian as women's economic power increases. In another example of how social change is eroding patriarchal gender attitudes, daughters are becoming more important than sons in many families, because many sons who migrate to the city to get work are losing their sense of responsibility toward their wives, children, or parents back home. As a result, parents are shifting their hopes for old-age security to their daughters, and there is growing pressure to educate girls and prepare them for good jobs (J. Harris 1985:31).

A recent symposium in Zimbabwe on women was sponsored by the African Development Bank and the World Bank and attended by representatives from numerous African countries. They concluded that men would not lose by gains in economic and social equality for women: "Increasing women's rights would expand opportunities for both men and women." Gender equality, in other words, is not a zero-sum game (Gittinger et al. 1990:37). Kenyan activist Wangari Maathai adds that development and change in Africa require "a partnership of men and women" and improvement not just in the position of women but "the economic and political improvement of the African economy, so that all people can move forward" (in Hultman 1992:3).

A partnership between men and women based on equality rather than the subordination and exploitation of women will be, in Africa as in every other region of the world, difficult to achieve. After all, many men do benefit—or think they do—from the privileges patriarchy permits them; and change in fundamental gender roles and identities is never an easy or quick process. As Eisenstein (1981:187) observes, gender equality does mean that men will lose privilege in a sexual hierarchy that divides home and work. They will have to share the responsibilities of child rearing and housework and give up freedom and privileges that exist because of patriarchal oppression. Therefore, male support for women's equality may be conditional on women limiting their agenda to what are perceived as family or community welfare issues rather than to fundamental challenges to patriarchy. In a telling discussion of the women's movement in Ghana, Nana Rawlings told an interviewer how men were beginning to appreciate the work women were doing. "At first, they thought we were like the European type of feminist group, looking for total equality and we wouldn't cook for them anymore and so on." The men were mollified when the women responded that "no, we aren't talking about that. We have basic problems and let us deal with the issues that affect us within our communities" (in Novicki 1995:54).

Obviously, along with raising consciousness and changing attitudes there must be major changes in social institutions organized on the basis of patriarchy—for example, the organization of work, the definitions of masculinity and femininity, and the relationship between home and work.

So, while men and women as individuals in their household or in organizations can address some issues and work toward more-equitable gender relationships, patriarchy is deeply embedded in economic and political structures linked to underdeveloped capitalism. These structures shape the social environment and limit what individuals and organizations can achieve—and what changes most men will accept. Promoting these structures as well as being necessary agents in their transformation are the African state and the development agencies and policies that are both shaping and responding to African societies. How the state and development community are linked with capitalism and patriarchy are the subjects of the next two chapters.

▲  Notes

1. I admittedly subscribe to a notion of universal human rights that includes women and reject the view that feminism and its concerns for gender equality are simply another form of Western cultural imperialism. See also Moghadam (1994:22), who notes that the UN Convention on the Elimination of All Forms of Discrimination Against Women views "cultural practice" as an invalid ground for the unequal treatment of women. "Discrimination against women is not derived from culture, but from power," she adds. Women need to be seen as human beings, not as cultural symbols, and women's rights as human rights. Western feminists must, however, as such writers as Mohanty (1991b) and Apfel-Marglin and Simon (1994) argue, pay heed to Third World women's concerns and interpretations of reality rather than imposing an exclusively Western hegemonic feminist discourse and program upon them.

2. Morna (1995:58) reports on an Economic Commission for Africa study of twenty-seven African countries that shows that in the last decade women's political participation at the national level has remained virtually unchanged, with less than 8 percent of offices held by women. The highest percentage of women in Parliament is found in South Africa, where women hold one quarter of the seats in the House of Assembly. This is mainly the result of an African National Congress quota in which one-third of the candidates were women. There are, however, only two women ministers and two deputy members in Mandela's Cabinet.

3. See ILO 1984:40; Tripp 1991:12; Staudt 1987:204, 1988:203–207; Stamp 1991a:827–828.

4. For instance, in Zambia women's groups rallied against a court decision forcing a wife to submit to her husband's sexual demands despite his history of wife abuse ("Domestic . . ." 1993). African groups such as the National Committee on Traditional Practices of Ethiopia and Mali's Action Committee for the Rights of Women and Children are using a combination of public education and political lobbying to end genital mutilation or female circumcision, to which an estimated eighty million African women and girls have been subjected (Press 1994:6). In Zimbabwe the International Socialist Organization (1994) is working to ensure women's right to legal, safe abortion as part of its overall struggle for African women's liberation.

5. In a 1992 Resolution on Women, the South African umbrella trade union COSATU advocated equality for women in the public sphere and sharing of housework between men and women.

# ▲ 4
# The State, Capitalism, and Patriarchy

Political theorists who study Africa tend to agree that while the state is closely linked to capitalism, it does not merely serve capitalist interests. That is, the state as an actor is "relatively autonomous" from the economy (see Fatton 1988). Although their actions frequently reflect pressures to cater to foreign capital, which largely owns or controls the formal economy, Africa's rulers have other agendas as well. That is, they must respond to multiple indigenous social forces and interest groups such as ethnic or religious constituencies, the military, domestic business and agricultural interest groups, and women's groups. Such interest groups must be appeased, co-opted, or repressed in order for the ruling class to maintain political stability and extract the economic surplus necessary for the regime's own activities (and often enrichment), and to facilitate capital accumulation.

Formal authority and control over economic, political, and cultural institutions in Africa, as elsewhere in the world, are mostly in male hands; and it is males who largely shape the interests to which the state and ruling class have been responsive. The state is patriarchal, Pringle and Watson (1992:56–57) argue, because "government is conducted as if men's interests are the only ones that exist." Even when governments incorporate women's interests (e.g., to get women's votes), they are using them to achieve their own ends. In reality, political differences become political differences among men, even if rulers are ostensibly acting on behalf of the people.

Marshall (1994:123–125) adds that the state is not capitalist or patriarchal inherently "but as a result of particular historical struggles." The interests or needs of patriarchy and capitalism are thus constructed through specific practices—and resisted. Rather than political actors such as men, capitalism, or women having objective unitary interests, we have a struggle of various groupings "to articulate their interests and hegemonize their claims." This hegemony is always partial and temporary (Pringle and Watson 1992:63). If we look at the state this way, Pringle and Watson claim, "we do not have to puzzle about why the state acts so contradictorily or, on

109

occasion, fails to act at all. We do not have to conclude in advance that it will act uniformly to maintain capitalist or patriarchal relations, or that this is its 'purpose.'"

The above perspective on the state has the virtue of allowing us to be sensitive to the process by which political interests are articulated, and to see that interests are subject to redefinition by political actors in an ongoing process of social construction. It also leaves open the possibility that the state is not invariably a tool of men or of capital. This implies as well that women can create alliances among themselves and influence the state to act on their behalf.[1]

It would be erroneous to conclude from this analysis that power arrangements and relatively stable structures do not exist and create parameters and constraints within which political actors operate. As Pringle and Watson (1992:65) point out, "the most powerful discourses have firm institutional locations." In Africa, it is the interactions among the economic, political, and cultural institutions found in specific underdeveloped capitalist societies that determine the parameters and constraints within which political interests are articulated and acted upon by various groups. Politics in turn shapes states.

Sangmpam (1993:86) argues that the characteristics of underdeveloped capitalism ("pseudocapitalism," as he calls it) are the decisive factors shaping politics and the African state. These include the partial or noncommodification of peasant agriculture by the capitalist sector, the marginal position of indigenous social classes in capitalist structures, dependency on the world economy and the West, and the "oscillation of social classes and groups between capitalist and precapitalist relationships." What Sangmpam ignores in his analysis is the centrality of African patriarchy to underdeveloped capitalism. It is through the patriarchal gender relations of the familial mode of production that the forces of production are mobilized to produce the economic surplus necessary for the regime's survival and for the enrichment of the bourgeois classes. This is one reason the state caters to pressures from men to maintain male dominance over women. The state also cannot afford to alienate the male chiefs, notables, and lineage heads who control the familial mode of production and benefit the most from it. This intersection of interests between the men who control the state and the men who dominate civil society is a formidable obstacle to galvanizing support for the equality for women through formal politics.

Another factor in the political hegemony of patriarchy is that access to economic resources and political influence depends heavily on patron-client relationships. For most men and women, patronage ties are an outgrowth of familistic ethnic and kinship ties with their roots in the familial mode of production. Thus, paradoxically, women as well as men depend on these relationships because they are perceived to be their best option for survival or advancement in underdeveloped capitalism, even if they also perpetuate women's inequality to men. Unless women have other means to influence the state (such as through strong women's organizations) or unless the state–African patriarchy political linkage can be weakened (e.g., through new democratic forces linked to capitalist transformation), efforts by the state to support equality for women are likely to remain halfhearted.

In other words, in the absence of "real" capitalism, most Africans, from the elites to the peasant masses, are bound to the familial mode of production and its specific patriarchal relationships. The state's unwillingness or inability to promote equal rights for women is part of this more general problem of the African state and African politics. Rather than the state's being a tool of capitalism, in Africa capitalism as a mode of production is ill-served by a politics and state constrained by the familial mode of production. By no logic of capitalism's interests can we explain the authoritarian, personalistic, patronage politics and states endemic to Africa. More-mature capitalism is based on equalizing opportunities in the competition for the social product, which in turn promotes liberal democracy with its emphasis on compromise and equal rights.[2] By contrast, where underdeveloped capitalism prevails

> the noncentrality of capitalist core relations prevents the equalization of opportunities by creating uneven patterns of linkage between social relationships and capitalist core relations and by stifling liberalism's contractual freedoms (the freedom to own, to buy, to sell, to enter in contractual arrangements), the very ideological base of equal opportunities [Sangmpam 1993:88].

The symmetry between the state, underdeveloped capitalism, and patriarchy is enhanced by the fact that the state and the economy are monopolized by males. As Fatton (1992:93) observes,

> male-dominated ruling classes have invoked gender ideology as a means of legitimizing their governance and enlisting the support of males from subordinate classes. By instilling fear of female economic competition and autonomy, ruling classes have reinforced sexism and eroded the solidarity of the oppressed. The relative hegemony of patriarchal ideology has tended to mollify women's resolve and confidence in their quest for emancipation.

Because the state is the source of legal, political, and economic resources and policymaking in Africa, capturing or influencing the state becomes an important arena for gender conflict and activism. Male control of the state, while generally preserving patriarchy of the familial mode of production, is not impervious to pressure and interest group politics, and, as discussed in Chapter 3, women's groups pushing women's issues are proliferating in Africa. As Herbst (1990:252–254) has shown, interest groups can influence the state if they use the right tactics. This is not necessarily dependent on how powerful or organized the group is but on how well it can focus on the issues that are of greatest concern to the government.

To date, the issues of greatest concern to the government are oriented around preserving ruling-class dominance, political stability, and the underdeveloped capitalist economy. But there are growing economic and political pressures on the state caused by the crisis of governance and economic stagnation in Africa. In order to understand the state's role in fostering patriarchy or gender equality we will examine first what the role of the state has been, followed by how capitalism poses a challenge to underdeveloped capitalism, the state, and African patriarchy.

## ▲ The State and African Patriarchy

Women were active in nationalist struggles all over Africa, and there was at independence considerable enthusiasm voiced by new African governments for women's rights and equality. Instead of equality, however, Western, even Victorian patriarchal views of women's place emphasizing women's domestic roles were perpetrated by Africa's Western-educated leaders (see Batezat and Mwalo 1989:53). While some new educational, legal, and economic rights and opportunities were extended to women, the emphasis was on stereotypic roles for women as teachers, nurses, secretaries, mothers, and wives. "Women's concerns" were typically defined in terms of their domestic and childbearing roles, and it was for these activities that women were to be trained and educated rather than for economic or political leadership roles (see Geiger 1987; Staudt 1987).

As mentioned above, one reason the African state has failed in its promises to women is that few women are in positions of power, nor do they have the resources necessary to cultivate the patron-client relationships crucial to political influence. Much of women's lack of political participation and influence is rooted in precapitalist and colonial structures. Although in some African societies women held formal political positions or participated in powerful women's associations, more typically women exercised influence indirectly as mothers, wives, or lineage daughters or sisters. During the colonial period many of the sources of female authority were ignored or undermined by colonial authorities, often in collusion with male elders and chiefs (see Okonjo 1976). Another disadvantage women faced as a result of colonialism and patriarchal notions of men's and women's proper spheres was that men were given most of the education and jobs that allowed them to assume leadership roles during the nationalist struggle and in postindependence states. Women were relegated largely to work in the fields and caring for the family, and their roles in the public arena were carefully circumscribed. The net result of these patriarchal biases has been, as Stamp writes, that the "community of men" has been systematically favored over "the community of women" in Africa.

> Outsiders from missionaries to colonial officials to contemporary government elites have recognized men's networks as the sole legitimate "public" that embodies "public interest." Consequently, the complex links between the male and female communities, which serve to make a village a functioning "public" whole, have been broken or distorted. Concomitantly, women's community has been relegated to the status of "private" or informal, to conform with Western ideology [Stamp 1989:116].

Parpart (1988:217–218) adds that the disadvantages women faced due to the colonial legacy have persisted since independence along with other handicaps. Women lack the economic power or professional jobs that allow entry into politics, the burden of women's work leaves them with little time or energy for politics, and gender stereotypes and patriarchal attitudes discourage women from challenging male dominance and male control of politics. As Oboler (1985:320) observed among Nandi women of Kenya, many women perceive that men have always held political power, so there is no break between the past and present. Because men control political institutions and males are the main constituents to which politicians must be responsive, women's interests and needs are typically ignored. The results, as discussed in Chapter 3, are that many women often have little interest in formal politics and seek to empower themselves through other means such as "kitchen politics," manipulating or aligning themselves with men, or self-help collective action (see Staudt 1987; Parpart 1988; Tripp 1991).

The African state has not been totally oblivious to women and issues of gender equity. In both socialist and capitalist states, Western liberal values of equality and fairness have been given at least lip service. With the passage of constitutions and common law legal systems based on European models, gender equality was, in principle, legalized in many areas; women were often given more rights in family and divorce matters, educational and economic opportunities were expanded, and so forth.[3] Unfortunately, discriminatory customary laws frequently are given precedence over such legal reforms. Women were also given some, usually secondary, political positions (often in stereotypic areas dealing with culture, family, and social welfare), and women's wings of political parties were formed (although subservient to men's politics and party platforms). In reality the state's embeddedness in underdeveloped capitalist society has rendered it unable or unwilling to radically transform gender relations or attack the systemic gender inequality and discrimination in society; the exploitation of women's labor and control over reproduction have been too vital to most male household heads, male wage earners, the state, and foreign capitalists who profit from the low wages and commodity prices the exploitation of women makes possible.

While the oppression of women is often blamed on capitalism, socialist regimes in Africa have not been much more successful than their quasi-capitalist counterparts in combating gender inequality. This suggests, as I have argued, that patriarchy and the economic mode of production are not one system, nor is socialism the antidote to so-called capitalist patriarchy. Socialist regimes as well as capitalist ones inherited patriarchal structures and ideologies with precapitalist and colonial capitalist roots. Those patriarchal structures can be very resistant to social change—even to changes in the economic system. As Robertson and Berger (1986:22) point out, socialist regimes may remove private ownership of the means of production, but it is men who have control of critical resources. Moreover, changing the mode of production may not change the relations of production in which men often have authority over women's labor and product and over household income.

Parpart's analysis of African socialist states is instructive. It is often said, she recounts, that women are fighting two colonialisms: European and African patriarchy. Although socialist states often have more avowed commitment to women's liberation than capitalist states, women in either system have little power at the national level and only limited power at the local level. Women are rarely in key central planning ministries. Instead, they are often marginalized in women's bureaus or health and social welfare ministries. Parpart (1988:216) concludes that the African state, whether capitalist or socialist, remains "a male preserve."

Socialist governments also have done little to improve women's access to land or improve their role in agricultural production. Croll (1986) reports that in socialist societies women still do most of the work on food crops, and often cash-crop work as well, yet they have little control over the allocation of resources or the products of their labors. Women continue to get access to land mainly through their husbands, and male household heads get most of the benefits. Haile (1985) found the same patterns in his study of Marxist Ethiopia. Even though land was nationalized, few women had direct access to it nor did they have a direct role in decisionmaking that affected collective production. Ostensibly democratic peasant associations restricted their membership to household heads, in other words, mostly to men. In Marxist Mozambique considerable effort was made by the FRELIMO government to empower women by promoting gender equality. Yet their efforts were stymied by such obstacles as traditional cultural stereotypes about gender relations, especially with regard to family labor in the home, and the lack of female education (Davison 1988a; Urdang 1985).

Scott's discussion of Angola and Mozambique is instructive. She argues that masculinist elements in Marxism led to contradictory statements and actions from the government that catered to male authority in the rural areas where patriarchal power is the strongest. Despite the concern voiced by the Angolan women's movement that "men in our country behave like chiefs with absolute and unlimited powers," the governments of both Angola and Mozambique sought to emancipate women by involving them in more agricultural production and wage work while ignoring patriarchal relationships in the household and insisting that women were still to be responsible as mothers for the welfare of children. Although Angola's government recognized the problem of the household division of labor and how it limited women's ability to participate in national reconstruction, there was no attention given to "the way in which male domination ensures the double burden, and no recognition of the inevitable male resistance that would accompany full-fledged attempts to collectivize child care and agricultural production." By the same token, although women's rights to reproductive freedom were argued, "men's power in imposing their sexuality upon women" went unexamined. Both in Angola and Mozambique, we see a faulty conception of equality: that women can be equal and individuals in the public arena of politics and the economy without changing the sexual division of labor and male dominance of women in the household (Scott 1995:107–112).

Eventually both governments were compelled, by patriarchal pressures to back away from their goals of gender equality. Opposition groups sought support from the populace on the basis of protecting "traditional tribal life" and African values, using "constructions of gender roles that attempted to preserve male power in the face of the modernizing ideology" of the regime. Government leaders found that proposed changes in family laws on divorce, brideprice (*lobola*), and so on were so controversial that they had to concede "the terrain of the household to male authority" (Scott 1995:107, 110).

The reason patriarchal relationships and the sexual division of labor in the home appear to be the most resistant to change is that they are the foundation of the familial mode of production and male dominance over women. Their resistance to change reflects the strength of African patriarchy and its ability to stymie or distort both socialist and capitalist development projects favored by ruling elites. When African patriarchy is combined with the patriarchal practices and stereotypes of the Western nations helping Africa "develop," neither the state nor the economy, whether socialist or capitalist, can be a very effective agent for the transformation of gender relations.

The experience of socialist Guinea under its first president, Ahmed Sekou Touré, as discussed by Renzetti and Curran (1986) illustrates these points also. As president, Touré, inspired by socialist egalitarianism, sought legal changes to improve the status of women both economically and politically. But at the same time, Touré called for the preservation of "traditional family values." His reforms failed because Touré was unable to confront the inherent contradiction between improving women's status within patriarchal family systems and the familial mode of production that are at the roots of women's subordination. Preserving traditional values resulted in educational discrimination against girls and their economic marginalization in gender-appropriate work such as sewing and crafts while mostly men received higher educational, technical, and professional training. The result of other family values was that women were still expected to fulfill their traditional roles in the home and marriage and to make marriage and childbearing their primary roles. Government agricultural programs oriented toward large mechanized collective farms largely bypassed women. Mostly men were hired, so they got all the benefits of development: technology, fertilizer, skills, better seeds, and so on. Women were still expected to produce most of the food, however, with no technological improvements. Western mining firms and development agencies compounded these problems with their own patriarchal biases. For instance, bauxite firms that hired women put them mostly in such sex-stereotyped jobs as secretaries and office clerks. Western development agencies imposed their own prejudices about the sexual division of labor by treating machines and large-scale production as a male domain, while women were relegated to low-skilled, small-scale income-generating projects.

Touré erred in thinking that the familial mode of production and Western socialist development were compatible, just as capitalist-oriented rulers err in the belief that they can have the familial mode of production and capitalism, too. The problem for each is that at the center of the communal extended African family are men who have authority over other family members and major factors of production as well. This situation makes changing the sexual division of labor as well as a just or economically rational allocation of productive resources for economic development impossible.

Even when women attempt to organize and press for change, the state often attempts to structure women's politics at the organizational level in ways similar to that of other groups in civil society; that is, the state tries to assure that women's politics and women's agendas are kept within politically acceptable boundaries. As in its treatment of other interest groups in Africa, corporatist strategies have been used to place women's groups under state sponsorship and control. Corporatism allows the state to claim to support civil society and pluralism by allowing labor unions, professional associations, or women's organizations to exist. Women's bureaus or ministries may even be included in the government; but this prevents their autonomy, subjects them to government control, and often eviscerates any real transformation in society or empowerment of the groups in question (see Nyang'oro 1989:132–134; Shivji 1990:65). Goetz (1991:136) sums up the problem corporatism poses to the advancement of women.

> These numerous tiny ministries, underfunded and staffed with weak political appointees, running handicraft projects and largely uninvolved with the broader affairs of government and development, represent precisely the sorts of token gestures that many states can trumpet while neglecting to do anything further to involve women in their agricultural, industrial, service and social sector development plans.

Shivji (1990:65) concludes from his study of Tanzania that Africa's economic crisis and growing challenges to the single-party, authoritarian states are resulting in even greater efforts by the state to bring all mass civil organizations such as women's groups under the state-party umbrella. By contrast, Woods (1992:93) argues that party-state control over labor, student, women's, and other groups and associations is ending in many countries. An example is the failure of the Kenyan government to keep Kenya's largest women's group, Maendeleo ya Wanawake, under the control of the Kenya African National Union (see Kabira and Nzioki 1993). In such countries as Côte d'Ivoire, Benin, Cameroon, and Zambia, the state is being forced to deal with increasingly vociferous and critical groups "no longer willing to abide by the quasi-corporatist rules defined by the ruling elite" (Woods 1992:93). As the underdeveloped capitalist economy continues to break down, the state has declining resources at its disposal to buy consent through the patronage system.

Women's groups are among those asserting their autonomy and confronting the state on a host of issues that directly and indirectly affect women. For instance, at the recent Regional Conference on African Women held in Dakar, women delegates hammered out an African platform for action that was presented to the fifth UN World Conference on Women in Beijing in 1995. Many delegates are demanding an end to customary law and many customary practices such as female circumcision, arranged marriages, and discriminatory inheritance laws. They are also speaking out against the misallocation of scarce resources on armed conflicts that cost the continent $8 billion in arms expenditures. As UN official Gertrude Mongella laments, "It is inexcusable that while African women are carrying water on their heads, the men are negotiating for arms" (Morna 1994). Disengagement from the state is also increasing as the state becomes less central in providing services and resources. This is reflected in the growth of self-help groups, opposition movements, and a diversity of other associational groups (see Chazan et al. 1988; Woods 1992).

Sara Longwe, co-secretary of ZARD (the Zambian Association for Research and Development), writing on women's efforts to get Africa's male-dominated governments to sign and implement the UN Forward-Looking Strategies, provides a revealing look at the uphill battle facing women trying to enlist the state in their fight for gender equality. Longwe praises the UN agreement on women's rights for going beyond welfare (practical gender needs) to empowerment of women (strategic gender needs). The main obstacle to the agreement in Africa, Longwe reports, is resistance from male-dominated government bureaucracies. As of September 1987, 51 percent of African governments had not even signed the accord, versus 42 percent of governments in the rest of the world. Many of those who have signed the accord have no serious intention or any program of action to implement it, Longwe claims. Even those in government who have expressed concern for women in development do not interpret this as requiring any effort to promote women's equality. Intergovernmental regional development agencies such as SADCC (Southern African Development Coordination Conference)[4] and the ECA (Economic Commission for Africa) have been indifferent as well. For example, in 1989 the SADCC Secretariat and Council of Ministers turned down a consultant's report that criticized SADCC's lack of focus on women's issues and recommended that officers from member countries be appointed to coordinate women in development (WID) strategies under an overall Regional Coordinator of Women's Development. According to the Progress Report for 1985–1987 of the ECA/MULPOV Project on the Integration of Women in Development, the group did little more than meet and hold seminars and workshops; consequently, it was likely to lose its UN funding. The group was supposed to produce a biannual regional report on WID but failed to publish after the first edition because of a lack of information from member states (Longwe 1990:4, 16).

Even where governments are committed to the principles of the UN Forward-Looking Strategies, the civil service bureaucracies are likely to obstruct efforts to improve the status of women. Longwe discusses ten strategies male bureaucrats use to resist and undermine efforts to promote gender equality:

1. *Denial.* Men deny that women have a problem or are discriminated against. They blame women themselves for their low status.

2. *Inversion.* They turn the argument upside-down. For example, evidence of women's marginalization by development projects is used to argue that women are not contributing their fair share to development and not helping their menfolk enough. Women are inefficient, incapable, and so forth. They must do better and do more—but not with any more control

or participation over the projects. This strategy "invites women to participate more fully in their own exploitation."

3. *Dilution*. Strategies intended to promote a higher level of control
and participation from women are reinterpreted to allow only access or
welfare rather than real empowerment.

4. *Selection*. Officials agree only to measures/projects that promote
lower-level (i.e., welfare) women's development, such as maternity clinics
or literacy programs.

5. *Subversion*. Bureaucrats carry out a project with such incompe-
tence or indifference that no progress is made; this may or may not be
done deliberately.

6. *Shelving*. The claim is "the time is not right" so that initiatives are
put off.

7. *Lip service*. Top government leaders and bureaucrats profess support but do little or nothing to carry out policies. This allows governments
and local offices of development agencies to claim projects support high-
level women's development when they do not.

8. *Compartmentalization*. This involves assigning responsibility for
women's development to a separate agency or ministry, then giving it little staff or money and no control over what other ministries do. These others are then absolved of responsibility for including women in their own
projects or planning.

9. *Tokenism*. A few women are put in decisionmaking positions with
responsibility for women's development. They are then outnumbered and
marginalized by men. Or the women appointees may have no experience
or previous interest in women's development or may have succeeded by
"acting like men." Real women's advocates would be "a nuisance."

10. *Commission of inquiry*. In response to efforts from women's
groups to end a discriminatory policy, the government appoints a commission to study the issue (with token women on it). After lengthy study and
no action, the issue is forgotten or nothing is done. If change is recommended, the government sits on the report or does not publish it (Longwe
1990:10–14).

Longwe's (1990:13–14) antidote to the above patriarchal biases, political
inertia, and foot-dragging is a coordinated effort by nongovernmental organizations at the national and regional levels to push governments to implement reforms and combat these strategies of resistance, which she believes are worse at the African national and regional government levels
than in international and bilateral agencies.

Scott's assessment of SADCC is somewhat more positive than
Longwe's. At SADCC's 1991 Annual Conference, delegates issued a state-
ment advocating equal access to land, credit, education, and services for

women along with the elimination of all legal, social, and economic barriers. The main emphasis was still, however, on making women more productive without challenging the sexual division of labor and women's responsibilities in the household. Scott (1995:82–85) saw some basis for hope in a 1988 SADCC conference on women and food technologies that recommended programs for men to sensitize them to "cultural constraints" on women, which could be "the beginning of a recognition of the sexual division of labor in the household."

The state has done so little to help women or transform gender relationships in Africa not because the economy is capitalist but because capitalism (or socialism) are too weakly established. Instead of a capitalist economy, there are enclaves of capitalism (or socialism) coexisting with the familial mode of production. It is the patriarchy of the familial mode of production that is often dominant even if this is detrimental to economic development efforts. Under the guise of preserving traditional culture and customs, male dominance in the underdeveloped capitalist political economy remains entrenched. By undermining male control over land, labor, and capital in the familial mode of production, capitalism is a threat to African patriarchy, just as African patriarchy is a constraint on a capitalist transformation of African societies.

This analysis leads to the question of whether and under what conditions the African state can be used to improve the status of women. This is not a question of eliminating all forms of patriarchy, because new forms of patriarchy are likely to evolve if African patriarchy is replaced (as discussed in Chapter 2). After all, patriarchy exists in some form or the other in both industrial and developing countries, in capitalist as well as socialist systems. It would be naive to think that Africans any time soon can achieve an ideal gender equality that eludes everyone else. Moreover, as was discussed in Chapter 1, there is no consensus even among feminists in Africa or elsewhere as to what gender equality is. To promote some clarity if not necessarily agreement, in the discussion that follows, I define gender equality as:

1. The advancement of women's access to political and economic resources (e.g., through equal rights laws and "affirmative action" policies)
2. The improvement of women's standard of living (i.e., materially as well as in improved health, education, and personal autonomy)
3. The empowerment of women in their relationship to men both in society at large and in the household (e.g., restructuring the sexual division of labor, expanding women's control over reproduction and sexuality, improving women's self-respect and self-assertion; the breaking down of gender stereotypes; and the strengthening of

women's activism in pursuit of both practical and strategic gender needs). Gender equality must also benefit the majority of women, not just elite women; therefore, it must address inequalities based on such things as race, class, and ethnicity, not gender alone.

State intervention is necessary to the promotion of gender equality as I have defined it both by breaking down institutionalized patriarchy and by facilitating or creating new institutions based on equal rights and gender equity.[5] Moreover, the state plays an important ideological function by informing women and men of women's rights, spreading the ideals of gender equality through the educational system and media under its control, and by expanding women's participation in government and other decision-making roles. The state will make only limited strides in promoting gender equality, however, without simultaneously improving the overall economic development of society. That is, underdeveloped capitalism must be transformed if African patriarchy is to be replaced by a more gender-egalitarian society.

This transformation will depend on the following developments, none of which is assured:

1. The replacement of the predatory, patronage-ridden African state with a developmentalist state
2. Reform of the economy that facilitates entrepreneurship and market forces
3. Democratization
4. State intervention to promote autonomous and equitable development (by gender, class, ethnicity, and region)

I will discuss each of these in turn.

## ▲ The Developmentalist State

Scott (1995:45) has criticized much of the recent scholarship on the African state for reading like "an advice manual to an imaginary African prince: African leaders are advised to display discipline, wield effective authority, and bolster their capacity." The state is treated as an organization of leaders independent of society with set boundaries that allow the state to mobilize resources and maintain insularity from particularistic social forces.

As I have pointed out, this insularity of the state in Africa hardly exists, nor does the capacity of the state to mobilize resources efficiently. Despite its hortatory character, much of the literature referred to by Scott does provide helpful insights into the reasons for the weaknesses of African states and what factors have enabled the state in some areas of the Third World to be a more effective agent of development.

Arguing against the position that Africa needs "less government," Sandbrook (1993) posits that a developmentalist state, similar to that found in such newly industrializing countries (NICs) as Taiwan and South Korea, is necessary if development is to occur in Africa. The state must be able "to engage in a directive, yet market-facilitating role" (Lall 1990: 272–273). This is similar to the view that the state needs to create "an enabling environment" for the expansion of the market, as currently espoused by the World Bank (e.g., 1990a; see also Hyden 1990b). Such liberal economic reforms as structural adjustments policies (SAPs) are not sufficient, claims Sandbrook (1993:54–58), to produce this enabling environment; it requires a favorable political administration, legal framework, and infrastructure—all of which depend on competent government. The developmentalist state is also able to insulate itself from the political demands of particularistic interest groups such as regional, class, or ethnic groups to achieve developmental goals. For similar reasons, Moghadam (1993:214) adds that only a strong, developmentalist state can counter patriarchal, precapitalist interests and promote capitalist development and women's rights.

One must agree with Clapham (1993:426–427) that few African states at the present time have the political or administrative capacity to run a developmentalist state. Because of the dominance of underdeveloped capitalism, the state is constrained in the policies it can pursue and the control it can exercise over the economy. With regard to reforms in gender relations, a case in point was Guinea under President Sekou Touré. As discussed above, Touré sought to advance the status of women as part of his government's development policies, but his efforts failed when patriarchal forces in Guinean society rose in opposition to challenges to the "traditional family" and "communal customs" of the familial mode of production (Renzetti and Curran 1986).

Because of these and other pressures on the state to favor powerful localistic and particularistic groups, public resources are often wasted to achieve political objectives. Capital accumulation is invested unproductively, the economy contracts rather than grows, peasants and other producers withdraw from the state-controlled economy because of a lack of incentives, and foreign investment dries up (see Boone 1990; Nyang'oro 1989; Hyden 1983). The ensuing economic crisis forces the state to turn to external sources of funding to maintain the patron-client relationships necessary for political stability. This increases the state's dependency on external capitalist forces, such as the World Bank–International Monetary Fund (IMF), who impose their version of capitalist economic and political reform as "conditionalities" for loans. While many of these reforms may be well-meaning and needed, they severely circumscribe the ability of African states to shape their own autonomous development goals or strategies (Fatton 1988:261; Amin 1990a, b).

While it is true that African states have not achieved the competency of the developmentalist states of Asia, there are signs in at least some countries that the grounds for such a state are being laid. Underdeveloped capitalism—although typically enclave, comprador, and dependent on a managerial bourgeoisie—is producing an indigenous business and professional class as well as a well-educated technocratic elite who are gradually replacing the autocrats and party ideologues who have governed Africa since independence. Many of the new technocrats have been educated abroad and have international financial, business, or diplomatic experience. Examples include Babacar N'Diaye, president of the African Development Bank; Prime Minister Allasane Ouattara of Côte d'Ivoire, former governor of the Banque Centrale des États de l'Afrique de l'Ouest; and Nicephore Soglo, a former World Bank official recently elected president of Benin. Internationally known financial figures also have been appointed to high posts in Gabon, Mali, Senegal, Congo, Zaire, and Cameroon ("Chance . . ." 1991:3). In Zimbabwe, competent technocrats are making the major policymaking decisions in the government ministries, virtually sidelining ZANU (Zimbabwe African National Union) party bureaucrats (Herbst 1990).

The technocratic elite are increasingly allying themselves with the forces of liberal economic and political reform in Africa. Although themselves products and part of the managerial bourgeoisie, some members of the technocratic elite are going into private business or have ties to international capital. In most cases, the growing capitalist business classes are comprador in nature (i.e., they are linked to and supportive of foreign capital), but Africa's indigenous business classes are in some cases gaining support, as in Kenya (Kennedy 1988; Kitching 1980; Bradshaw 1990), Zimbabwe (Herbst 1990), Côte d'Ivoire, Nigeria, and Botswana (Riddell 1990).

Africa's bourgeoisie is not, as is commonly discussed, a hegemonic class able to enlist the state's unequivocal support for a capitalist transformation of society (see Fatton 1988; Kennedy 1988). The familial mode of production and its culture continue to permeate the state, the business class, and the general populace. As Sandbrook (1985) writes, Africa's bourgeoisies are too small and weak to enlist the state or the masses in a radical project of structural change to promote real development. Although personal ambition and greed associated with capitalism certainly exist in Africa, and wealthy businessmen and politicians are envied, the individualistic and instrumental ethics of capitalism are usually lacking—that is, individual competition, personal accumulation, thrift, efficiency, innovation, and hard work. Even the bourgeoisie has weak bourgeois values, what Sandbrook (1985:69–70) terms a "precapitalist mentality."

Clientelistic relationships based on kinship and ethnicity are major impediments to the individualist and instrumentalist ethics of capitalism to which Sandbrook refers. In the case of Kenya, for instance, a country where the indigenous capitalist class is among the strongest in Africa, Himbara (1994:89–90) discusses the reasons so many African businesses fail. Many reasons are rooted in the ethnic and kinship norms of the familial mode of production, for example, unwise loans to relatives from kin; family obligations that hinder development of enterprises, such as obligations to share income with extended family or employ relatives whether competent or necessary; bonds of ethnicity/kinship that block partnerships with "outsiders" or pressures to form partnerships with kinsmen regardless of business efficiency; and running businesses alone like "chiefs" rather than hiring competent managers.

Because capitalism is underdeveloped, the state may support development and capitalist expansion on the one hand while seeking to protect the familial mode of production and its social relationships at the same time. This prevents the state or societal actors from embracing the universalistic norms and rules of liberal capitalist society that sustain both capitalism and liberal democracy as opposed to the particularistic and personalized relationships still hegemonic in Africa (see Woods 1992:92–94).

This contradiction between universalism and particularism pervades African legal systems where universalistic European common law has been adopted but is often ignored in favor of ethnic or religious customary law. As legal scholar J. W. Van Doren (1989) writes,[6] capitalism and Western values have given common law its present character. But Western liberalism's individualism and equality are at odds with traditional values of communitarianism and ethnic group loyalty. African states are apparently not ready or able to reject the communitarian and particularistic African values of customary law in favor of the Western values that undergird capitalist society. These universalistic values of individualism and equality are not only necessary for capitalism and democracy to thrive but for women's rights to be asserted as well. Traditional society and customary law, Van Doren (1989:130) concludes, validate male dominance and sex discrimination.

Among Africa's growing bourgeois classes, insofar as they are becoming less dependent on kinship/ethnic ties and are creating a transethnic and even transnational class cohesion, universalistic, capitalist behavior and norms are implanting themselves (see Bates 1989; Sklar 1987:30–31). Kennedy (1988) discusses, for instance, how the rise of Africa's technocratic, professional, and business elites are conducive to a deepening of capitalism in society:

- They are educated and likely to be involved in their own businesses
- Intergenerational transfers of wealth and resources between parents and children is creating a professional middle class less tied to rural or ethnic kin than to others of their class
- The managerial bourgeoisie and ruling elites who gained their assets from access to the state now have secure wealth to invest in productive activities
- There is a growing class consciousness and sense of class interest reflected in part in greater intermarriage among ethnic groups
- There is a deepening of material values, technical training and education, and more financial collaboration occurring

Overall, Kennedy (1988:187) concludes, the climate for Africa's capitalist classes is improving.

The elite of Africa's business class are hoping to make that point by promoting trans-African and international business investment. In 1991 the African Business Roundtable (ABR), cosponsored by the U.S. Overseas Investment Corporation and USAID (U.S. Agency for International Development), held a conference in Dakar. U.S. investors were taken to Côte d'Ivoire, Ghana, The Gambia, and Senegal to encourage foreign investment in Africa and to enhance the image of the African business community abroad. The ABR is a high-powered millionaires' club of entrepreneurs whose credo is that the future of Africa in terms of development and growth rests not with the overburdened and incapable public sector but with the creative genius of the private sector (da Costa 1992:42). Babacar N'Diaye (founder of the ABR and president of the African Development Bank) expressed the group's consensus that economic freedom and an entrepreneurial ethic are needed in Africa and that economic progress depends on democratization and new public policy management that promotes entrepreneurship. While foreign investment should be encouraged, indigenous African businessmen are needed to develop the continent. It is time, stated Nigerian businessman Alhaji Abulaziz Ude, "to take on the political establishment" that has hindered indigenous capitalists who are often seen as a threat to those in power" (da Costa 1992:43).

One conclusion to be drawn from the above discussion is that the African state needs to be transformed into a developmentalist state that can promote the entrepreneurial and productive forces in society that have been stymied by the familial mode of production and underdeveloped capitalism. The only force that can do this is the market, which promotes the rise of a local bourgeoisie and other classes and interest groups who will benefit from the removal of the constraints on entrepreneurialism imposed by the familial mode of production (Hyden 1983:197–198; Nyang'oro 1989:134–136).

This transformation is also necessary to provide the grounds for women's emancipation from subordination and exploitation by the patriarchal relations that undergird underdeveloped capitalism. Women's claims to be treated as individuals with human rights and equal rights, which are fundamental to any feminist agenda, are universalistic demands rooted in capitalist society; as we have already seen, such values have too few adherents in the kinship/ethnic-based political economies that dominate in most of Africa now. As Scott (1995:113) observed in Mozambique, even among women it is difficult to enlist support for radical reform in gender relations without changing the material conditions that sustain them.

## ▲  Support for Capitalist Market Reforms

Economic and political liberalization can play an important role in promoting gender equality and breaking down African patriarchy. Economic reforms are needed that will encourage the development of private investment (both local and foreign) and market competition and that will reward innovation, risk taking, and entrepreneurship in order to rapidly improve economic productivity and growth. Only this will transform the familial mode of production and create the basis for greater gender equality. As Kennedy (1988:188) concludes,

> capitalism is nothing if it is not expansionary. Without productive investment wealth consists of little more than bits of paper chasing around in ever-decreasing circles capable of benefiting fewer and fewer people. Despite the potential for short-term gain, this kind of capitalism is not satisfactory even from the perspective of political elites and entrenched commercial interests.

Socialism or delinking are currently unfeasible options to some form of capitalism. Socialism has been largely abandoned all over the continent, as Sandbrook (1993:149) points out; delinking from the global economy in order to promote economic self-reliance and autonomy does not work in societies as weak and peripheral as those of Africa. Although underdeveloped capitalism has hitherto relegated African economies to the role of exporters of primary goods, Bloom and Brender (1993) find that developing countries that integrate into the global economy have greater income growth and material well-being than those that do not, although internal income inequality may increase. The solution may not be for African countries to withdraw from the international economy but to devise successful ways to create a market economy that meets developmental goals as well, a subject to be discussed below.

Market reforms could benefit women in several ways. Capitalist-oriented economies can, Nafziger (1988: 65) writes, reduce poverty, increase equality, and meet basic needs—as in Taiwan and South Korea—but this depends on state policy, not laissez-faire or trickle-down capitalism. If it addresses problems of institutional sexism, economic liberalism can benefit women by giving them more support as entrepreneurs in the private sector. In the current system, business opportunities largely depend on holding positions in government or having patrons who do. Since few women are in the managerial bourgeoisie or can work the patronage system (because most patronage resources are under male control), women have had little access to the economic spoils of state capitalism and patronage systems. Economic liberalism would, some claim, undermine the patronage system by giving less scope for bureaucrats to interfere with producers through the controls over the economy they currently have. The market would also reward efficiency and productivity more, rather than allowing mostly males to prosper because of patriarchal privilege (see Nafziger 1988:65, 74). A final benefit of market reform is that it partially reorganizes the sexual division of labor. This is a threat to African patriarchy insofar as it reduces or eliminates male and family control over women. As more women get paid work or control their own businesses, their options and power in relation to men can increase as well. Some industrial firms actually prefer to hire women because they are cheaper than men, which is a form of capitalist exploitation of women made possible by patriarchal sexist discrimination. However, women's employment can still help to erode at least private patriarchal control over women (i.e., that exercised by male family members), as is discussed in Chapter 2.

The danger for women is that men who fear losing control over women as a result of the expansion of capitalism may seek to reestablish that control through political means (Walby 1986:110). For this reason, among others to be discussed, there is no cause to believe that markets alone will result in gender equality; men can use patriarchal privilege and the male-dominated state to maintain gender inequality. Similarly, liberal democracy can promote women's equality, as in the West, but it does not guarantee it. Indeed, democracy can be a means of reestablishing or maintaining patriarchal systems.[7] Although not a panacea, democratization does have the potential to be beneficial to women's equality by creating a more open, pluralistic environment for women's organizations and politics. Democracy also may be a positive force for economic liberalization, which can help women to acquire more economic resources and independence from patriarchal control. But democracy's benefits to women may depend to a large extent on how powerful the patriarchal resistance to gender equality is. Even the liberal democracies of the West are far from achieving gender equality and ridding themselves of institutionalized patriarchy.

## ▲ Democratization

There is no one-to-one relationship between capitalism and democracy. Although today's mature capitalist countries are also democratic, most were not when the process of capitalist industrialization began. In today's developing countries, those that have developed the most, the NICs, have done so under authoritarian, developmentalist regimes. The NICs are now becoming more democratic because their economic success has spawned a growing middle class and has eliminated the rationale for authoritarianism. The experience of the West and the NICs suggests that a viable democracy is built on a base of sustained economic development and industrialization. Qadir and coauthors (1993:419–420) may be correct in their claim that in Africa the prospects for democracy are not good unless it can produce sustainable economic benefits for the masses. While democratization movements have grown all over Africa, there are legitimate doubts as to whether democracy or a developmentalist state can flourish without changing the social, political, and economic systems of Africa's underdeveloped capitalist societies. As Sandbrook (1993:98) observes, "Africa's stunted and dependent capitalism shapes stunted and dependent class relations" that do not disperse power (i.e., there is no bourgeoisie with an independent economic base to balance or limit the holders of political power).

There are also grounds to support the assertion that, given the conditions of underdeveloped capitalism in Africa, democratization is necessary to implement economic and political reform in Africa. Reciprocally, economic reform may promote democratization and political reform. Clapham (1993:431–432, 437) argues that market-oriented structural adjustment reforms imposed by the World Bank–IMF will succeed only if democratic reforms are in place that prevent the government from sabotaging reform to protect its own interests. Democratization will also force the government to rely more on popular support to stay in power, partly because external political, economic, and military backing has eroded. Sandbrook (1993:98–99, 118–119) contends that economic and political reforms may limit the patronage resources available to the state, thus helping to rejuvenate the private sector and political pluralism. Democratic reforms can also give more influence to the poor (and women), but, as Sandbrook admits, Third World democracies, including African examples such as Botswana, provide few models of equitable development. C. S. Whitaker

(1991) disagrees with those who think that, due to the sacrifices borne by the citizenry under SAPs, democracy will undermine economic reforms (see Fatton 1992). Using cases of labor union layoffs in Senegal and Côte d'Ivoire, Whitaker (1991:348–349) asserts that democracy is necessary for SAPs to succeed, because it promotes cooperation and bargaining among major interest groups, strengthens political interest groups, promotes government accountability for its decisions, and opens up the deliberation of national issues beyond particularism. Based on his study of SAPs in Tanzania, Kiondo (1992:37–38) makes similar points in favor of democratization. Democracy is needed so that the elites instituting liberal reform measures are responsible to the masses. Otherwise, the elites, under the guise of privatization and agricultural reform, are likely to use their political connections and money to accumulate most of the privatized land and other economic assets for themselves and cut services to the poor while sparing the rich.

Perhaps the most important argument in favor of democracy is that its liberal values are necessary in capitalist or socialist systems if they are to avoid "the authoritarian trap" into which most of them have fallen. Democracy forces the ruling class to seek legitimacy from the governed and be accountable for its actions rather than resorting to brutality and repression to stay in power (Sklar 1991c:221). Socialist Claude Aké agrees and proposes that socialists should temporarily put aside their socialist goals and support democratic and political rights in Africa. While liberal democracies in the Third World do little to address issues of inequality, poverty, or injustice, liberal democracy does protect some civil and political rights for the poor as well as the middle classes. It also allows progressive (i.e., socialist) elements to survive and organize against capitalism or to promote the economic reform of capitalism (in Sandbrook 1993:132–133). Democracy is also necessary for a fully developed civil society that, while tolerant of ethnic and cultural pluralism, can limit particularistic norms that violate such universalistic norms as equal rights and human rights.

It is these universalistic norms that must first and foremost be established in Africa as the basis of gender equality. As discussed by feminist scholar Eisenstein (1981:222), liberal democracy makes it possible for women to push the state as far as it can go toward equality of opportunity for women, although the state and reform alone will not allow for women's equality with men. Women can, however, make real gains. These gains plus the realization of the limits of this strategy will result in a women's politics that goes beyond liberalism. Such a position is a better starting point than one that must build on a society predicated on privilege and unchallenged oppression.

## ▲  The Interventionist State

Let me stress that market-oriented reforms and the deepening of capitalism in African societies *can* be beneficial to women and help to promote gender equality, but this largely depends on the extent to which feminist forces are able to organize and pressure the state to end sex discrimination and actively promote gender equality within the political system, the economy, and society as a whole (especially in education and the family).

As Sklar (1991a:325–326) writes, capitalist success stories in the Third World are not based on laissez-faire: "there is no substitute for an actively interventionist state"; otherwise, capitalist "efficiency" and economic growth often ignore human needs and inequality. In other words, political remedies are necessary to balance the need for efficiency and growth with equity and an ethic of social responsibility (see also Nyang'oro 1989:155–156). Sandbrook (1993:120) adds that without a welfare-oriented state, market relationships tend to favor those already richer and better endowed. In Africa, that would mean mainly the managerial bourgeoisie, their families, and cronies—and mostly males.

This elite class formation is already beginning to take place. In Côte d'Ivoire, for instance, from the 1960s to 1980s at least two-thirds of Ivoirian investors or promoters of small industries were members of the civil service or held political positions (Nafziger 1988:104). In rural Cameroon, a new rural elite of "big men" is developing as a result of privatization of land. They are able to combine positions of authority in precapitalist society (e.g., formal roles in traditional politics, titles in secret societies, regular visits with the *fon* [king]) with access to the state. This facilitates access to land and other resources for private accumulation. Although women are legally able to get land allocations, their applications are rarely approved (Goheen 1991:248). Patriarchy, not capitalism per se, is the problem. Instead, as Goheen (1991:250–251) remarks, "local norms and ideology perpetuate static ideals of male-female roles and spheres of influence," even though material conditions have changed due to increasing market penetration and commoditization. Especially difficult to overcome are norms that only men can own land through the patrilineage, while women have only usufruct rights. Women end up being unable to get land either through the family or the government.

Without state intervention, norms and values associated with patriarchy are likely to subvert the universalistic norms and values of democracy as well as capitalism. Sandbrook (1993:95, 144–145) notes that African political traditions were usually hierarchical and heterogeneous and, in many ways, not conducive to Western pluralistic democracy. Therefore, such liberal-sounding reforms as "empowering people" and "promoting civil society" may not be necessarily liberating. The empowered groups and organizations may reinforce existing ethnic, religious, and gender inequality and divisions. Moreover, the already powerful (e.g., males) tend to dominate local organizations and groups and divert benefits to themselves. Only the state can protect the interests of the poor and powerless and promote equality for all.

Olofin (1991:322–323) adds that another role for the state is to create the conditions necessary (i.e., entrepreneurs, skills) for the success of market incentives (e.g., profit motive). The private sector alone cannot be relied upon to create the conditions for technological innovation and acquisition of skills. This is especially true given the role of patriarchy and underdeveloped capitalism in determining human resource development and resource use in Africa. Elson (1989:64) underscores the fallacy of assuming the neutrality of the market. "If greater reliance is to be placed on private enterprise, we need to ask: whose enterprise? The enterprise of the woman farming or trading on her own account, or the enterprise of agribusiness and merchants with monopoly power? The enterprise of a woman's cooperative or the enterprise of a multinational corporation?" Women's enterprise, she argues, requires support from the state—training, credit, and services that free women's time from domestic duties.

All of this contradicts what Crow (1988) refers to as the simplistic definition of "more capitalism, less state" that has permeated the formulation of World Bank–IMF austerity measures and structural adjustment in the 1980s. As will be discussed in the next chapter, SAPs and other market-oriented development strategies pursued in Africa have typically neglected or been oblivious to the fact that patriarchy negates the goals and theory of free enterprise capitalism. Instead, they "can be viewed as policies that simultaneously reinforce the capitalist, liberal, and bureaucratic aspects of the African state while at the same time reinforcing, in general, masculine privilege" (Scott 1995:77). In other words, without taking into account the operation and effects of African patriarchy on the current economy and on the market reforms being pursued, women will likely end up losers. But it will not be the result of the "impersonal" market!

The challenge for the African state is, according to Amin (1990b:183), to avoid development strategies that maximize "the consumption of a minority, even at the price of a sacrifice of the material interests of the masses and of national and cultural values." While this sounds desirable, we must not forget that some traditional cultural values oppress women and undermine the universalistic values of equality and dignity of the individual that underpin capitalism, socialism, or the "delinking" espoused by Amin (1990a, b).[8] The challenge is to pursue development that focuses not only on equity but nurtures the talents, ambitions, and entrepreneurial spirit of all Africans, females as well as males, for the betterment of their societies.

Woods (1992:95) points out correctly that the demand for economic democracy among Africans is not so much a demand for a laissez-faire economy but rather for the establishment of nonarbitrary rules and an end to incessant political and personal intervention in the economic affairs of African businesspeople. The state's arbitrariness has largely been the result, as we have discussed, of the political and economic interests of Africa's ruling elites who, on the one hand, are enmeshed in underdeveloped capitalist and patriarchal structures while, on the other hand, embryonically embarking on the path of capitalist development and class formation.

While they remain loathe to attack patriarchy, under the rubric of respecting African tradition, there is a dawning realization by at least some African rulers that the long-range development, and perhaps survival, of their nations depends on transforming underdeveloped capitalism. This cannot succeed, nor can the capitalist (or socialist) and democratic reforms in Africa succeed, without a significant liberation of women from African patriarchy. This liberation will entail the consent and involvement of men as well as women; women cannot force gender equality on a recalcitrant male power structure, nor can the state (at least while it remains controlled by the male power structure). Men's advocacy of gender equality depends on both their acceptance of universalistic human values of equality and equal rights and on gender equality's being seen as in their interests, not just at their expense.

The task of the developmental state is to selectively intervene in the economy to support both growth and equity as the measure of development. Promoting gender equality will require overcoming deeply entrenched patriarchal institutions, practices, and attitudes. This cannot be accomplished through gender-neutral policies that, by ignoring patriarchy or expecting women to be like men, assure patriarchy's perpetuation. This is true of other forms of class, ethnic, or racial inequality as well. While some men will never accept the goal of gender equality, under the right conditions there are men who will support gender reform. As C. S. Whitaker (1991:347–348) writes about reforming the familial mode of production in general, "The state capable of breaking through this impasse is one that is able to be convincing about a claim that redeployment of resources acquired, at the immediate expense of groups and individuals, will eventually yield a positive sum, a boon in some sense for everyone."

## ▲ Notes

1. Pringle and Watson (1992:68) and Marshall (1994:125) argue against an essentialist conception of women's interests, but they also see that women need to embrace a common core of identity as women as a political tactic of empowerment

if they are to successfully forge alliances among women across class, race, and ethnic lines.

2. In many cases, capitalist development is associated with authoritarian regimes in much of the Third World, not with liberal democracy. This appears to be more true in the early stages of capitalist development but less so as capitalism matures and an educated middle class is created. In the long run, capitalist "command economies" are no more efficient than socialist ones; nor can they indefinitely expand through coercion, lack of popular political participation, or the denial of some redistribution of economic benefits to workers. The experience of the NICs indicates that this trend toward liberalization is occurring in almost all of them. It is interesting to note that even in Third World autocracies, liberal ideology, symbols, and formal political-legal institutions are maintained, even if there is little substance behind them. This often sets up expectations for what should ideally exist, which becomes the basis for political movements to demand real democracy, equality, and rights (see Monshipouri 1995; and Pinkney 1994 for good analyses of these and other issues related to democratization and capitalism in the Third World).

3. Most African governments have made their constitutions conform to the UN Universal Declaration of Human Rights, but only thirty-three of fifty-three African nations signed the 1979 Convention on the Elimination of all Forms of Discrimination Against Women (Morna 1994).

4. In 1992 SADCC became SADC, the Southern African Development Community.

5. I refer the reader to the discussion of equality in Chapter 1. Equality for women must recognize the differences between men and women and avoid the pitfall of requiring women to be like men to be treated equally.

6. Van Doren was writing in response to the famous Otieno burial controversy in Kenya in the late 1980s. Wambui Otieno challenged her husband's kinsmen for the right to bury him. The case opened up a Pandora's box of controversial issues surrounding women's rights, ethnic rivalry, and traditional versus common law. See Gordon 1994, 1995; Cohen and Odhiambo 1992; and Stamp 1991a).

7. As in Algeria, for instance, where Muslim fundamentalists, who wish to roll back the advances women have made, would likely win in a democratic election.

8. Delinking is associated with what Amin calls "autocentric" development in which the imperatives of a nation's own internal development determine development strategies rather than the dictates of the world capitalist economy. The market relegates Africa to the position of dependency and unequal underdevelopment and prevents local control of the economy.

# ▲ 5
# Development and Women

Colonialism introduced dependent, peripheral development to Africa, which bound African economies to producing primary products for export in exchange for capital, technology, and manufactured goods from the West. The African familial mode of production, along with patriarchal gender relationships that had evolved in precapitalist economies, were maintained in modified form to serve colonial capitalism. But colonial capitalism also introduced Western patriarchy to Africa in the form of stereotypic notions of men's and women's spheres (the public vs. the private), the monogamous nuclear family headed by men, and new notions of femininity and masculinity. Even now gender relations and women's status in Africa continue to be molded by these three influences: African patriarchy (with its roots in precapitalist Africa); underdeveloped capitalism (the distorted form of capitalism that results from the articulation of capitalism with precapitalist modes and relations of production); and Western patriarchy.

Contrary to the position of scholars who view capitalism and patriarchy as either one system or who aver that capitalism requires patriarchy, my position is that the relationship between patriarchy and capitalism is contingent, changing, and in some respects adversarial. The reason is that patriarchy takes more than one form, just as capitalism does; therefore, patriarchal relationships that evolved in precapitalist societies may be incompatible with capitalist development. By the same token, capitalism introduces new economic and social changes that can undermine existing patriarchies. Indeed, capitalist expansion may be hindered by patriarchal practices that undermine capitalism's control over the rational use of land, labor, and capital. Capitalism remains underdeveloped capitalism, neither capitalist or precapitalist but an unproductive, exploitative hybrid capable of producing only limited capital accumulation or development.

In the underdeveloped capitalist environment of Africa, both men and women are exploited, but patriarchy maintains structures of male privilege and allows men and capitalism to exploit the labor of women. In fact, more than capitalism, it is the social relationships and discriminatory barriers

135

erected by patriarchy that make it more difficult for women than men to gain the economic and political resources necessary to improve their lives. As Afonja (1986a:134) has argued, capitalism has opened up new occupations for women in commercial agriculture, new forms of trade, and informal and formal sector occupations, but "women's tasks of reproducing and nurturing the family, which were established in the subsistence economy, have primarily determined their subordinate position in new production roles."

## ▲  Patriarchal Bias in Development

Although underdeveloped capitalism has benefited from and used gender inequalities, the results have been unsatisfactory and unsustainable. African economies are in crisis and threatened by environmental and population problems. The African state is mired in corruption, ethnic strife, and authoritarianism. That efforts to develop Africa have failed is acknowledged by Africa's leaders and Western development agents alike. The importance of women to the development effort has also been acknowledged. Yet despite all the attention paid to "integrating women in development" and formal laws and international agreements that espouse equality of the sexes, patriarchal biases have permeated the development strategies pursued in Africa from independence to the present.

Newland (1991:130) believes women in development (WID) policies take the form they do in part because they are set within male-dominated institutions in which women's issues are instrumental to such male concerns as lower population growth, higher economic growth, or successful political mobilization rather than being ends in themselves. WID organizations and programs are also handicapped because they cannot afford to offend host countries by proposing controversial initiatives. Therefore, deeply entrenched and strongly defended patriarchal institutions and practices are rarely challenged. Instead, WID must work within "the constraints of purdah, machismo, unequal division of labor, restrictive interpretations of religious teachings," and so on.

Stamp (1989:59) discusses the role gender bias in African government policies has played in the marginalization of women from technological advances introduced into Africa. In general, she points out, development planning ignores women's relationships with technology and the fact that new technology has mostly benefited men. One example involves the promotion of "appropriate technology" without taking gender issues into account, that is, who decides what is appropriate and who benefits. Stamp cites, for instance, cases where women were given carts to carry water and wood but men took them for themselves. She notes other problems as well:

(1) "income-generating projects" often trivialize women's role as food producers while reinforcing a "home economics" stereotype of appropriate women's activities that disregards whether there is a market for the resulting products; (2) women lack access to finances for acquiring productive technologies; (3) they lack secure rights to land or control over management (including technological inputs); (4) technological inputs (if controlled by or benefiting men) can disrupt gender relations and undermine women's power in their families—thus women may resist innovations from which they do not benefit; (5) some new agricultural and health technologies increase women's work but at the same time women lose decisionmaking power (Stamp 1989:50–51).

Part of the explanation for the marginalization of women is that development planning in the Third World is permeated with sexist assumptions, as Moser (1991:85–87) demonstrates. These include the assumption that households are basically nuclear (i.e., with a husband, his wife, and children) and that there is a uniform sexual division of labor. That is, the husband is the main breadwinner who works outside the home, while the woman is primarily a housewife; women's subordinate position with regard to control over resources and decisionmaking in the household is typically ignored. These gender relationships are seen as natural and reinforced by legal and educational systems, the media, and family planning programs. Such stereotypes shape development thinking and policies despite the fact that one-third of the world's households are headed by women—in urban area as many as 50 percent or more may be female-headed. In rural areas where male migration is common, women are the de facto heads of families and often managers of farms as well. Male unemployment is also not uncommon, while female farming and informal sector activities may be the main source of family survival. The result of these assumptions is that, despite a formal commitment to women in development, WID policies and programs have so far had little positive impact (Stamp 1989:26).

In fact, the status of women in many cases has worsened. Gittinger and coauthors (1990:3–4) report that women grow 75 percent of all the food in Africa, do all the food processing, fetch most of the water and fuel, do 60 percent of the marketing, and do at least half the work in storing food and raising animals. Women also do much of the work on cash crops, work on other people's crops to earn cash, and do nonagricultural work for cash while still finding time to work in community self-help activities. But as a result of the combination of patriarchal cultural factors and the biased policies of governments and development agencies, the social and economic gap between men and women has widened. Women own the least property and goods, have the poorest nutritional status, and are the most overworked group in Africa. Households headed by women are the worst off, having the least access to resources and the labor of others. And such households are growing: over one-third of rural households in Malawi, 40 percent of small farms in Kenya, and more than half of rural households in the communal areas of Zimbabwe are now headed by women. Most rural women have to supplement farming with nonagricultural work such as beekeeping or raising small animals, crafts, or beer brewing. Women are often the main source of income for food, school fees, and medical expenses for their families.

Capitalist demands for efficiency or profit do not create or require these excessive demands on women's labor and other forms of bias against women. While it has been a capitalist-inspired choice that the most efficient use of development resources is to invest in farmers with land, cash, and a willingness to innovate, it is institutionalized patriarchy that has determined that these farmers will be mostly men. Moreover, even women farmers and managers who fit the criteria often do not get the services or resources to which they are entitled, reports Staudt (1987). Such gender biases obviously distort the market and efficiency, rather than reflect market forces at work.

One of the most common problems in shaping development policies that affect women is the assumption that such policies are gender-neutral whereas in reality they greatly favor men at women's expense. This bias is observable in many World Bank publications. For instance, in the Bank's (1989b:92) market-oriented report on achieving sustainable growth in Africa, it advocated such things as allowing comparative advantage to decide whether farmers produce food or export crops, rather than government policy. The assumption that an impersonal market will determine such production choices ignores the fact that in the familial mode of production men, who control and benefit mostly from cash crops, usually have more control over the use of the land than women, who produce food crops. This bias obviously favors cash-crop production over food crops. If food crops become major sources of cash income, men can redefine them as cash crops and take them over for their own benefit. This can discourage women from growing some marketable crops. In both cases, patriarchal power, not the market, is determining production choices.

The Bank (1989b:45) also advocated "a neutral structure of incentives" and "getting prices right" as ways of using the market to encourage greater production for the market. This, too, ignores structured gender inequality that makes it difficult for women to respond to market incentives. One problem, Palmer (1991:157) points out, is that price incentives will not work if most of the benefits of increased production or prices go to male household heads rather than to the women actually doing the work. Another problem is that the sexual division of labor that requires women to do almost all the child rearing, food provisioning, and housework may dictate women's "choice" of where to put their labor regardless of market incentives to the contrary (see Gittinger et al. 1990:7).

The treatment of the household as a unit, and ignoring women's subordination within it, results in often fallacious assumptions. One is that market forces and structural adjustment will reduce expenditures on luxuries in favor of household necessities such as food. But as Elson (1992:36) notes, men who control the household budget tend to maintain expenditures for themselves on such goods as alcohol, cigarettes, and socializing in bars at the expense of their families. Similarly, improving household income may provide few benefits for women or children in the household. Recommendations that small farmers need more resources, assuming that some of these resources will reach women in the household, ignores the fact that men often control who gets such resources, and they often create barriers that prevent help from reaching their wives. Efforts to increase the efficiency and output of small farms also can be harmful to women if this extra output is produced by even more labor of women rather than by improved inputs. As Palmer (1991:156) writes, higher land yields sometimes result from overexploitation and undercapitalization of female labor. In Kenya, for instance, women's productivity is very low—women maintain yields by more and more work.

There is also a major contradiction implicit in the World Bank's approach to promoting agriculture and industry. On the one hand, the Bank believes quite rightly that farm prices need to go up to provide incentives for farmers to produce for the market. At the same time, the Bank declares that wage costs in Africa are too high and must be brought down to induce multinational firms to invest. Apparently, from the Bank's standpoint, a laudable goal would be for average wages for the subcontinent to approach those of Madagascar where the hourly wage of 29 cents is, not surprisingly, beginning to encourage foreign firms[1] (World Bank 1989b:3–7, 117). It does not seem to occur to the Bank that higher prices for food crops accompanied by falling wages may have disastrous consequences for the standard of living of the urban poor who must purchase food with their meager wages or for the rural poor who depend on the remittances of urban wage earners. Moreover, the results for women, given the patriarchal power structure, may be demands on women's time to grow even more food for the family, to keep prices for food crops low (thus lowering production for the market), or to work even harder at extra jobs to earn cash (see Bennholdt-Thomsen 1988:54–55). It is not clear what the Bank would see as the way out of this impasse or whether it perceives this situation as a problem for women at all.

Finally, the Bank discusses the need for secure land tenure and title registration as a means of promoting commercial farming (which would most assuredly over time undercut the familial mode of production and produce a class of capitalist commercial farmers). The Bank is also aware of the need for women to have secure access to land. It is, therefore, difficult to comprehend why the Bank advocates "codifying customary land rights" (World Bank 1989b:8), apparently oblivious of the fact that customary land rights most often stipulate that only men can own land. The Bank's proposal here would guarantee what is already happening: men are gaining almost all the titles to land, although women provide most of the unpaid or poorly paid labor.

Another contradiction can be found in the Bank's calling on the state to "enable women" to play a full role in economic and social development and remove all obstacles to this participation. At the same time, the Bank urges the state to play a neutral role and minimize intervention in the economy (Scott 1995:76–77). Obviously, the state cannot provide an enabling environment for women without substantial intervention in current discriminatory economic and property relationships to include such things as legal reforms; bureaucratic policy reforms and regulation; and new "affirmative action" programs in education, employment, and credit.

Finally, the Bank never challenges the sexual division of labor that results in women's being called upon "to bear the costs of capitalist state policies by generating more income. Meanwhile, they are expected to continue their sex-specific nurturing activities within the household" (Scott 1995:78). This strategy, which is a modification of existing efforts to base development in part on women's unpaid labor in the home plus wage work, is, as Scott (1995:78, 18) recognizes, not "woman friendly."

Perhaps the Bank's insensitivity on these gender issues can be explained in part by the fact that, as Charlton (1984:206, 212) reports, the Bank's staff has been overwhelmingly male: only 12 percent of the professional staff was female in the early 1980s. While WID units with mostly female staff are now more widespread in the Bank and other agencies, Moser (1991:84) argues that development planning is still dominated by men who fail to recognize the importance of gender or who attempt to "graft" gender planning onto existing planning.

Others maintain that, in general, the Bank is ill-equipped to support projects, policies, or organizations that benefit the poor—men or women. Hellinger and coauthors (1988:125–138) contend that the main goal of the World Bank is to make countries "safe" for foreign direct investment and creditworthy for commercial bank lending. To do so it has consistently pursued the same export-led development strategy that encourages the exploitation of primary goods and cheap labor and in the process marginalizes the poor. Hellinger and coauthors also suggest that the Bank's liberal-sounding rhetoric on such issues as women or the environment may be largely public relations.

Development projects, especially women's projects promoted by the World Bank and the U.S. Agency for International Development (USAID), also take their share of criticism. Stamp (1989:40, 61–62) argues, for instance, that such projects are popular with male policymakers because they do not challenge the sexual division of labor that gives prerogatives to men in the sphere of commercial enterprise. Instead, women's projects are often ancillary to mainstream development initiatives that focus on men and are an extension of women's domestic roles (e.g., sewing or crafts activities). Thus they serve to maintain the sexual division of labor rather than encouraging women to learn new skills and advance with new technology into areas that provide better opportunity and remuneration. Women's projects also ignore women's main economic activity as farmers and their need for full-time employment; instead they often simply add to the heavy burden of work women already carry.

## ▲ Capitalist Development and Women

The conclusion I draw is that the patriarchal biases and male control of social institutions are among the reasons development strategies have failed to serve women—not that they are capitalist and market-oriented. Capitalist expansion in Africa is severely constrained, not aided, by the patriarchal gender relations and structures found in Africa. There are at least two major ways that capitalist development in principle is a threat to African patriarchy and of potential benefit to women. First, both Western and indigenous policymakers are increasingly realizing that gender relations must be changed for capitalist development to succeed in Africa. Women need more resources, opportunity, and liberation from customary forms of male dominance. Second, by introducing social change and new egalitarian ideologies, legal reforms, and social relationships, capitalism undermines the familial mode of production and African patriarchy. Although capitalism is far from perfect, feminists must deal with the present reality that more market-oriented economies are inevitable and, if properly managed, can offer hope for a renewal of growth and development that can benefit women as well as men.

While many African governments are tepid, at best, in their enthusiasm for such reforms, socialist alternatives to some form of mixed market economy have failed and been abandoned on the continent. Moreover, sub-Saharan Africa's best economic performers, Botswana and Mauritius, are unequivocally procapitalist, export-oriented economies. Sklar (1991a:323) aptly assesses the present triumph of capitalism on the continent. "Few sophisticated socialists today rate the 'development merits' of socialism above those of capitalism; fewer still would dispute the short term advantages of capitalism for societies at early stages of industrial development." Socialism has become more a moral critique of inequality, Sklar claims, than a practicable blueprint for development.

Although the degree to which African economies are embracing capitalism varies, several themes relevant to women in development stand out:

1. One theme is that entrepreneurship and individual initiative in the private sector need to be encouraged and rewarded at all levels of society. Since the late 1980s, World Bank publications have been emphasizing the importance of the informal sector, called a "seedbed for entrepreneurs" (see, e.g., World Bank 1989b:5), and the need for more local medium-sized businesses (i.e., "the missing middle" between small-scale informal sector business and large enterprises). Among the virtues of SMEs (small-medium enterprises) is that they create jobs at lower cost, use more local resources, and provide affordable goods and services to local consumers (World Bank 1989b:137). This represents a major change of emphasis from earlier World Bank–IMF development strategies that focused on large-scale projects, enterprises, and multinational corporations (MNCs) (see World Bank 1981), or what Crow (1988:338) refers to as the "development is nasty" approach. The development is nasty approach is characterized by the view that peasant farmers and small enterprises are inefficient and less productive than large ones that can employ economies of scale. Development necessitates that land and other productive assets be in the hands of productive capitalists (i.e., large-scale producers) whereas inefficient peasants become increasingly proletarianized.

2. Another theme, related to the above, is that peasant agriculture, which employs most Africans, must be made more productive, rather than eliminated. As the Bank points out, governments and development planners alike have neglected peasant agriculture and implemented counterproductive policies that are the major culprits behind falling agricultural output. Declining production and export volume is the major reason for falling revenues in Africa, not declining commodity prices, the Bank claims. For African economies to recover, they must grow by 4.5 percent per year—mostly from agriculture (see, e.g., World Bank 1989b:3–4).

3. Africans must be more self-reliant and build up local capacities. African economies are becoming increasingly marginal in the global economy. Many of its traditional exports are becoming obsolete, and Africa is losing market share to other LDC (less developed country) producers (World Bank 1989b:304). Foreign investment and local investment in manufacturing as well as Africa's share of global manufacturing exports have declined so far that scholars such as Nyang'oro (1989:95–99) and Chazan and coauthors (1988:256) argue that Africa is fast de-industrializing.

As Africa loses its attractiveness to large-scale foreign capital and foreign exchange becomes a greater problem, Africa is able to import less, must diversify its exports, and manufacture more using local resources; in other words, be more self-reliant (see Riddell 1990; Kennedy 1988:189–190; Chazan et al. 1988:256–258, 297). Much current development thinking is that the state must interfere less in the economy while providing an "enabling environment" for ordinary Africans to "do things on their own—individually, as entrepreneurs, or organized in groups or communities" (Hyden 1990a:47). Kennedy (1988:189–190) writes that central to this strategy must be a "concerted and deliberate attempt to foster local initiative and effort at all levels and in all sectors of the economy." Kennedy provides an example from Kenya, where small-scale rural businesses engaged in food processing, metal fabrication, and producing inputs for farming are being promoted; small, informal sector businesses have access to loans through the Kenyan Commercial Bank (funded by USAID). Hyden (1990a:57), writing for the World Bank, acknowledges that top-down, state-directed development and dependence on imitating the West has failed in Africa. Instead, "grass-roots development" which relies on indigenous institutions and know-how and local initiative and action is needed. He also argues for support of the informal sector as the key to reversing Africa's economic decline because it employs so many Africans and is a major source of technological ingenuity and innovativeness (i.e., appropriate technology). Self-reliance and efficient use of local resources also have environmental benefits, as Hyden (1990a:49) envisions greater reliance on intercropping, agroforestry, and biological means to aid agricultural production and soil fertility.

4. "Growth with equity" has recently become the mantra of the development community, including the World Bank (see, e.g., 1989b:1). Partly in response to the outcry over the suffering of the poor under World Bank–IMF structural adjustment programs, the World Bank has been emphasizing concern for Africa's most vulnerable groups. The Bank's 1990 *World Development Report* stressed poverty alleviation as a major goal of development. Government policies were to be evaluated in terms of their impact on the poor, and countries whose policies were not geared toward alleviation of poverty could expect only moderate aid from the Bank (see also Feinberg 1991). Equity issues affect the operations of other development agencies whose efforts to help the poor have often fallen short. In a book on U.S. development aid to the Third World, for example, Hellinger and coauthors (1988:29–31) offer the following criticisms:

- U.S. aid too often has been used to maintain unequal wealth and power with relatively few benefits going to the poor
- Despite congressional mandates that USAID projects involve and assist the poor, this is rarely reflected in AID's mainstream operations

- The aid lobby uses such idealistic rhetoric as "basic needs" and "growth with equity," but instead needs are decided and implemented by outsiders and Third World bureaucrats using a top-down approach that results in little self-sustaining development for the poor
- Too much aid is a subsidy to U.S. business interests, rather than benefiting the poor

Lovell (1989:168–170) offers similar criticisms of the NGO (nongovernmental organizations) community. She accuses NGOs of addressing the symptoms of poverty but not the causes. NGOs encourage the poor to think they can escape poverty through petty capitalist income-generating activities without transforming exploitative economic and social relationships. Such activities do little to increase the productive capacity of the economy. She adds that too few resources reach the poor because of waste, inefficiency, and corruption by government officials and others.

5. Concern for the poor is largely the result of the realization that development cannot occur without the poor. They are the overwhelming majority of the population. But for the poor to contribute more to development and reap its benefits, efforts to improve human capital are necessary (see, e.g., World Bank 1989b:45; Chibber and Fischer 1991). This requires making education and training available to more people and at a higher level, as well as improving health and nutritional levels. In part, developing human resources, or "investing in people," is a job for the state, but in Africa where government services or subsidies have been cut, individuals, groups, and communities must provide more for themselves (see section on self-reliance above). Ironically, World Bank–IMF structural adjustment reforms designed to liberalize African economies have combined with existing economic problems to worsen the human resources environment in much of Africa. The United Nations reports that between 1986 and 1991 expenditures on health and education fell sharply, school enrollment declined, and malnutrition among children increased ("Controversy . . ." 1991:4). In response to the problem, the World Bank, the African Development Bank, and the United Nations have reportedly made human resource development an important priority (Shepherd 1992:37).

In all of the above areas, women's needs have been largely neglected, as the World Bank (1989b:86–87) admits:

"Modernization" has shifted the balance of advantage against women. The legal framework and the modern social sector and producer services developed by the independent African nations (and also most externally sponsored development projects) have not served women well. Legal systems have discriminated in land titling. . . . It is often more difficult for women to gain access to information and technology, resources, and credit. Agricultural extension and formal financial institutions are biased toward a male clientele. . . . There is a wide gender gap in education. . . .

As a result, women are less-well equipped than men to take advantage of the better income-earning opportunities. . . . In industry and trade women have been confined to small-scale operations in the informal sector; . . . despite the trading empires built up by the most successful female entrepreneurs, women's average incomes are relatively low. Women are also handicapped in access to formal sector jobs by their lower educational attainments, and those who succeed are placed in lower-grade, lower-paid jobs.

Neither the World Bank nor the donor community have had an impressive record of helping African women, despite such pronouncements. Hellinger and his associates (1988:143) contend that between 1975 and 1985, the Bank's Women in Development policy office was dragging along with little real action. Uma Lele, manager of the Agricultural Policy Office of the Technical Department in the World Bank's Africa Region, acknowledges the Bank's problems and sees the role of big donor agencies in helping women as limited by the fact that they are too centralized and too distant from the scene to make appropriate rural development programs. Their role is mostly "improving the capacity of national, regional, and local governments, voluntary agencies, and private agents" (Lele 1991:61). Lele (1991:68) also feels that the main help for women will be derivative of an improved general "macroeconomic and sectoral policy and institutional environment," the assumption being that the benefits of a freer economy will trickle down to women.

UNDP (United Nations Development Programme) programs in the 1980s also failed to do much to help women. In an assessment of UNDP projects from 1985 to 1986, Goetz (1991:140) reports that project evaluations mentioned women in income-generating projects, but "no evaluation suggested improving the economic status of women in a way that would not reinforce the traditional division of labor." Sixty percent of the sample did not mention women at all. Another problem Goetz found was that women were absent from the process of setting national development priorities in development plans, the level where the main decisions about resource allocation are made.

In its 1990 report on women in development, the World Bank (1990b: v) vowed to do substantially more to help women because opportunities for women are not only an issue of justice but a "sure route . . . to faster and more sustainable development." This new emphasis on women was preceded by the establishment in 1987 of a Women in Development Division and in 1989 the inclusion of a coordinator for women in development in the Bank's four regional complexes, including Africa. With help from

UNDP and several Bank member countries, research on women and agriculture was launched, and more than one-third of all the Bank's 1989 operations in Africa included actions specifically addressed to women (World Bank 1990b:10).

A major concern of the Bank is helping women grow more food for the household, thus reinforcing the traditional sexual division of labor. An awareness of the importance of women to feeding Africa is not lost to African policymakers either. A 1990 World Bank Symposium on Household Food Security and the Role of Women, which included forty-seven senior African policymakers, academic specialists, and the staff of several international agencies, concluded that "improving household food security in Africa means focusing on the role of women. . . . Unless the production and productivity of these women is increased, efforts to improve household food security in Africa will not succeed" (Gittinger et al. 1990:1).

But women's role in agriculture is not restricted to food production. The World Bank recognizes that women are major cash-crop producers as well. If production of cash crops, the main source of exports for most African countries, is to grow, women—not just men—must receive more resources. Moreover, some studies show that when women do get more help, they outproduce men. For example, a World Bank study of women in Kenya reported that the women are producing most of the country's cash (e.g., tea, coffee, pyrethrum) and food crops, although men usually hold title to the land and women get little access to formal credit and less extension help than men. Women farmers also must work much harder than men, having child care and household responsibilities on top of running a farm. Despite these disadvantages, extension agents find women are more productive and willing to adopt advice than men (World Bank 1989a:xiv–xv, 4). In a later report, the Bank added that when female farmers are given the same access to inputs, extension, credit, and education as men, they produce about 7 percent more per acre (World Bank 1990b:5). In essence, African economies are paying a substantial economic cost for discrimination against women.[2]

As with the World Bank, the large body of literature published by USAID in the 1980s and 1990s shows a significant evolution in orientation toward WID and a growing awareness of the deficiencies of the past. In part this changing awareness is due to growing pressures from women's groups to improve the agency's focus on women and the growing number of female (and male) staffers with a more feminist outlook on gender issues in development. But it also reflects the growing awareness of the aid and donor community that economic development cannot take place without greater assistance to women and the elimination of many patriarchal barriers.

Beginning in 1973, USAID for the first time was required by law to promote WID,[3] but an internal assessment of WID activities between 1975 and 1984 revealed that WID had mainly been addressed as "an economic issue that can increase the success of main A.I.D. projects" (AID 1984:ii). It has become increasingly obvious, however, that women's roles, especially their productive roles in farming and the development of women's productivity, are crucial to development. Rather than "women-specific projects" or "women-integrated projects," the emphasis should be on addressing women's needs and talents from the beginning of the project design through the completion of the evaluation of project effectiveness. Among the WID goals should be

- private sector employment
- management training
- education and skills training
- credit and technical assistance
- agricultural development
- technology transfer

Successful WID strategy would include identifying and overcoming the barriers that limit women's benefits from assistance programs, increasing women's role in the programs, and providing technology to lessen women's burdens (e.g., fetching fuel and water, and food preparation and storage) so they can participate in other aspects of the projects (AID 1984:2–3, 9).

In a 1988 AID publication, Grosz (1988:11) reiterated a point made by the World Bank: helping women is not just an equity or welfare issue; structural adjustment and other market-oriented reforms cannot succeed without "addressing gender issues." Optimal use of productive capacity is necessary for economic recovery in Africa, and a large proportion of that productive capacity, largely underutilized, is women and girls. In a 1989 AID publication on gender issues in development, Sandra Russo and others (1989:A3) add that "the use and expansion of women's productive capacities is a necessary condition for social and economic progress."

A major gender bias in both World Bank and USAID WID frameworks is that women are visualized as being either in smallholder farming or small-scale enterprises. This suggests that little may be done to promote women's involvement in larger-scale enterprises, thus leaving the "commanding heights" of the economy in the hands of men. The results of this would be an economy similar to that in the West in which men dominate the economy, while women are active but in subordinate economic roles. This has to be actively combated if it is to be avoided.

There is some recognition in the AID/WID literature of this growing gender gap. In 1987, for instance, in a manual for AID staff, Otero (1987: 7–8, 15–16) discusses gender issues in the promotion of SMEs. She notes that women's SMEs are usually the smallest and least remunerated and typically an extension of women's household activities. This is a reflection of the fact that women are more limited than men by a lack of education, skills, and capital. Women need greater access to such resources, especially credit and technical assistance, to break out of such subsistence activities. In recognition of women's importance in the informal sector, Otero adds that helping women entrepreneurs is necessary if SMEs are to make much of a contribution to development.

Following up on this theme, Ernst and Young (1988:19) discuss the deficiencies of AID's PRE (private enterprise) and other business programs. They charge that "the institutions that support business communities in developing countries rarely address the needs of women in business. Frequently, they may increase the barriers to women's involvement in private sector activities." Referring to AID specifically, they maintain that the agency does not know if its programs, except PRE micro-enterprise programs, are even reaching women.

In its 1989 annual report to Congress, AID defends its PRE/WID strategy and claims that it is working to ensure that PRE resources are equally available to male and female members of project target groups. Moreover, through its Bureau of Science and Technology, AID is working to improve the preparation of women for participation in the labor force through literacy programs, technical and professional training, and training in developing and managing small businesses (WID 1989:16–18).

But WID efforts to reach women will not succeed without attacking the institutional sexism in many African countries. As the World Bank (1989b:137–139) notes, in its discussion of the need for medium-sized enterprises in Africa, it is patriarchal biases that are to blame for women's inability to move beyond small-scale informal sector businesses. Major problems are government discrimination, such as in access to credit, and cultural and legal obstacles that require women to get their husband's permission for licenses or loans or that allow men to expropriate women's profits or businesses. These practices must change, the Bank declares.

Recent AID/WID research also faults the sexist attitudes of Western aid personnel as well as Africans for failure to deal effectively with gender issues. Poats and associates (1989:4) write that effective inclusion of gender issues in development projects requires overcoming cultural attitudes from professional disciplines, development agencies, the "native culture," and project team members alike. The patriarchal cultural biases of the project team, especially those involving basic constructs about appropriate gender roles, often go unexamined, while the culture of the target group is seen as the obstacle to be overcome. Referring to AID's PRE programs, Ernst and Young (1988:1–3) add that PRE officers tend not to be very aware of the significance of gender issues in their programs and are sometimes even "skeptical" about how gender is even relevant to their work. Without such awareness, patriarchal biases in current and future programs are unlikely to be rectified.

Not all of the problems of gender bias rest with the development agencies. Host country gender bias hampers WID efforts as well. Longwe (1990:5–7, 14) laments the fact that in Zambia most women's projects are mainly "concerned with improving women's performance in their sex-stereotyped domestic role" while doing little to improve women's access to productive resources; raise their consciousness on gender issues; involve them in decisionmaking or planning; or enhance their control over factors of production, the sexual division of labor, or their own lives and labor. She adds that progressive bilateral agencies often find it difficult to find NGOs or government agencies to work with because most are seeking funding for welfare projects to "lessen the discomfort of women's subordination" but not to promote "the process of women's *empowerment* to escape from subordination."

## ▲ Development Aid to Benefit Women

While capitalist-oriented reforms and development initiatives in Africa can benefit women and lessen gender inequality, this will necessitate the state and development community's removing patriarchal barriers to women's entrepreneurial and productive activities and making positive efforts to get resources to women and improve their educational and technical skills (rather than relying on gender-neutral policies that simply reinforce preexisting male advantages over women). The following discussion focuses on several specific areas where change is needed. Also included are some examples of development projects that have helped women, and some that have failed, and the reasons for these results.

### Women's Role in Agriculture

Although women are heavily involved in cash-crop production, the familial mode of production has allowed men to control the land and most of the benefits, reducing women to unpaid or underpaid family labor. Women's primary agricultural role has been in subsistence food production. The underdeveloped capitalist economy has heretofore largely attempted to exploit the sexual division of labor and to make it more productive rather than changing it. As I have argued, however, this system of farming is exploitative and unproductive. If agriculture is to be the engine of economic recovery in Africa, the neglect and exploitation of women must change. As Cloud and Knowles (1988:260) write, it is cash crops that generate income that can be invested in technological inputs or the hiring of labor. As data from Zimbabwe show, households that produce market crops have much more income than those that depend solely on subsistence agriculture (Gittinger et al. 1990:14).

Women's food crops, however, hold great potential as cash crops (see Cloud 1986:27–31). They could also promote badly needed diversification away from the monocrop agriculture inherited from the colonial period, as is being attempted by Uganda (Banugire 1989:108–109). Investment in food crops, long neglected by African governments and Western donors, could greatly benefit women—and men too. Ajayi (1991) reports on a project by the International Institute of Tropical Agriculture (IITA) in Nigeria that achieved these and some additional positive outcomes. Over the past twenty-five years, IITA has been working to improve food crop production (such as maize, yams, cassava, cowpeas, and rice) and food-processing technology and lessen women's work load. Gender issues have been a major concern because, as Dr. Lukas Brader, director-general of IITA states, "If Africa is to develop a more productive, sustainable, and equitable agricultural sector, it cannot afford to neglect women" (Ajayi 1991:28). Processing cassava used to take twenty-five hours per ton; with new technology from IITA, this has been reduced to six hours. In one Nigerian village where the technology was installed in a community processing center, women's average income increased 337 percent. Men's income also increased, by 126 percent. In another village, labor was reduced 70 percent and losses due to processing declined 50 percent. For the first time, women reportedly had some leisure time. IITA is also using "affirmative action" to get more women in its training programs, and hopes to get more women agricultural scientists.

Without addressing patriarchal dominance over women and other gender biases, women may not benefit from strategies to improve, diversify, or commercialize agricultural production, as studies indicate (see, e.g., Davison 1988b, c; ILO 1984; Gladwin and McMillan 1989). If, for instance, title to land, access to credit and inputs, and decisionmaking remain in the hands of male household heads, women will have little control over their own labor, nor are they likely to be fairly compensated. They may even be worse off. An example of this is the Isoya Rural Development Project in Oyo State, Nigeria, discussed by Pittin (1985). The project began in 1969 to help men farm yellow maize as a cash crop sold through the men's cooperative. Women grew white maize as a food crop. Within two years, the women's land was largely taken over for the men's crop. The men gained income, while the women lost income. Some of the women were forced to seek money from their husbands to meet household expenses. The men were also trained to be more economically productive as farmers while the women were given a home economics program

focusing on nutrition.[4] Another example comes from a Senegalese land reform program researched by Ba and others (1984). In this case, women
greatly outnumbered men (heads of households), but men were over-
whelmingly elected to the Rural Councils. The men ignored women's interests: they did not inform women of their legal rights or about reforms
that affected them, they controlled the land, and they used plows and other
agricultural inputs for their cash crops rather than women's crops.

The patriarchal family structure can even undermine efforts to get land
to women, as shown in Carney's study (1988) of The Gambia's irrigated
rice plots project (funded by the International Fund for Agricultural Development). The project was designed to get land to women in order to increase rice production, traditionally a woman's crop. Male heads of households managed to get control of the land by declaring it compound land,
over which they could exert authority. The entire project was undermined.

Some scholars maintain that export-oriented agricultural development
and large-scale agribusiness schemes are risky for both men and women
because they subject farmers to all the attendant risks of integration into
the global economy. These risks include international control versus autocentric control over the uses of the land, inputs, rewards, and the labor
process (see Amin 1990a, b; Knowles 1985; Samoff 1992). This is indeed a
risk, one that every country faces that is subject to international market
forces. However, inward-looking strategies have not been successful in
Africa (see Mahjoub 1990), while research, such as that of Bloom and Brender (1993:29–30), indicates that the per capita income of less-developed
countries who have integrated their economies into the world economy has
grown much faster than that of those who have not.

Moreover, it is sexist biases, not capitalist market forces, that are primarily responsible for women's disadvantages in commercial agriculture.
As Ernst and Young (1988:27, 32) point out, agribusiness and other agricultural projects can potentially benefit women by providing opportunities
for income and employment, including processing, packaging, and marketing of agricultural commodities. New labor-intensive crops can also
generate jobs and income for women. Elson (1989:73–74) adds that agribusiness can be the entry point for women into their own manufacturing
enterprises that process locally produced crops into food and drink products (see Chapter 3 for examples of such businesses started by women's
groups).

*Education*

Whether women benefit from agricultural or other projects depends on the
existence of policies that lessen the barriers women face due to institutionalized sexism both within and outside the family. "Price incentives"

provided by the market will not by themselves work. One important barrier to women's ability to gain power over their lives in the household and in the economy is the lack of education and the gender-biased education women receive. While both male and female illiteracy or undereducation are problems in many parts of Africa, females are far more likely to be illiterate than men, and the higher up one goes in the educational system, the larger the gender gap becomes.[5] This creates real disadvantages for women in competing for jobs, improving agricultural productivity, or managing a business. Moreover, it lessens women's ability to promote women's issues in the political process or to improve their status in their households.

While lack of education is a problem for women, gender bias in the kind of education girls receive is more insidious. As Robertson (1986) concluded, women's education is a means of keeping women subordinate and trained for domesticity and dependence on men. When women are trained for productive roles it is usually in sex-stereotypic jobs such as teaching, nursing, or clerical positions (see also Mukarasi 1991:7–8).

Much to their disadvantage, women are greatly underrepresented in technical and scientific education. According to the ILO (International Labour Organisation), from 1970 to 1983 in thirty-nine African countries studied, the proportion of women students receiving technical and scientific education grew from 27 percent to only 28 percent of the total. Only 5 percent of secondary students receiving vocational and technical training were women. In late 1980s projects in nine English-speaking African countries, the ILO found that only about 12 percent of students in purely technical programs in polytechnic and technical schools were women— and most of these were in science, environmental studies, and agriculture. Very few women were in engineering. Especially at the higher educational levels, there were few female instructors, administrators, or clerical workers. Most of the female instructors taught nontechnical subjects, such as art, culture, or business. Not surprisingly, only 4 percent of technical employees in the countries studied were women (based on data from 176 industries and parastatals). Male employer bias toward women was a major problem despite the fact that employers admitted that women performed as well as men. The ILO concluded that the main reasons women are so poorly represented in technical and scientific fields are: (1) stereotypic attitudes about women's roles and capacities; (2) lack of mathematical, scientific, and technical/vocational education in school; and (3) lack of government support (Leigh-Doyle 1991).

In its 1989 study of women in Kenya, the World Bank (1989a:32, 47) confirmed the existence of the gender education gaps reported by the ILO. Although there is almost educational parity between boys and girls at the primary level, at higher educational levels and especially in science and technical areas, girls become increasingly disadvantaged. In fact, it has been only recently that girls were admitted to technical schools—but mostly in home economics. There are very few women in science, engineering, or architectural programs.

The gender biases in education reflect and reinforce the sexual division of labor and patriarchal structure of African society and of the European cultures whose educational systems Africans have adopted. Among the ways patriarchal relationships are reinforced by biased educational attitudes and practices is that, in agricultural projects, men receive most of the technical training and access to machinery and therefore benefit more. Women are relegated mainly to stereotypic female jobs. This can be seen in Smith's (1987) study of four agricultural cooperatives in Zimbabwe. In the allocation of tasks and training, men took over most of the management and skilled jobs, such as building, welding, mechanics, driving, and livestock husbandry. The women learned sewing, knitting, typing, and cooking. Few men chose to learn or engage in these "female" jobs or skills, although a significant number of women were interested in management, driving, and mechanics—tasks the women knew had more prestige and were better compensated. Similar findings are reported by Koons (1988) in his study of the MIDENO (Northwest Development Project) in Cameroon.

The obvious ramifications of the above gender biases in education and training is that men are learning skills that are likely to lead to better jobs or to the development of capitalist enterprises with much greater potential for growth and remuneration than those of women. Although we saw in Chapter 3 that women have launched successful businesses in such extensions of their domestic tasks as food processing, beer brewing, or restaurants, most of these enterprises remain microenterprises or are likely to be eventually eliminated by larger male-owned breweries, franchises, or factories. Moreover, there are likely to be greater economic rewards in a developing economy for people who can repair or build automotive engines than for someone who can crochet tablecloths.

Also important to consider is that control of technology and the uses of technology is a source of power that can have profound effects on social relationships. For instance, technology can and has been used to improve male cash crops and income from farming while women's food crop farming remains hoe agriculture with few technological inputs. Women's arduous and time-consuming jobs as gatherers of wood and water can be lessened by the provision of more fuel-efficient cookstoves and carts or by waterpoints and wells, or these needs can be ignored in favor of laborsaving devices for men. Men can be the ones taught to drive and repair trucks, thus leaving women dependent on men when it comes to taking their crops to markets. Admittedly, as Gittinger and coauthors (1990:31) maintain, women do not have to control technology to benefit from it. For instance, mechanical maize mills are often controlled by men, but women who take their maize to the mills save hours of pounding, thus freeing their time for more economically productive activities. As Stamp (1989:2) observes, however, too often in Africa technology transfers have not been used to empower women, lessen their work load, or strengthen their community involvement and decisionmaking authority either in the family or the village. Instead, African women find themselves with increased work loads, a more subordinate role in the family, and access to fewer resources.

In business as well as agriculture, women's lack of education or appropriate education handicaps them. The World Bank (1990b:22), for example, finds that while almost half of those in informal sector businesses are women, they are underrepresented in formal small- to medium-sized enterprises. Lack of education, technical training, and business training are part of the problems women face in developing and expanding successful businesses.

Women's groups (as discussed in Chapter 3), NGOs, and some development agencies are attempting to address some of these problems. In Kenya, the Anglican Church has opened a training center for girls in motor vehicle mechanics to help girls learn technical skills and compete in the job market. The program is also designed to help the girls start their own businesses ("Girls Set . . ." 1993). A program funded by Winrock International (a U.S. development organization) is training African women for leadership roles in agriculture, for example, as scientists and extension managers. Many countries are also training more women as extension agents to work with women farmers (Blumberg 1994).[6] USAID's BEST (Basic Education and Skills Training) project in Zimbabwe and the ROSH rural development program show what can be done to help women overcome some of the gender gap in education and training. Although not focused specifically on women, the BEST project is reported to be having more impact on women than men. More women are enrolling in education and training programs and in fields not previously open to women. For instance, the 2,500-student teacher training college developed by AID emphasized training secondary teachers in science and vocational and technical subjects. Between 1982 and 1984, the enrollment of women teachers grew from less than ten to over one hundred. Technical colleges financed under BEST are being designed to cater to women trainees in automotive, mechanical, electrical, and business fields (AID 1984:28–29). The ROSH program is designed to promote rural, private sector, smallholder industrialization by improving skills and technical and entrepreneurial abilities and to create linkages among manufacturing, domestic raw materials, and local labor. It is hoped that such rural industries will produce hand tools and other implements (e.g., plows and planters) and generate more rural, nonfarm employment. The acquisition of new technological skills and innovations could provide the basis for greater industrialization in the future. The model for ROSH is China, where similar rural industrialization led to increasingly sophisticated small-scale manufacturing enterprises that produced an array of goods from electric motors to fans and bicycles. An expansion of entrepreneurial skills and growing ability to assimilate more-complex technology are other beneficial spin-offs ROSH hopes to achieve in Africa (Olofin 1991:322–323). Such programs could benefit women if efforts such as BEST were used to ensure the participation of women.

## Credit

The entrepreneurial capacities of African women are well documented, as is the need to encourage private sector initiative and productivity for both men and women. Access to credit is essential for farmers or business entrepreneurs to start, expand, or improve the productivity of their enterprises. Here, as well as in education and training, women suffer disadvantages due to institutionalized sexism.

Basic to the familial mode of production in most African societies is the fact that only men can own or inherit land. Capitalism has compounded the discriminatory impact of traditional land tenure practices. Privatizing land in order to turn peasants into capitalist commercial farmers, in the overwhelming majority of cases, means giving land titles to men, even though women are often doing most of the farming.

Because they do not own land to offer as collateral, women find it difficult or impossible to obtain credit. This is compounded by legal discrimination against women (e.g., denying women the right to get loans or engage in business activities without their husbands' consent) and prejudice among mostly male lenders (see Davison 1988c; Palmer 1991; World Bank 1990b). As Palmer (1991:155) relates, because women inherit less, they have less chance of accumulating capital, thus they lack collateral for loans that would allow them to expand their productive activities. This results in women having fewer assets and less capital, with the result that male privileges become more and more entrenched.

Such biases do not just hurt women; they hamper and slow the entire development process. By preventing women from obtaining the resources they need, efforts to increase agricultural productivity and expand the number of small to medium-sized businesses are being undermined. By contrast, providing women with credit (and technical assistance) would, according to Otero (1987:15–16), enable women entrepreneurs to break out of subsistence activities, which is necessary if small enterprises are to contribute to economic development. Economic efficiency is also undermined because male bias in credit often results in poorer payoffs both to lenders and to societal development. Studies from Africa and other areas of the Third World as well indicate that women are often better savers and more responsible borrowers than men (see, e.g., Lovell 1989:27). Guyer (1986:401) writes, for example, that African women work harder, are less inclined to spend money on ceremonial expenditures, and are inclined to save, invest, and innovate when resources are available. When their income improves they are also more likely to spend it on their children's health, nutrition, and educational needs—an investment in human capital.

In Chapter 3 I discussed how women have developed informal self-help credit sources among themselves as a result of their lack of access to formal credit sources. International organizations are also increasing their efforts to make credit more available to women. In Zimbabwe, for example, the FAO (Food and Agriculture Organization) set up a credit program for women (although men were included as well) drawing on African traditions of labor sharing. Credit was provided to groups of ten to twenty (at least half of each group had to be women). Groups farmed collectively but also had individual plots. They planned all activities and managed their loans jointly. If groups were successful, they were encouraged to borrow from the Agricultural Finance Corporation (AFC). No collateral was required for the loan; Zimbabwe's Marketing Board pays back the loan to the AFC from the group's crop proceeds. Not only does the program teach men and women about credit and how to get it for their own enterprises, it promotes group cohesion and common interests among both males and females. Also, since the group was at least partly removed from the patriarchal African household structure, women were able to retain much greater control over their share of the profits (Gittinger et al. 1990:27).

In conjunction with its PRE program, AID's WID office has cofunded Women's World Banking (WWB), with branches in twenty-four African countries. WWB works with commercial banks to make loans available to low-income women for women-owned or women-run small businesses. In 1990, after six years in operation, there had been only one default on a loan! WWB affiliates emphasize training women in economic skills and use of credit, with support from such international agencies as the World Bank, the African Development Bank, UNICEF, and SIDA (the Swedish International Development Agency). An example of the kind of program WWB supports comes from Kenya. The Kenyan Women Finance Trust, an affiliate of WWB, got money from SIDA to train women traders in the two largest markets in the country in business management, accounting, and marketing. The women were then given loans from a commercial bank (AID 1984; Gittinger et al. 1990:27–28; Morna 1991:31).

Rather than setting up separate credit systems, another approach to getting loans to women is to remove the barriers women face in seeking institutional credit. Uganda decided to waive the collateral requirement for women and used the woman's reputation and an analysis of the proposed enterprise instead to determine creditworthiness. Uganda also waived the requirement that women had to be previous customers to get a loan, simplified the loan application, gave women extra assistance in making applications, and made loans and special training in credit and record keeping available to women's groups. Women's repayment record was excellent (Gittinger et al. 1990:25–26).

## ▲ Empowering Women

While the above approaches to helping women compete in a capitalist economy can help promote greater gender equality, entrenched patriarchal barriers are very difficult to overcome. And, as I have suggested, although capitalism would benefit from greater gender equality, the market alone cannot create equal opportunity or a level playing field. Contrary to the assumptions and beliefs of some free marketers, there is no "magic of the market" where patriarchy is concerned. As Palmer (1991:158–159, 165) recognizes, women need "counterbalancing policy instruments" if the benefits of a more liberal capitalist economy are to be more than an empty promise to women. Some measures suggested include low, subsidized interest rates for credit; a tax on men's produce to finance investments in improving women's productivity; quotas for females in educational and training facilities; and making women a priority, rather than a marginal element, in informal sector services (e.g., information, training, credit). Palmer also recommends counterbalancing taxes and expenditures for things like child care to counteract the unpaid domestic labor of women and give it market value. Access to maternity leave, tap water, and electricity would release women from other domestic labor (not shared by men), allowing them to compete more equitably.

Rather than being reverse discrimination, as some might charge, the justification for these policies is that any alleged distortions that result from favoring women are efforts to counter the effects of existing distortions that favor men. These measures to support women would only be temporary, according to Palmer; the long-term objective is efficiency of resource use (made impossible by current gender relations). Palmer also argues that the view that confronting gender inequality must wait until market inefficiencies are reduced elsewhere in African economies and economic growth is under way is also misguided, because structural adjustment programs and other economic reforms will not succeed unless gender issues and gender bias are addressed from the outset.

As Palmer's suggestions imply, development planning that truly integrates women must also begin to move away from trying to meet practical gender needs (PGNs) while tiptoeing around strategic gender needs (SGNs); that is, transforming patriarchal institutions and gender relations that subordinate, exploit, and oppress women. While such projects as providing milling machines can lessen time spent grinding grain and give women more time to grow food or earn cash from other activities, it does not alter the sexual division of labor or male control over productive resources or women's lives (see Newland 1991:130–131; Moser 1991:90–91). Making women more productive and increasing their earning opportunities, while laudable goals, may also further entrench the dual work day, as found in many Western countries, where women work outside the home but still do most of the child care and housework. This subsidy from women to men, which frees men to pursue economic gain without domestic burdens, makes a mockery of the notion of equal opportunity or development.

Examples of this problem abound in the literature, and it plagues both capitalist and socialist states. In formerly Marxist Mozambique's Cooperative Farm Projects, for instance, efforts to promote gender equality led to women's assuming more-productive work loads, but men largely refused to share more of the domestic and child care work (Davison 1988a). In socialist-oriented Zimbabwe, Dorothy Smith's study (1987) of rural cooperatives revealed that men took most of the decisionmaking roles, dominated in the skilled jobs, and had more free time to attend (and control) co-op meetings in part because women, after a full day of other work, did almost all the child care and housework. Unexamined biases about men's and women's roles are also part of the problem. The Northern Wells Project Phase I in Cameroon was designed to make access to water easier for women, along with providing women health and water-use hygiene education so that they could better meet their family's needs and have more time for productive activities (AID 1984:40). The obvious bias here is that the sexual division of labor that makes fetching water and family welfare women's jobs rather than shared responsibilities of both men and women is simply reinforced.

Moser (1991:96–106) writes that WID has evolved over time and shifted its emphases since its inception. During the 1960s the welfare approach dominated, which assumed that motherhood was women's main role in development while men were the producers. In the 1970s, with the UN Decade for Women and Plan of Action, equity concerns gained prominence. Such SGNs as women's need to make a living and legal reforms (e.g., in divorce, custody, property, credit, and voting) were accepted, although many Third World governments and development agencies were hostile to any "radical" interference with countries' traditions. Next, also during the 1970s, the emphasis of WID was on fighting poverty, with a focus on women's productive roles as necessary to this effort. SGNs such as women's access to land and capital, and sex discrimination in the labor market were also examined. There was still a reluctance, however, to deal with such "sensitive issues as women's subordination to men as a root cause of their poverty." "Efficiency" is the main emphasis now, according to Moser. Women are seen as a wasted human resource, and increasing their productivity is seen as essential to the development effort. The danger of the current WID focus is, however, that, with cuts in government spending on health, education, and food subsidies and growing pressures on households to earn income to purchase these basics, the burden will be shifted to already overworked women.

Blumberg (1995:6–11) agrees that WID is evolving in a progressive direction. WID is now being called "GAD" (gender and development), to emphasize how gender is constructed by the ways men and women participate in production and reproduction. GAD challenges the view of the household as a unit sharing resources, focusing instead on differential power and privilege and its effects on development efforts. Past development efforts have demonstrated that directing more resources to women produces not only economic gains but improves family and community well-being. Often women have been more responsive to even modest productive incentives, they are willing to work longer and harder than men, they produce more, protect the environment, and devote more of their income to their children, education, health, and nutrition. Other positive signs Blumberg sees are the 1990s emphasis on development with equity in policymaking and the growing numbers of gender-sensitive men and women in national and international bureaucracies and governments. While many problems remain in the development field, Blumberg believes these changes "should provide building blocks for a stronger, more gender-equitable foundation for development."

We still need to avoid what Goebel and Epprecht (1995:16–19) call a naive confidence that WID alone can empower women. WID can result in greater economic independence, a sense of freedom and personal pride, class consciousness, and new forms of solidarity among women. But WID, without more far-reaching changes in women's disadvantaged position in society and in both the domestic and international economies, can also leave women vulnerable economically and subject to continued oppression and exploitation, rather than empowered.

Some Third World feminists and women's organizations are creating their own alternatives to the WID efforts to date. The new emphasis is on empowerment, that is, on women's challenging all forms of oppression that affect their lives—be it patriarchy, race, class, colonialism, or peripheralization in the global economy. Empowerment is based on women's increasing their own self-reliance, and their right to make choices and influence change through control over political and economic resources. It means critically questioning the value and direction of Western-designed development and having a greater voice in shaping their societies. The most effective organizations, according to Moser (1991:106–110), are those that focus on meeting women's PGNs, such as health, employment, and basic services, then using these concerns to meet women's SGNs, as identified by women themselves. Successful organizations, where possible, also enlist the support of men. For example, in Bombay, India, in 1979 a feminist group worked with women to combat homelessness. At the same time, women became more conscious of patriarchal biases in inheritance and hiring. The group sought to raise men's consciousness about these problems and to make housing needs a mainstream issue, not just a concern of women.

Similar approaches could be applied to Africa, where many problems affecting women—poverty, land scarcity, lack of basic services, and political and economic oppression—affect men as well. The problem, of course, is that while men and women may both suffer from class oppression and poverty, patriarchal oppression is suffered only by women. Therefore, the struggle against patriarchal oppression will also at times require the intervention of the state and organizational efforts on the part of women, even at the risk of alienating men, as discussed in previous chapters. The difficult challenge facing women everywhere, as well as in Africa, is to convince men—husbands, brothers, fathers, employers, and policymakers (i.e., the current holders of power)—that men have more to lose than gain from subordinating women, denying them basic rights, and obstructing the contributions women could make to the betterment of their societies, contributions that would benefit men as well as women.

## ▲ Notes

1. This compares to the average hourly wage in India of 40 cents and $1.89 in Hong Kong (World Bank 1989b:117).

2. According to World Bank data, 50–60 percent of farmers now regularly contacted by extension agents are women, and women's groups are often valuable contacts for extension information. Agents report that women often adopt innovations more readily than do men (Gittinger et al. 1990:28; World Bank 1990b:21).

3. In 1977 the World Bank created the post of adviser on women, and the president of the Bank promised to monitor the impact of Bank activities on women and ensure that women's role in development was taken into account. By the end of the 1970s, almost all major foundations had active women's programs, although mostly marginal and poorly funded (Newland 1991:124).

4. Eventually the women complained about their lack of income and, with the help of project workers, started their own co-op. Their husbands gave them some support but resented women's owning their own machinery, and some gave their wives poor land. Nonetheless, the women did gain in self-confidence and self-esteem and added education courses to their other activities (Pittin 1985:236–237).

5. Yearly World Bank *Development Report* data on education is one source of facts on the gender gap in education.

6. Blumberg (1994) reports that currently in Africa only 7 percent of extension services are devoted to women, and only 7 percent of extension agents are women —and some of these are providing home economics rather than farming services.

# ▲ 6
# Capitalism, Class Formation, and the Future of Patriarchy

Underdeveloped capitalism, as I have discussed, has maintained, albeit in distorted and modified form, the African precapitalist familial mode of production. The familial mode of production depends on distinctive social relationships based on kinship, ethnicity, and gender. Paradoxically, over time capitalism has created a tug of war between social forces that work to maintain these social relationships and social forces that are slowly eroding them. The first of these social forces are associated with ethnicity, extended family systems, and communal values; the second with classes, more nuclear families, and individualistic values. The future of patriarchy in Africa is closely tied to which social forces dominate.[1] This in turn will largely be decided on the basis of whether and how capitalism expands on the continent.

## ▲ Kinship, Class, and the Transition to Capitalism

Because capitalist expansion in Africa has been largely uneven and based on exploiting rather than transforming the familial mode of production, both men's and women's reliance on kinship and ethnic ties has in many ways been reinforced. Ethnic groups and lineages jealously control most of the land allocated to their members. Urban migrants largely retain ties to their kin in order to receive help in the city and to maintain claims to land back in the rural areas (Gregory and Piché 1983). Political solidarity is also closely linked with ethnic and regional identity (see Chazan et al. 1988:120–123).

In part, ethnic ties remain strong because of underdeveloped capitalism's close association with the African state. As discussed in Chapter 4, access to resources and mobility in Africa occur more often through the state than through the private sector and ownership of the means of production. Africa's indigenous bourgeoisie is small, and with so little industrialization in Africa and most people working as peasant farmers, there are few proletariat. Therefore, the basis for class consciousness and organization is weak, while ethnicity becomes the main source of solidarity as individuals and groups seek to influence the state.

Pringle and Watson (1992:62) argue that classes do not arise automatically out of the mode of production, nor do members of classes or other interest groups simply know their material interests or have a sense of identity with others. These are constructed, maintained, and even reconstructed from within the context of the specific time and culture. The same is true of ethnicity. Both contemporary class and ethnicity in Africa are identities that have been constructed from within different locational positions in colonial and postcolonial underdeveloped capitalist societies. In Africa, Chazan and her associates (1988:110) point out, ethnicity is more a political than a cultural phenomenon; it is not an archaic representation of tradition. Ethnicity is similar to socioeconomic class, in that both are modern state-linked concepts used by groups to place claims upon the state and to which the state normally responds. Ethnicity mobilizes interests in competition with other ethnic, occupational, and business groups.

Ethnicity has more than political significance, however. The potency of ethnicity as an identity and a basis for group interests must be understood within the context of growing competition and inequality in underdeveloped capitalist society. In some ways, ethnicity tends to undermine class consciousness and solidarity among all socioeconomic groups because ethnic consciousness cuts across class lines and includes the rich as well as the poor. Ethnicity is often the basis of patron-client relationships that obligate the rich to redistribute some of their wealth to their more needy kin. This allows, for example, rural peasants to get resources such as loans, school fees, jobs, burial or wedding expenses, or development projects for their communities that they could not afford otherwise. Ethnic-kin ties also obligate urban wage earners to send remittances home to support the elderly and other kin or to provide financial capital and other resources for new businesses (see Hyden 1987:131; Sklar 1991b:306; Sottas 1992). Sennett (1970:107–108) has even argued that those who maintain strong extended kin ties are more upwardly mobile than those who do not.

As economic crisis has gripped underdeveloped capitalism, investments in kinship and communal ties have become even more important for many Africans. Competition for scarce resources, both political and economic, have intensified, claim Bates (1989:43–44) and Stamp (1991a: 835). Capitalist expansion is contributing to this trend. Schoepf and Schoepf (1988) found that in Zaire, for example, as peasants lose access to land and adequate food and must sell their labor in low-wage agroindustry, the poor are forced to remain in the traditional agricultural sector in order to have some land to grow food. This results in their remaining tied to the village and subject to chiefs.

Other scholars have suggested that, for some, ethnic and kin solidarity is a form of struggle against capitalist penetration. For instance, Lonsdale (1992b:213–214) argues that migrant workers use their tribal membership as a way of struggling to avoid proletarianization by maintaining their right to land and thus some control over the means of production. Peasants seek to preserve kinship and ethnic structures in order to maintain communal land tenure against the forced introduction of private property in land and the appropriation of land for commercial export production. As Caulfield (1993:443) points out, capitalism seeks "to eliminate the corporate power of kin groups," especially where organized around lineages. Preserving these family networks is a form of rejection of capitalism's efforts to isolate the individual worker in his/her productive relations.

Kenyan professor S. O. Kwasa points out another function of ethnic identity. Ethnic obligations and solidarity can help keep fragile African societies from disintegrating in the face of social change. "Tribal traditions" serve as an anchor as well as a means of redistributing resources from the haves to the have-nots. Tradition provides a sense of continuity with parents, ancestors, and the precolonial, precapitalist past. Finally, Kwasa notes, until change brings about a more complete capitalist and social transformation of society, there is nothing to replace ethnicity and kinship for most Africans (in Harden 1990:120–123).

Because of the unevenness and partial nature of capitalist transformation in Africa, most Africans are caught somewhere between the social relations of the familial mode of production and those of capitalism, which are gradually emerging as commercialization and privatization of land and industrialization advance, haltingly perhaps, on the continent. Along with this advance is the emergence of social classes whose existence is at present embedded within ethnic-kin structures. As Lonsdale (1992a:301) writes, class formation occurs within, not apart from, ethnic groups. An example of this can be seen in the way the ideology of lineage rights in property is being used by elders (and men) to consolidate property in their hands at the expense of juniors, nonkin, and women. In some cases emerging capitalist elites straddle both arenas—they manipulate and comply with the demands of ethnicity while also forging alliances and relationships based on class interest.

The sometimes uneasy balancing act between ethnicity-kinship and class interests is becoming more strained, however, and in some cases tipping in favor of class. Most African governments have moved slowly to expand and consolidate private ownership of land because of fears of the massive landlessness and inequality that would result. However gradual, the trend toward privatization appears to be inexorable. Harrison (1990:55) points out that secure title to land appears to be a requisite for long-term investment. In Africa, "rights to sell, rent, forfeit, and inherit land may be introduced gradually, as land scarcity increases, although they are probably necessary for rational use of land and mobility of labor."

Currently, only Côte d'Ivoire has unrestricted private landownership, but the process of privatization and commercialization of land is growing elsewhere (Harrison 1990:55). In Kenya land scarcity is increasing as the best land becomes concentrated in the hands of the small, politically well-connected elite (Bradshaw 1990:14–16). Shipton (1992:371) reports that 25 percent of the agricultural finance loans made in Kenya went to government officials or to the kin or supporters of such officials. In Cameroon a rural elite of large landowners is emerging as a result of policies designed to promote privatization and commercial agriculture. Government policies were supposed to help small farmers, but "the new professional class," those with money, are investing in suburban areas and land speculation is widespread (Goheen 1988:4). Similar trends are occurring elsewhere, although the speed of change is variable from region to region and country to country.

In some areas, agribusiness expansion is also beginning to transform the rural economy and promote growing rural stratification. In Nigeria, for instance, the Funtua Agricultural Development Project has helped large, "progressive farmers" receive over two-thirds of extension visits and most project credit and inputs. Few of the benefits of the project have gone to small farmers; instead the project has helped to further concentrate resources in the hands of capitalist farmers, foreign and local agribusiness companies, traders, and moneylenders. Other beneficiaries of agricultural projects are retired generals, chiefs, civil servants, and businessmen and their companies. By contrast, massive land alienation and rural unemployment, especially in project areas, is growing. At the current rate of land alienation, the 1990s will see the emergence of a largely landless rural work force and the complete dominance of foreign technology in large-scale agriculture (Bonat and Abdullahi 1989:157–158, 166–168). While the pace of change may vary widely across the continent, "capturing the peasantry" is well under way in Africa, bringing rural class stratification with it.

In the nonagricultural economy change is also occurring, although the small size and weakness of Africa's bourgeoisie remains a constraint. African economies continue to be dependent on foreigners in many areas that normally spawn entrepreneurship and technological innovation. Lall (1990:97) reports that the most successful businesses in Africa are joint ventures or have non-African managers because there continues to be a shortage of trained, experienced African managers. The availability of trained Africans has not changed much in thirty years, by some estimates. Part of the problem is the decline of higher education in Africa (Green 1994:205). In addition, in what amounts to a major brain drain, many thousands of Africa's best-educated people are migrating to Europe and North America (see Skinner 1985). As late as 1982 in Côte d'Ivoire, once considered a model of capitalist development, Europeans were 68 percent of all directors, managers, and administrators; only 22 percent were Ivoirians. For the foreseeable future, there will continue to be a shortage of technicians and skilled shop floor workers as well as managers—although there is a surplus of unskilled and white-collar office workers. Lall (1990:97–98) finds similar problems in Zimbabwe, where in 1984, 72 percent of professional employees were of European origin. While the number of managers, professionals, and skilled workers is growing, African-owned enterprises tend to be smaller-scale and, as we have seen, informal sector businesses. What is needed, concludes Lall, is for Africans to launch more larger-scale and technologically complex enterprises.

As was discussed in previous chapters, an indigenous bourgeoisie capable of developing such enterprises has been gaining strength in Africa (see Kennedy 1988), but it has been hampered in part by the familial mode of production. In general, Africans themselves, according to Sottas (1992: 284), acknowledge that investments in kinship networks are good for social insurance but "not good for saving any money," which is especially an obstacle for those in business. Himbara's study (1994:89–91) of Kenyan entrepreneurs illustrates many of the problems extended kinship creates for capitalism. African entrepreneurs are expected to share their incomes with members of the extended family, aid them during financial hardship, and employ relatives whether qualified or needed. The result is that too much capital is withdrawn from enterprises, and they fail. Bonds of family and ethnicity also block the formation of partnerships and limited liability companies. Finally, rather than investing profits back into their businesses, Kenyan entrepreneurs have a "sentimental value for land," often of little economic value, and a "fascination with rural homes," even when they are no longer residing there. Such practices are expensive and wasteful, and they retard economic development. In a similar analysis, Kayongo-Male and Onyango (1984:44–59) contrast the African businessman's mentality with that of Asian businessmen. Asians identify family welfare with business, Africans with land. Therefore, unlike Asians, Africans often use their business profits to purchase land rather than expanding their businesses. This, along with the expectation that business profits must be shared with relatives, is one reason that in Kenya Asians own most of the successful large enterprises, while many African-owned enterprises have failed (Himbara 1994).

## ▲ Kinship and Patriarchy

As the above discussion shows, extended kinship and ethnic ties are simultaneously contributors and impediments to capitalist development. Ethnic group and kinship membership entitles people to resources, but that very entitlement drains enterprises of needed capital or results in wasteful, unproductive investments. These complex and contradictory relationships affect women differently than men because patriarchy dictates the different resources to which men and women are entitled and the obligations they must fulfill. For one, appeals to ethnic ideology and tradition sanctify men's right to land in the face of capitalist encroachment and are also used to maintain control over women. Fatton (1992:97) contends that such ideologies "invent patriarchal traditions that reduce women to subordinate peasant producers and protect male migrants' rural status." That is, as long as women remain in the rural areas and work the land, the man's claims to that land are safe. Men also use their patriarchal prerogatives to gain greater control over land, labor, and capital at women's expense as land and other resources become more scarce and pressures for commercialization of agriculture intensify. In Kenya, for example, Hay (1982:110) finds that limiting women's access to property has been a principal means of social control for the Luo, Luhya, and Gusu. These limits are imposed primarily through customary shifts of property control in marriage, separation, and inheritance.

In both traditional land tenure systems and where privatization of land exists, women's survival is often dependent on men because so few women have land of their own. In both situations women must subordinate themselves to lineage and kinship demands in order to maintain what access to resources they have. In Kenya over 90 percent of privately held land is titled to men, but women do most of the farming while men are often working in town. However, if men default on their agricultural loans, women face dispossession. Therefore, women must do everything possible to insure that loans are repaid to protect their own interests in continued access to their husband's land (Hay 1982).

Earlier in this chapter, I mentioned that women sometimes ally themselves with their extended families and menfolk against capitalist transformation of communal land tenure and kinship relationships—regardless of the disadvantages women face from African patriarchy. The reason for this is not necessarily that capitalism exploits women (more than it exploits men); rather, patriarchy leaves many rural women with little or no opportunity to compete against men in the capitalist market economy. Women are often denied land, credit, extension services, and other resources. They do not have the education, skills, or resources to compete for most salaried jobs or to go into anything but small, informal sector enterprises—or if they do have the ability to compete, they must overcome sex discrimination from the legal system, financial institutions, or employers. For many such women, Hay (1982:117) explains, the spread of individualized land tenure is seen as a threat rather than an opportunity. They know that individualized landownership usually means male ownership with no assurance that women's rights or interests will be protected. At least the communal system provides women some security, as the norm is that women must be provided for by the lineage. In fact, Hay (1982:120) notes, "Married women who have borne children for the lineage are almost impossible to dislodge" even by a husband seeking a divorce.

Many African women are also dependent on the intergenerational wealth/resource flows of the familial mode of production. In Sangree's (1992:356–357) study of Tiriki, Kenya, and Irigwe, Nigeria, he found that the power of the extended family and male elders was weakening—with some negative effects for women. Educated young men were now handling most community and pantribal matters formerly managed by male elders. By comparison, young women were often disadvantaged by lower education, child care responsibilities, and "androcentric prejudices." Local elders once ensured the proper care of female dependents, but women were now losing that protection. The problem is that, as women lose the security the extended family has provided, it is not being offset by new equal rights laws or job opportunities. In Irigwe, for instance, the decline of secondary marriages has favored men at women's expense because men are no longer responsible for their lovers or outside children. In Tiriki, grandmothers are becoming the de facto managers of their wage-earning sons' farms, but grandfathers exercise supervisory authority.

The increased demand on women's labor to grow cash crops along with performing their other responsibilities also ties women to the kinship system because it makes women more dependent on their children's labor to assist them. Moreover, as women become more economically vulnerable, they are even more reliant on their children, especially sons of the patrilineage, for old-age security. Palmer (1991:4) writes that "with diminishing chances of surplus economic accumulation and of ability to plan for a better future, women retreat into their traditional role of motherhood for securing labour assistance and their old age."

As we can see, under the conditions of underdeveloped capitalism many people—both males and females—remain closely bound to kinship and ethnic groups in part because their access to land or other resources are threatened by the capitalist transformation of their societies, or they have few opportunities outside the familial mode of production. Inequalities of class mean that the benefits of capitalism go to a small strata of the population, and it is who you know, not what you know, that too often separates the winners from the losers. Patriarchy gives men the edge over women under these circumstances, which in turn keeps women under male control within extended kinship systems by keeping them economically dependent on men and the family.

## ▲ Capitalism and Family Transformation

Capitalism has created countervailing forces in Africa that are weakening the extended family and ethnic group identities. Social classes, the nuclear family, and individualism are growing in Africa among those exposed to Western education and culture, urban life, and the benefits of capitalism (e.g., better jobs and pay, science and technology, higher material living standards). Among this strata of society, there is a tendency to reject what Ojwang (1989:5) refers to as the solidarity of kinship that precludes individual distinctions of fortune and status. For the more successful, as Bates (1989:42) writes, kinship is being transformed "from an open system of lineage relations . . . to a closed system of family property, which protects the rise of privilege."

Bates (1989:41–42) describes the societal circumstances that give rise to individuals and families who begin to disassociate themselves from extended kinship systems. Bates posits, based on Marshall Sahlin's model, that family segments that control dominant economic niches no longer have the incentive to invest in the maintenance of kinship ties with those in other niches. When this occurs, rights to assets based on kinship begin to weaken. As some kin segments become wealthy and possess private assets that generate high income, they no longer share with the poor. Similarly, nuclear families become more prevalent among couples who have the economic resources to loosen ties with extended kin. Such families prefer to spend their money on their own children rather than to support distant kin (see Vock 1988).

Sottas (1992:291) suggests another factor important in the weakening of extended kinship systems; that is, the waning control of lineages over land. Although most Africans still get land from their fathers or other relatives, this can continue only as long as land is not scarce or overly fragmented and off-farm income remains available to supplement farm income. All of these are becoming problematic in many areas of Africa, thus diminishing the resource flows that have traditionally bound people to kin and ethnic groups and to male elders.

In the cities as well as the countryside, individualism and acquisitiveness are competing with the communitarian values of the familial mode of production. Especially among the more privileged, there is a desire "to restructure kin relations: to exclude and to accumulate, rather than to purchase social insurance" (Bates 1989:43),[2] and some Africans are finding that kinship and ethnicity are no longer the best or only source of access to resources or security. One sign of this is that, as Sottas (1992:290–291) found in Kenya, nonkin associational groups are spreading as migrants join together away from their home regions. Also in Kenya, Bates (1989:69) refers to data that show that many Kenyans are rejecting communitarian ideals; they want high incomes and wealth—to accumulate, invest, and prosper. They want good clothes, homes, and other consumer goods, and the idea of limits on accumulation has little appeal. In their study of the Tswana, Ingstad and coauthors (1992) report that the extended family is breaking down among the young who see themselves as less socially embedded in family and community. Instead, young people are becoming more individualistic and achievement-oriented. Rather than poverty's reinforcing reliance on kin, young Tswana are responding by withholding resources from relatives including their elderly parents. To a growing extent, members of the younger generation are detaching themselves from reciprocal, extended family relationships, preferring to strive for success in a narrower (i.e., more nuclear) family context.

Some observers emphasize that Africa is in a transitional period between its communitarian (precapitalist) past and a more individualistic (capitalist) future. As a transitional stage, the present is characterized by variations in the degree to which and by whom ethnicity and kinship values and norms are upheld or rejected. Although as a generalization, younger, more educated, urban, affluent Africans are likely to be more individualistic, transethnic, and less kinship-oriented, among all groups there is ambivalence about both the decline of "traditional life" and the attractions of the modern capitalist economy. Odera Oruka (1989:87), for instance, laments the growing acquisitiveness and self-interestedness he sees in Kenya and "the rush for imaginary plenty and happiness." Among Kenya's Luo, although this is applicable to many other Africans as well, this ambivalence is personified in two famous men—Tom Mboya and Oginga Odinga, both leaders in Kenya's independence and postindependence periods. Mboya was a flamboyant exemplar of individualism and achievement through education and occupational success, if necessary to the neglect of the extended family and ethnic group. Mboya was transethnic in his politics and associations, often working in alliance with Kenya's dominant ethnic group, the Kikuyu, while, according to his critics, neglecting his Luo tribal community.[3] Odinga represented "gerontocratic and geneological authority" and tribal solidarity. Both men were admired by the Luo, but Mboya aroused considerable ambivalence, as is indicated by the Luo term *sunga* applied to him. *Sunga* means a proud person and is used to refer to someone who neglects his relatives in favor of friends. At the same time, the term also carries with it a certain admiration, for a sunga is not only someone who neglects his relatives but also someone who is such a big man he does not need them (Parkin 1978:29–30). Parkin (p. 215) adds, "It is as if the term's ambivalence represents the private uncertainties most Luo have regarding the advantages and disadvantages of adhering to collective Luo customs as against the possible benefits of individual achievement."

Many Africans of every social class are, like the Luo, ambivalent about social change. As journalist Harden (1990:101–102) reports, many of the best-educated and most influential people who live in Africa's major cities still see themselves first as members of their villages and tribes, not their nation, and major areas of life (e.g., marriage, children, divorce, death) are governed by these traditional fealties. On the other hand, Harden also notes the growing number of "modernists" who reject "tribal law" and thinking for "bourgeois values." Modernists believe that "education, professional achievement, and property ownership are the stuff of a successful life."

The slow shift taking place from a communitarian/ethnic-based society to an individualistic/class-based society is having a corresponding effect on the family. Western-style, nuclear, conjugal families are becoming more common in Africa, especially among those who have adopted more-individualistic achievement goals and are benefiting more from the new opportunities associated with capitalism.[4] In Kenya, for instance, among the Kikuyu, the country's most populous and prosperous ethnic group, the extended family is weakening the most in favor of the nuclear household family structure (Bates 1989:42–43; Parkin 1978:255–261). Even among such groups as the Luo, who have as a group benefited less from capitalism and been more resistant to change in the familial mode of production, there is growing recognition that economic security and prosperity are best achieved through monogamy and few children, who can be well educated (Parkin 1978:271).

These changes in the family, while gradual and not usually a complete break with the traditional extended family, are clearly in line with the development of family institutions more conducive to capitalist expansion in Africa. They reflect the growth of individualism and geographic and social mobility and the declining hold of the extended family and the familial mode of production over the forces of production. Or in other terminology, the nuclear family is a concomitant of privatization and commercialization of the means of production (vs. extended family and communal ownership) and proletarianization of the population (i.e., the expansion of a "free" labor force, either by choice or necessity).

The nuclear conjugal family has important functions for capitalism, as Caldwell (1982) discusses. Spouses typically pool their assets and use them to accumulate more assets (through investments in business and homes) and to secure advancement for their children (e.g., education, trust funds). This helps to strengthen the class system by differentiating families economically as well as in terms of life-styles and becomes a basis for new nonkinship associational groups (e.g., groups related by occupation, education, common interests, and lifestyle). This process is especially important for the development of a capitalist class able to invest and accumulate capital and pass on its assets and class position to its children. This perpetuates the values and norms of the capitalist class as well as assures that succeeding generations will have the means to further the process of capital accumulation and expansion. Intergenerational heredity of assets allows for the steady building up of assets that can be mobilized for large-scale investments (Kennedy 1988:169–177).[5]

African common law legal systems, in place but not always well enforced in many countries, favor the nuclear conjugal family and capitalist development. This includes laws affecting marriage, divorce, custody, marital property, and inheritance. Such legal reforms can play an important role in expanding women's rights, improving their status, and changing gender relations within the family. As early as 1967 in Kenya, for example, the Commission on the Laws of Marriage and Divorce was set up. Cotran (1989:163) writes, "The Commission stresses again and again the importance of the nuclear family . . . as the important unit in present day Kenya" and the need to prevent "the depradations of extended family members after a person's death to deprive widows of their rightful place and share." More recently, efforts are under way to protect women's rights to marital property. The Women's Bureau of the Ministry of Culture and Social Services is proposing joint ownership of land for married couples and individual ownership for single women. And the Kenyan government's 1994–1996 national economic program calls for joint family decisionmaking on land use and an equal distribution of economic benefits between spouses. Kenya's attorney general has also set up a task force to review all laws affecting the status of women (Munyakho 1994:8–9). Ghana's 1985 Intestate Succession and Property Laws require that all customary marriage and family property be registered and distinction made between self-acquired and family property. If a man dies intestate, his wife and children now get three-fourths of his property; one-fourth goes to his matrikin. Women are now inheriting property from their brothers as well as husbands; others are buying their own farms. Some men are getting prior consent from their matrikin to offer a share of family property to their wives and children. Although elite women have been most able to use the laws and courts to assert their rights to land, there is a marked shift toward women's acquiring more land either through their husbands or from their own earnings. As a result, rural property relations and relations of production within the household are changing to become less patriarchal (Dei 1994:132–133). Similar reforms are under way in other countries, such as Zimbabwe (Batezat and Mwalo 1989).

These changes in the family are consistent with the capitalist development agenda. The World Bank (1992:173) favors related reforms, such as the privatization of land and measures to intensify production on small family farms, not only because they promote growth with equity but because they are part of the process of change necessary to create "enterprising, commercially minded nuclear families,"[6] the bedrock of capitalist society.

## ▲ Family Change and Patriarchy

The nuclear family is becoming more common in Africa, especially in the towns among the young, the more educated, and the affluent, although agricultural policies and the commercialization of agriculture are encouraging this development in rural areas as well. Gender relations are changing along with them, and in some ways becoming more egalitarian. Stichter (1987:158–160) found in Kenya, for instance, that gender relations in urban, middle-class families are becoming more like those in Western middle-class, nuclear families. They are less male-dominated and there is more joint decisionmaking between husbands and wives. Polygyny has greatly declined as well, although housework largely remains women's work. In affluent Kenyan rural households, research by von Bulow and Sorenson (1993:43–44) indicates that women have more decisionmaking power, leisure time, time to pursue their own income-earning businesses and participate in women's groups, and less work than poorer women.

Oppong (1981) reports similar trends as those in Kenya among the middle classes in such countries as Ghana, along with a tendency for men to share tasks with their wives. Kayongo-Male and Onyango (1984:105–107) agree, but add that the convergence of the Western and African family systems are unlikely in the near future, despite the advance of more-Western decisionmaking and leisure patterns among married couples. This is largely due to such hangovers from the patriarchal African family as husbands and wives continuing to maintain separate budgets and bank accounts and tendencies toward authoritarianism among husbands when domestic disputes occur.

Women in middle-class households are leading advocates of efforts to ensure access to marital assets for wives, widows, and divorced women—and to weaken the extended family's claims to such assets traditionally defined as rightfully belonging to the lineage.[7] This is a crucial aspect of the struggle for the class and gender interests of bourgeois women. Most affluent women's class position is dependent on that of their husbands (see Bujra 1986:134–136; House-Midambá 1990:16–17), even though wives often have jobs themselves or engage in business activities such as trading or running shops or bars. As Parpart (1988:224) points out, "divorce and inheritance customs continue to undermine the class position of all but a small number of independently wealthy women." To protect their economic interests, wives are exerting more influence over their husbands to keep resources within the nuclear family. Bujra (1986:134–136) finds in Kenya that affluent educated couples are becoming more linked to others of similar class and occupational interests while losing interest in helping their relatives. In Botswana, Ingstad and associates (1992:384) find that after marriage sons often live apart from their families of origin and reduce or eliminate their support for relatives. This is largely due to the influence of daughters-in-law who do not want to share with their in-laws.

The affluent and educated become models who influence the behavior and choices of others who wish to emulate their success. This provides an impetus for changing family and gender relationships among them as well. An example of this is provided by Parkin (1978:10–11, 29–30) in his discussion of the Luo of Kenya. Luo culture values polygyny, segmentary patrilineal descent, and large families, but these values are increasingly in conflict with the perception that a monogamous family with few children can result in more parental investment in children's education and greater personal and family success. The change from polygyny to monogamy would involve, however, "a radical change in the status of Luo women" by lessening the whole system of controls men currently have over women.

As families invest more in the education of both their daughters and sons, patriarchal relationships become more difficult to sustain (see Moghadam 1993:199–202). Female illiteracy and lack of education are currently key factors in the lack of power and awareness of their rights suffered by African women. Again using the Luo as an example, Parkin (1978:30–31, 269–273) found that highly educated Luo women reject the polygyny that undergirds the Luo segmentary lineage system. As more Luo women become educated and have opportunities for economic independence through trade or careers, the Luo system will break, Parkin maintains, including such institutions as polygyny, bridewealth, and marriage laws that give custody over children to men and their kin. Other changes women are likely to promote are the decline of ethnic endogamy, more mixed marriages, and more matrifocal units (similar to their Kikuyu counterparts).

Even among Africa's conservative Islamic groups, education of girls is beginning to be a threat to patriarchal norms. Ver Eecke's (1989:62) study of Fulbe women in West Africa's Adamawa region is instructive. In the past girls usually received little or no education and were married at age twelve to sixteen. "In recent years, this has been complicated by education and now the desire to work and, of course, the girls' insistence on finding or choosing their own marriage partner, as well as an appropriate time for marriage." Men still make these decisions for girls, and most girls still see themselves in domestic roles with education primarily a means to secure a well-off husband. For the small group of highly educated women, however, men are more likely to be supportive of their daughters' or wives' career ambitions (but in such "safe" areas as teaching and nursing), and polygyny is declining (ver Eecke 1989:64–67).

Women's educational prospects are currently mixed because of Africa's economic crisis and cutbacks in government educational subsidies resulting from structural adjustment. On the positive side, Joan Harris (1985:31) reports that in Kenya daughters are becoming more important than sons to many families. Boys migrate and often feel little responsibility to their wives, children, or other relatives. As a result, parents' hopes are shifting to their daughters to get a good job and provide them with old-age security; therefore, more importance is attached to education of girls. Kenyan rural activist Julia Mulaha argues, by contrast, that educational cuts have been so drastic that the rate of female illiteracy is going up; many girls must drop out of school at an early age because their families cannot afford the cost (in Gellen 1994a:11). Another problem with educational investments in daughters, or sons for that matter, is that such investments currently do not in many cases pay off as they once did. In her study of women traders in Senegal, Mullings (1976:255–256) found that, for many families, their educated children could get only lower-level jobs. This problem is likely to be worse today. As a result of structural adjustment reforms, many salaried jobs in the public sector have been eliminated, and the pay and perks for remaining jobs have been drastically reduced.

Oddly enough, the current economic pressures on families resulting from structural adjustment—most of which result in more work and economic vulnerability for women—can also alter gender relations in ways conducive to more gender equality. In Tanzania, for instance, women are becoming the main providers in many families through their projects. Salaried husbands have lost their jobs or found their salaries cut so low that most wives have started informal sector income-generating businesses that provide most of the family's income. This new reality is challenging the power relationships in the family—with varying responses from men. Some men downplay their wives' economic contribution, while others fear their wives will become too independent or leave them. Some men are so threatened they refuse to allow their wives to have their own projects or restrict the kinds of projects they can have. But most men encourage their wives' income-generating projects (Tripp 1992:170–171).

More-equitable gender relations can also be an advantage for social class mobility, as demonstrated in Orvis's (1993:30–33) study of Kenyan families. In Kenya, "straddling" (i.e., combining female farming with male wage earning) has become the economic strategy that provides the greatest opportunity for social class mobility for most families. Straddlers are most likely to have the resources to purchase land, accumulate capital, or make other productive investments such as in education. Straddling depends on men providing capital from their cash earnings for women to farm. Successful straddling requires cooperation between husbands and wives. If men fail to adequately invest in women's farming and in the household, women reduce their labor on the farm and increase their activity in their own income-generating businesses. Because of the necessity for cooperation and the interdependence of husbands and wives, the conjugal relationship among straddlers is stronger, straddler marriages are more stable, and the gender tensions that affect other households are lessened.

The growing class formation and differentiation in Africa holds some troubling implications for patriarchy in the future. For one thing, more-affluent and educated women (and men) are likely to be most in favor of changes that support the nuclear, conjugal family and a women's rights agenda. They are also in the position, because of their class, to assume most of the better economic and political opportunities that open up to women in an expanding capitalist economy. While desirable from the standpoint of more-privileged women, such an eventuality may not be conducive to achieving gender equality for lower-class women. Parpart (1988:223) discusses this issue and expresses her concern that women who achieve positions of power and privilege will promote the interests of women and men of their own class rather than those of poor women. The gap between elite and mass living standards is already enormous and could intensify if capitalism becomes a guise for entrenching the power and greed of the privileged rather than a strategy for releasing the productive and creative energies of all of Africa's people for social, political, and economic change.

Another possibility is that the Western dependent housewife model may gain in prominence among the bourgeois classes, with its promotion of female domesticity, the male breadwinner role, and the cult of femininity and domesticity. This model can be seen in many magazines in Africa directed toward more-affluent women. Like their Western counterparts, such magazines focus on cooking, sewing, fashion, beauty, and romantic love—even dieting![8] Such images of femininity and domesticity are troubling to those of us who recognize how "the beauty myth" and "the feminine mystique" have been used in the West to control female sexuality and divert women's talents and energies to getting and keeping a man as their primary goal in life. This is a powerful and seductive tool of nuclear family patriarchy in advanced capitalist societies that relegates many women to the home or to second-class status in the public arena.

These concerns are also expressed by some Africans, including two of Africa's most famous male writers, Ngugi wa Thiongo (Kenya) and Chinua Achebe (Nigeria). In his novel *Devil on the Cross* (1982), Ngugi denounces the subordination and exploitation of African women by men, including in the workplace and marriage. He bemoans the fact that affluent women may be reduced to superfluous roles as ornamental wives as Africans aspire to become like their Western counterparts. Ngugi (p. 125) parodies the attitudes of the Kenyan elite when he writes,

> I would like to remind the women here, whether they are wives, mistresses, or girlfriends that . . . there will be a fashion parade, a chance for you to show off your jewelry. . . . We must develop our culture, and you know very well that it is the way women dress and the kind of jewelry they wear that indicates the height a culture can reach.

In the same vein, Achebe, in *Anthills of the Savannah* (1988:89), condemns the treatment of women in precapitalist Africa but also decries the dependent "woman on a pedestal" model from the West.

> So the idea came to man to turn his spouse into the very Mother of God, to pick her up from right under his foot . . . and carry her reverently to a nice, corner pedestal. Up there, her feet completely off the ground she will be just as irrelevant to the practical decisions of running the world as she was in her bad old days. The only difference is that now man will suffer no guilt feelings; he can sit back and congratulate himself on his generosity and gentlemanliness.

Among the more affluent, African patriarchy could be transformed into its Western counterpoint since elements of Western patriarchy, such as female dependency and the male provider-leader dichotomy introduced by colonialism, already permeates many African societies. This is clearly evident in Batezat and Mwalo's (1989:26–28, 56–57) discussion of the sexist attitudes that buttress discrimination against both white and black women in Zimbabwe. Despite the government's commitment to equal rights for women, lower wages for women are common and justified by the attitude that men are the breadwinners; women only supplement their husbands' wages. This also justifies giving men priority in access to jobs. Also, given the current scarcity of jobs, the attitude is, "Why should women get a job when men are unemployed?" Such views overlook, among other things, the fact that as many as a third of women are household heads with no male breadwinner. The concept of femininity held by many in Zimbabwe is that women should stay at home and not compete with men. Moreover, women are weak and delicate, and therefore unfit for positions of authority and responsibility. They should be content to be "sugar cookies." First and foremost, women are regarded as wives and mothers with any other activities secondary. These attitudes reflect men's fear of losing control over female labor and sexuality and of having to compete with women in the labor force.

Such stereotypic dependent roles for women do filter down to influence poorer classes of men and women, although poor women do not have the economic means to be delicate sugar cookies or economically dependent housewives. Nonetheless, development policies to date have reinforced the notion that family and household tasks are women's work by directing home economics extension services and health and nutritional information almost entirely to women. The male breadwinner stereotype is reinforced by programs that provide productive agricultural extension services and resources to men, teach men to run and maintain machinery, and train men in scientific and technical fields. Any mention that men are responsible for child care or domestic tasks or actual education for men in such tasks is neglected. Moreover, even when income-generating projects are introduced, women's and men's projects often reflect the sexual division of labor with the result that women's projects are often limited to such extensions of their domestic roles as handicrafts and food processing. If such concepts of integrating women into development remain the norm, the housewifization of women that scholars such as Mies and her cohorts (1988) warn about is likely to persist, along with the exploitation and subordination of women within the family and society as a whole.

## ▲ Capitalism and Patriarchy: Toward Gender Equality

The rather pessimistic assessment of women's prospects I have given is not the whole story, of course, and the future is not predetermined by the past. As I have argued, there are grounds for concluding that capitalism can be a force for greater gender equality in Africa. Through the introduction of new forms of property and productive relations, liberal values such as individualism and individual rights, education, new economic opportunities apart from the familial mode of production, geographic and social mobility, and the nuclear conjugal family (insofar as it encourages more cooperation, sharing of tasks and assets, and intimacy between husbands and wives), capitalism erodes the familial mode of production and the patriarchal gender relations inherent to it. But in the process of breaking down African patriarchy, new forms of patriarchy based on the male breadwinner–female housewife model and the nuclear family can be erected in its place. This is the form of patriarchy found in Western industrial capitalist societies at the present time. The Western model of "the modern family" and "modern woman or man" is penetrating societies all over the world (although distinctive elements of the indigenous culture are retained as well).

In the form of underdeveloped capitalism, patriarchy and capitalism combine in ways that are exploitative of most men as well as women, although they have encouraged the superexploitation of women both within and outside the household. Women lost much of the status and rights they enjoyed in precapitalist societies while only a privileged few have gained the affluence or opportunities afforded by capitalist development. Underdeveloped capitalism does not work, however. It is unsustainable and will either collapse into chaos and misery, such as we see in countries like Zaire, or will simply perpetuate economic stagnation and poverty. This does not benefit the global capitalist economy or Africans. In the current economic and political environment of the virtual demise of socialism and the hegemony of global capitalism, Africans have little choice but to liberalize their economies if they want to move beyond the present impasse.

Providing more rights, opportunities, and resources for women is essential to this effort, and there are reasons for concluding that African women will not simply recapitulate the housewife model of the West. For one thing, the dependent housewife of nuclear family patriarchy is inconsistent with most African cultures and is no longer the norm in the West itself as capitalism draws more and more women into the labor force. Moreover, feminist organizations and other women's groups are challenging the sexual division of labor and the inequality of women in every institution of society including the family. Although discrimination against women and inequality have not been vanquished in the West, progress has been made and will assuredly continue through the efforts of women and men of conscience.

These changes and challenges to patriarchy are influencing Western capitalism just as capitalism modifies patriarchy. More women are entering the labor force and rising within the ranks. The capitalist economic climate, although it has a long way to go, is becoming more friendly to women as it becomes more dependent on women's labor force participation. Women are entering and transforming other institutions as well, including the political system and the international development community that influences development policy and planning in Africa. These trends are global. Women's labor force participation is growing, women are becoming more educated and organized, and their voices are being heard even within the male-dominated institutions that shape and control the international economy, and in policymaking bodies like the World Bank and United Nations. Fewer women are accepting the limitations of housewifization in the West or in Africa. As articulated by women's groups across the world, women want to be full and equal participants in the development of their countries, and they are demanding equal rights with men and an end to their oppression as women. As Moffett (1994) observed in his report on the UN Population Conference in Cairo, "women's groups have coalesced into a powerful worldwide movement," and the pressure they exerted on largely male policymakers changed the whole focus of global population concerns to the importance of empowering and developing women as a precondition to population control and economic development itself (see also Laclau 1994).

Such efforts by women's groups to put women at the center rather than the periphery of development are growing in Africa. Soukeyna N'Diaye Ba, founder of Senegal's Femme Développement Enterprise en Afrique (FDEA), writes of her organization's efforts to see that the needs of women farmers are central concerns in development policy in her country. To ensure this, the FDEA is educating women to fight for their rights to land and the income from their labor, and teaching, to women from grassroots nongovernmental organizations (NGOs), leadership and business skills (in Gellen 1994b:5).

Such efforts are beginning to pay off. According to Comfort Olayi-wole, principal of Nigeria's Samaru College of Agriculture, the pressure of women's NGOs on policymakers and donors is changing things for women. "Women's groups and projects are no longer isolated ventures, easily ignored by governments or community members. Women are organizing themselves into a formidable political and social movement" (in Gellen 1994:43). The results are evident in Kenya, where for the first time in the 1994–1995 national economic program, gender issues were linked to development, and Kenya's attorney general has created a new task force to review all laws affecting the status of women. In another positive move, Kenya's Women's Bureau has produced a Gender and Development policy document that argues for joint ownership of land for married couples and individual ownership for single women. The government is also now advocating joint family decisionmaking on land use and equal distribution of economic benefits between spouses, as well as investing more money into supporting women's agricultural production, including access to land. In South Africa women's groups are working to guarantee that gender equality, as outlined in the Women's Charter, is enshrined in the new constitution and enforced in the legal system (Madlala 1994). These are not isolated cases, as a new level of awareness of the importance of women and the need for change in gender relations is occurring all across Africa.

Women are making their needs known, and at the top of the list is the need to be productive so that women can support themselves and their children. African farmers, both male and female, generally support the principle of market reform and liberalization of the economy. They want to be free to produce, prosper, and own or control their own land. But current economic reform policies are another story. Some farmers, often the larger commercial farmers, have benefited, but smallholders, especially women, often find it difficult to gain market access or to benefit otherwise from current market-oriented structural adjustment policies.[9] Opposition to flawed policies is not the same thing as opposition to a more open and competitive economy, however. What most people, including women, want is a more level playing field and assistance, where needed, that makes it possible for people to be productive (see Harsch 1994; Putterman 1994).

Recognizing this, the World Bank in its 1994 *Development Report* began to reassess its policies and to acknowledge the role of the state in creating markets and helping farmers. This includes assisting farmers to market their produce or supplying them with reasonably priced inputs, ensuring food security, and promoting the market—for example, by investing in marketing facilities and rural feeder roads and improving credit, market information, and training. But more must be done if women are to benefit. In its recent report on structural adjustment in Africa, the World Bank (1994a:168–169) acknowledges that market-oriented reforms and economic growth may benefit women less than men because of the patriarchal organization of the African household, where "labor and income are allocated according to the status, bargaining power, and options of individual household members; which in turn are related to control over assets and income." Since most of women's production is in nontradable food crops for home consumption or in low-profit income-generating activities, price incentives and other market reforms may do little to improve women's economic well-being. Expanding education for girls and promoting women's involvement in the production of export crops or tradable food crops are viewed as key elements in raising not only women's income but in achieving overall economic growth (World Bank 1994a:162, 169).

Such proposals will not be enough by themselves to overcome the market distortions created by patriarchy. Owoh (1995:183–184) contends that while structural adjustment programs are not "inherently pro male," "they reflect an underlying male bias in society and the development process that operates in favor of men as a gender and against women as a gender." They falsely assume that both men and women exercise individual sovereignty in the marketplace while neglecting the realities of unequal power based on gender. Until women have equal access to land, equal rights with men, control over their labor and the benefits of their labor, equal access to nonstereotypic education and development resources, and an equitable sharing of domestic tasks with men, there will be no free market operating in Africa.

There are also psychological obstacles to overcome. Rowland and Schwartz-Shea (1989) argue that equal rights for women and greater access to the market arena, while laudable, are not the same as the empowerment of women. Because of the history of patriarchy and cultural conditioning of women within it, women are often ambivalent about feminism's equality agenda and doubt their own power to shape their lives. Moreover, it is difficult for many women to overcome "powerless responsibility," that is, to value themselves as autonomous persons rather than dutifully caring for others out of subordination to them. Autonomy does not mean that women should become selfish or uncaring toward their families or others. It involves expecting others to be responsible also for nurturing and caring for themselves rather than placing the responsibility for these activities exclusively on women. Women's autonomy, in Rowland and Shwartz-Shea's analysis, promotes cooperation and empowering others in families and relationships. Women's empowerment requires that the responsibilities of home and child care be shared by men and society at large and an end to the fundamentally unequal sexual division of labor. Sharing the jobs of nurturing and caregiving among men and women could also help reduce male violence against women so prevalent in the patriarchal male-female relationship and in society in general (see Mies 1986:221–223; Rowland and Schwartz-Shea 1989:1).

African women such as Batezat and Mwalo (1989:66) have come to similar conclusions. They write that an economistic view of African women's liberation is inadequate. Alleviating poverty and enabling women to earn a cash income will not end women's inequality. While the eradication of poverty is desirable and necessary,

> economic well-being alone cannot solve the problems of women. Discrimination on the basis of gender cuts across class as well as race and ethnic group. Policies aimed at transforming women's lives both economically and socially must also address the sexual division of labour and men's control over women within the household.

Batezat and Mwalo (1989:65) also point out the fallacies of development programs that put total responsibility for children's health and nutrition on women while ignoring men's responsibilities to their families. No one, they observe, addresses fathers' alcoholism or failure to provide financial support for their families, nor does anyone mention the health needs of women themselves as crucial aspects of overall family health, nutrition, or well-being.

At a recent symposium in Zimbabwe sponsored by the African Development Bank and the World Bank, gender issues in development were discussed. Male and female African participants at the symposium agreed that both men and women would gain from the expansion of women's rights and women's economic and social development (Gittinger et al. 1990:37). Stamp (1989:66) adds that the current distortion in gender relations and male dominance over women only appears to benefit men, when in reality women, men, families, communities, and the nation are better off when women are able to participate in all aspects of their societies. It will be a formidable task of the development community and women's groups to make this case persuasively to African men and to employers and others who exploit and discriminate against women. But such an effort to enlist men in the cause of gender equality is essential to its success. As Mies (1986:223) writes, women cannot break out of patriarchy unless men do. Changing the international division of labor or other structures of gender inequality can start at the individual man-woman level.

Yet it must be acknowledged that in some ways men will lose in the short term from greater gender equality. As Eisenstein (1981) points out, men will lose sexual privilege in the sexual hierarchy that divides home and work. They will have to share the responsibilities of child rearing and housework. They will lose privileges and freedoms that exist because of patriarchal oppression. Moreover, the destruction of a system of power and oppression does not mean that everyone gains equally or in the same way.

Social changes associated with capitalism will continue to undermine the economic, political, and social foundations of African patriarchy. The extent to which this occurs depends on whether capitalism can expand and erode the familial mode of production and the complex of social and political structures tied to it. There is, of course, no guarantee that this will happen. But those societies that are more extensively transformed by capitalism will see the emergence of social classes and social forces with a stake in modifying gender relations in ways that provide more rights and opportunities for women—partly because they will see it as in their interests to do so and partly because women will no longer be willing to accept their exploitation and subordination.

This process of change will be gradual and will likely be associated with backlashes from both men and women who feel threatened by changes in what they accept as the proper, natural, or divinely ordained relationships between the sexes. While this phenomenon is most dramatically noticeable in association with Islamic fundamentalism, it is also found in the West, as Faludi (1991) has so cogently documented for the United States. Despite such obstacles to change, in the West and in Africa, women are sharing their experiences, articulating their needs, and pressing for changes both from within and outside the corridors of power. While capitalism has directly and indirectly helped to precipitate these changes, women's demands for equality and a world that values women and their contributions as workers, wives, mothers, caregivers, and community workers are beginning to and will in the long run help to transform capitalism itself.

This transformation of capitalism is only in its embryonic stages but its outlines are already apparent. A predatory, laissez-faire capitalism has few advocates left in the world, and most advocates of the market economy, including the World Bank, recognize the need to intervene in the economy to provide a safety net for the poor and other economically vulnerable members of society, to protect the environment, and to spread the benefits of economic development to the poor. Rather than undermining the bottom line, such measures are needed to maximize the social, physical, and political climate for the success of global capitalism itself. In its 1992 *Development Report*, for example, the World Bank concludes that economic efficiency and sound environmental management go hand in hand, and there is now "near unanimity on the central importance of markets and human resource investment for successful development" (p. 178). Flavin and Young (1993) add that ecological pressures are becoming a more important influence on economic decisions as governments reform the global corporate economy by setting environmental guidelines within which business must operate.

Improving the status of women will play a key role in ensuring that the interrelated issues of population, environment, and economic development are successfully addressed, because patriarchy and the oppression of women are so closely tied to poverty, environmental degradation, and rapid population growth. This was a major theme of a 1993 workshop, Sustainable Development: Population and the Environment, sponsored by the Africa Bureau of the U.S. Agency for International Development (USAID) (C. Green 1994). Poverty compels many Africans to overexploit natural resources and to have large families, but the fact that men have more power than women over natural resource use, production decisions, resource allocation, and reproduction makes these problems worse. As Jacobson (1993:62) comments, patriarchy "prevents women from transforming their increasingly unstable subsistence economy into one not forced to cannibalize its own declining assets."

In her discussion of WEDNET (Women, Environment, and Development Network), Kettel (1995:242, 250–253) examines the difference between women's and men's "landscapes" (i.e., the gender-based distinctions that people have of the environment) and the impact this has on environmental problems in Africa. Women's landscapes typically arise from their responsibilities as mothers involved in the production of life and nature to benefit their families. This differs from men's landscapes as fathers and, increasingly, as autonomous individuals. Coupled with Western outlooks on the environment as a multiplicity of exploitable resources for human use and profit, men's landscapes tend to ignore the needs of women and children for sustainable resource use. At the male-dominated policymaking level, the same problems arise, and male needs with respect to the environment tend to be favored over women's. Environmental degradation results. An example of this difference in landscapes was provided by Harrison (1990) at the Sustainable Development workshop:

> If women had the power to plant trees in most parts of Africa, then trees would have been planted very much sooner and we would not have needed to wait for the development of a market in fuelwood. For example, in Kenya, I have met men who did not care in the least that their wives were walking for four hours a day to collect fuelwood. But when shortages developed and men had to pay their own hard-earned cash to buy fuelwood, they began to be interested in planting trees.

Similarly, high fertility is affected by the fact that male policymakers make the decision about whether or how much to invest in family planning. In addition, at the household level reproductive decisions are not equal. Dasgupta (1995:42) argues that men have more power over many reproductive decisions than women do; and they get most of the benefits of children while not having to bear most of the costs. The extended family tied to the familial mode of production allows many women also to not bear the full costs of childbearing. As women's work load increases with poverty and environmental degradation (e.g., the hunt for fuelwood and water as resources become more scarce), children are desirable assets. Norms of fosterage and shared child care allow women to share the burdens of child rearing, usually with other women.

Just as women's and men's environmental landscapes may differ, so do their reproductive landscapes. But both are subject to change if the relative situations of males and females change. For instance, when men had to bear more of the costs of environmental degradation (e.g., the shortage of fuelwood), their interest in conservation increased. Similarly, when men have to bear more of the costs of childbearing or women's decisionmaking power increases, men's interest in or control over family size often changes.

The World Bank and USAID refer to studies that show that education for both boys and girls may be the main ingredient in both protection of the environment and population control. Education is correlated with conservation-oriented attitudes; support for family planning; healthier and better-educated children; and improved agricultural production, enterprise development and wage employment (World Bank 1992:173; C. Green 1994:182–183). Dasgupta (1995:42) adds that income-generating activities on the part of women, even more than education, affects childbearing because women's power in the household increases with income, and the costs of children to men rise if procreation limits their wives' ability to bring in cash income.[10]

Capitalism and the market on their own are unlikely to solve these broad issues of development, poverty alleviation, gender equity, and environmental protection. For this reason, it is the job of governments to structure the market so that profitable investment, gender equality, and environmental sustainability coincide. Unfortunately, as experience shows, economies can grow and businesses can prosper for some time by exploiting the poor, women, and the environment. Moreover, governments are unlikely to act and businesses are unlikely to change unless pressured to do so. For this reason, women's groups acting locally, nationally, and internationally are essential to change the political economy of capitalism to lay the foundation for a sustainable global economy. In addition, women must increase their numbers within policymaking and decisionmaking institutions so that the impetus for change can come both from within as well as from outside the system.

For those who would argue that this is not capitalism but "social engineering" or interference with the market, we must remember that purely free markets are a useful fiction of economic theory and political ideologues, not a picture of reality. Markets always operate within the context of social, political, and economic institutions, constraints, and choices that regulate, modify, or distort them. To date, the context in which capitalism has operated in Africa and elsewhere has been a patriarchal one. Policies that favor women and women's rights are in reality corrections of a major source of distortions in the market; that is, patriarchy and male privilege that have denied women the ability to compete on an equal basis with men. Such gender bias must change if capitalism and genuine development are to occur in Africa.

In his book on Africa's current economic crisis, Adebayo Adedeji (1994:216–217), former executive secretary of the United Nations Economic Commission for Africa (ECA), discusses "the central role of women" in African economies and the need to invest in women as part of Africa's effort to support entrepreneurship and economic growth.

> Any sustainable renaissance requires the acceptance of gender equality in economy, society, and polity. . . . African women should occupy leading technical and managerial positions in large numbers. . . . Where traditions and laws impede their economic and political empowerment, these should be repealed. . . . Africa can simply not afford to marginalize women.

## ▲ Conclusion

The real issue in Africa now is not whether Africa will become more capitalistic but what kind of capitalism will develop. As mentioned above, a pure market economy exists only in theory; markets are always regulated or modified by values, choices, and power arrangements in society. For this reason, economics is always political economy; capitalism is constructed, not a given based on abstract market principles. Currently, there appear to be basically two models of capitalist development that can act as guides for African capitalist development: (1) top down, which is characterized as elitist, marked by gross inequality in wealth and income, dispossession of the masses, and a trickle down of benefits from the top of the socioeconomic pyramid to the bottom; and (2) grassroots, which is based on a concern for equity and empowering the masses to be more productive and in control of the economic choices and benefits occurring in their societies.

Admittedly, African societies face considerable constraints on their freedom of choice, the result of pressures from the global economy and the structural adjustment conditionalities being imposed on them. Just as important are internal constraints in the form of powerful elite interests that benefit from exploiting rather than empowering the poor. In underdeveloped capitalism, as we have seen, a small elite has parasitically thrived on the surplus produced by Africa's farmers and workers. For the most part they have gained income and wealth not by merit or by their productive contributions to society but by speculation, corruption, and access to state resources. Structural adjustment, while ostensibly designed to lessen such predatory activity and promote market forces and entrepreneurship, has created some negative, unintended consequences. Among these, as Adedeji (1994:7, 216) discusses, is an "adjustment-induced elite" that has grown up in many countries. This class of "speculators and wheelers and dealers in currencies, cars, and drugs" has come to symbolize market forces. At the same time, there has been a "massive decline" in productive entrepreneurs and their organizations. This form of elitist, top-down capitalism will not empower most women or men and is likely to perpetuate male dominance at the top of the economic and political hierarchies. The danger is that without a concerted effort by grassroots organizations and the state to promote democratic capitalist development, receding public control over the economy may simply be replaced by established oligopolistic interests or new mafioso-type gangs to fill the void (see also Shaw 1994: 82–83).

That African states have hitherto shown little capacity for promoting grassroots capitalism is uncontestable; yet that should not dissuade us from proposing what changes are necessary or desirable. Moreover, examples do exist in Africa of successful programs, such as Women's World Banking, from which African policymakers can draw considerable satisfaction (see Chapter 5). The fast-growing economies of Asia—the so-called NICs (newly industrializing countries)—also offer some lessons from which Africa can learn. Although Africa cannot copy their experience, and these countries are far from perfect, Taiwan, Thailand, Indonesia, and Malaysia in the 1960s were, according to the World Bank, similar to Africa now. Between 1930 and 1960 they had almost no economic growth and were widely seen as poor prospects for development. All four countries were very poor and experiencing rapid population growth as well. Indonesia, like Nigeria, became an oil-exporting country; between 1973 and 1981 both got 20 percent of gross domestic product from oil revenues. Indonesia's economy has grown, however, while Nigeria's has stagnated. Among the important differences between the NICs and Africa, according to the World Bank, is that in the NICs (including also Hong Kong, Singapore, and South Korea) the state intervened in the economy to promote more equitable development and human resource development. Indonesia invested heavily in infrastructure, agricultural development, and labor-intensive industries directed to rural areas. Nigeria spent its oil revenues mostly on the cities and large-scale, capital-intensive agricultural projects with low rates of return. Other NICs, such as South Korea and Taiwan, invested in labor-intensive industries and basic services such as universal primary education. The results have been "the fastest sustained growth of any group of countries in history, but also highly equitable growth thus enjoying the most rapid reduction of poverty ever" (World Bank 1994a:163).

If managed capitalist development can promote equity, growth, and poverty reduction, it can also promote gender equality if this is made a priority. As I have argued, gender issues in Africa are not peripheral issues to be dealt with once sustained growth and development are well under way. Improving the status of women in Africa both in the household and society at large is a vital component of sustainable, capitalist development. It is patriarchal resistance and bias (both African and Western) that must be overcome through a combination of education, legal reform, enlightened political action initiated by women's organizations and the state, and gender-sensitive development policies. Without these, Africa's future—not just women's—will be grim indeed.

## ▲ Notes

1. I am not suggesting that African cultures and family systems will disappear or be replaced by "modernization." Cultural change is always gradual, and many elements of the past are retained and incorporated into new institutions and relationships. It is still useful to make conceptual distinctions between types of social orders. These conceptual distinctions allow us to compare societies in terms of degrees of dominance of one type or the other.

2. See also Kayongo-Male and Onyango 1984:41–42.

3. Odinga was also an ally of the Kikuyu but broke with them in the 1960s because he felt Luo and other smaller ethnic group interests were not being well served.

4. The relationship between the nuclear family and capitalism is complex and variable across and within societies. Marshall (1994:53, 61–62) points out that in much of Europe, the United States, and Canada the nuclear family was not the creation of capitalism, as is sometimes thought. The nuclear family was already the

dominant household form. She adds that capitalism does not just take over the pre-existing patriarchal organization of domestic life for its own purposes; this is actively created and recreated—and contested. Still, the nuclear family appears to be crucial to the development of capitalism. Where it does not exist as the dominant household form, as in Africa, efforts are often made to encourage its evolution. Also where capitalism's impact is greatest, more nuclearization of the family begins to evolve spontaneously, and gender relationships within the family evolve, too—although earlier family forms and gender relationships do not in most cases disappear entirely.

5. Kennedy (1988) writes that business expansion in Africa is impaired by the demands of extended families. One of the major needs is the successful transfer of business assets (e.g., farms, businesses, houses) to the next generation; otherwise, reinvestment and growth of firms is prevented.

6. The life-style of these families is also expected to lead to lower birth rates. The World Bank (see 1986) has made lowering the birth rate and supporting family planning in Africa a major priority, and improving the status of women in the family and society at large is recognized as crucial to these efforts (see, e.g., World Bank 1992:173). This theme is also echoed in the 1994 UN Population Conference in Cairo and the 1995 UN Conference on Women in Beijing (see Jacobson 1993).

7. The notorious Otieno burial controversy in Kenya is a prime example of the conflict between "modern" families and extended families and the efforts of some elite women (and their husbands) to expand women's rights and keep wealth within the nuclear family (see Stamp 1991a; Gordon 1995).

8. An example is a recent edition of the southern African women's magazine *True Love* (June 1994) with its fashionable, Westernized models, couples, and articles with such titles as "Erotic Power: How to Turn Men On!" and "Young Married Bliss."

9. Hellinger and Hamond (1995) join a lengthy list of critics of structural adjustment programs (SAPs) who assert that current policies not only have failed to solve the continent's economic problems, they have been devastating to the poor, and especially to women. There is growing evidence that poverty is worsening despite stated SAP objectives of poverty reduction, gender equity, and growth with equity. Among the negative impacts of SAPs on the poor in general are tight credit, cuts in social and extension services, withdrawal of subsidies on agricultural inputs, deterioration of roads and other infrastructure, stagnant rural wages, and higher prices, including food prices. Women and children have been especially hurt by cuts in social services and new user fees on services. Oxfam reports that in Zimbabwe maternal mortality has tripled at Harare Central Hospital since user fees were introduced. Infant mortality and undernutrition/malnutrition among children are also rising. See also Adedeji 1994; Gordon 1991, 1992; Onimode 1989; Palmer 1991; and Chakaodza 1993 for a sample of other critical works on structural adjustment reforms.

10. See also Blumberg 1995.

▲

# Bibliography

Abu-Lughod, Lila. 1993. *Writing Women's Worlds: Bedouin Stories*. Berkeley: University of California Press.

Achebe, Chinua. 1988. *Anthills of the Savannah*. New York: Anchor.

Adams, Paul. 1995. "Cycle of Dependency?" *Africa Report* 40 (March–April): 34–37.

Adedeji, Adebayo. 1994. Outlook: Africa's Strategic Agenda. In *Africa within the World: Beyond Dispossession and Dependence*. London: Zed.

Afonja, Simi. 1986a. Changing Modes of Production and the Sexual Division of Labor Among the Yoruba. In Eleanor Leacock, Helen I. Safa, et al. *Women's Work: Development and the Division of Labor by Gender*. South Hadley, MA: Bergin & Garvey.

———. 1986b. Land Control: A Critical Factor in Yoruba Gender Stratification. In *Women and Class in Africa,* edited by Claire Robertson and Iris Berger. New York: Africana.

Africans Seek Homespun Remedies in Kampala." 1991. *Africa Report* 36 (July–August):8–9.

Agheyisi, Rachel Uwa. 1985. The Labour Market Implications of the Access of Women to Higher Education in Nigeria. In *Women in Nigeria Today*. London: Zed.

"AID (Agency for International Development). 1984. *Women in Development: The First Decade 1975–1984*. A Report to Congress. Washington, DC: WID/AID.

Ajayi, Femi. 1991. "Food for Thought." *Africa Report* 36 (September–October): 25–28.

Ajulu, Rok. 1993. "The 1992 Kenya General Elections: A Preliminary Assessment." *Review of African Political Economy* 56:98–102.

Amalric, Franck. 1994. Finiteness, Infinity and Responsibility: The Population-Environment Debate. In *Feminist Perspectives on Sustainable Development*, edited by Wendy Harcourt. London: Zed.

Amin, Samir. 1990a. *Delinking: Towards a Polycentric World*. London: Zed.

———. 1990b. *Maldevelopment: Anatomy of a Global Failure*. London: Zed.

———. 1990c. Preface to *Adjustment or Delinking? The African Experience,* edited by Azzam Mahjoub. London: Zed.

———. 1974. *Accumulation on a World Scale*. London. Monthly Review Press.

Apfel-Marglin, Frederique, and Suzanne Simon. 1994. Feminist Orientalism and Development. In *Feminist Perspectives on Sustainable Development,* edited by Wendy Harcourt. London: Zed.

Ampofo, Akosua Adomako. 1993. "Controlling and Punishing Women in Ghana." *Review of African Political Economy* 56 (March):102–111.

191

Atkinson, Ti Grace. 1974. *Amazon Odyssey*. New York: Links.

Ba, Fama Hane, Aminata Mbengue Ndiaye, Marie-Angelique Savane, and Awa Thiongane. 1984. The Impact of Territorial Administration Reform on the Situation of Women in Senegal. In *Rural Development and Women in Africa*. Geneva: ILO.

Badri, Balghis. 1990. A Profile of Sudanese Women. In *The Long-Term Perspective Study of Sub-Saharan Africa*. Washington, DC: World Bank.

Banugire, Firimooni R. 1989. Employment, Incomes, Basic Needs and Structural Adjustment Policy in Uganda. In *The IMF, the World Bank and the African Debt: The Social and Political Impact*. Vol. 2. Edited by Bade Onimode. London: Zed.

Barrett, Michele. 1992. Words and Things: Materialism and Method in Contemporary Feminist Analysis. In *Destabilizing Theory: Contemporary Feminist Debates,* edited by Michele Barrett and Anne Phillips. Stanford, CA: Stanford University Press.

———. 1988. *Women's Oppression Today*. London: Verso.

Barrow, Nita, 1985. "The Decade NGO Forum." *Africa Report* 30 (March–April): 9–12.

Bates, Robert H. 1989. *Beyond the Miracle of the Market*. New York: Cambridge University Press.

———. 1981. *Markets and States in Tropical Africa*. Berkeley: University of California Press.

Batezat, Elinor, and Margaret Mwalo. 1989. *Women in Zimbabwe*. Harare: SAPES.

Becker, David G. 1987. Postimperialism: A First Quarterly Report. In *Postimperialism: International Capitalism and Development in the Late Twentieth Century,* by David G. Becker, Jeff Frieden, Sayre P. Schatz, and Richard L. Sklar. Boulder: Lynne Rienner.

Beneria, Lourdes, and Gita Sen. 1986. Accumulation, Reproduction, and Women's Role in Economic Development: Boserup Revisited. In Eleanor Leacock, Helen I. Safa, et al., *Women's Work: Development and the Division of Labor by Gender*. South Hadley, MA: Bergin & Garvey.

Bennholdt-Thomsen, Veronika. 1988. "Investment in the Poor": An Analysis of World Bank Policy. In Maria Mies, Veronika Bennholdt-Thomsen, and Claudia Von Werlhof, *Women: The Last Colony*. London: Zed.

Berman, Bruce. 1992. The Concept of "Articulation" and the Political Economy of Colonialism. In Bruce Berman and John Lonsdale, *Unhappy Valley: Conflict in Kenya and Africa*. London: James Currey.

Bernal, Victoria. 1988. Losing Ground—Women and Agriculture in Sudan's Irrigated Schemes: Lessons from a Blue Nile Village. In *Women, Agriculture and Land: The African Experience,* edited by Jean Davison. Boulder: Westview.

Bernard, J. 1987. *The Female World from a Global Perspective*. Bloomington: Indiana University Press.

Bienen, Henry. 1974. *Kenya: The Politics of Participation and Control*. Princeton, NJ: Princeton University Press.

Blomstrom, Magnus, and Bjorn Hettne. 1988. *Development Theory in Transition*. London: Zed.

Bloom, David E., and Adi Brender. 1993. "Labor and the Emerging World Economy." *Population Bulletin* 48 (October).

Blumberg, Rae Lesser. 1995. Introduction: Engendering Wealth and Well-Being in an Era of Economic Transformation. In *Engendering Wealth and Well-Being: Empowerment for Global Change,* edited by Rae Lesser Blumberg et al. Boulder: Westview.

————. 1994. "Reaching Africa's 'Invisible' Farmers." *African Farmer* (April): 14–15.

Bonat, Zuwaqhu A., and Yahaya A. Abdullahi. 1989. The World Bank, IMF and Nigeria's Agricultural and Rural Economy. In *The IMF, the World Bank and the African Debt: The Social and Political Impact.* Vol. 2 Edited by Bade Onimode. London: Zed.

Boone, Catherine. 1990. "The Making of a Rentier Class: Wealth Accumulation and Political Control in Senegal." *The Journal of Development Studies* 26 (April):425–449.

Boserup, Ester. 1986. *Women's Roles in Economic Development.* Aldershot: Gower.

Boyle, Philip. 1988. The Socio-Economic Effects of Structural Adjustment on Women. Paper presented at the meeting of the OECD Development Assistance Committee, April 18, Paris.

Bozzoli, Belinda. 1983. "Marxism, Feminism, and South African Studies." *Journal of Southern African Studies* 9 (April):139–171.

Bradshaw, York W. 1990. "Perpetuating Underdevelopment in Kenya: The Link between Agriculture, Class, and State." *African Studies Review* 33 (April):1–28.

Brooks, George E., Jr. 1976. The Signares of Saint-Louis and Goree: Women Entrepreneurs in Eighteenth-Century Senegal. In *Women in Africa: Studies in Social and Economic Change,* edited by Nancy J. Hafkin and Edna G. Bay. Stanford, CA: Stanford University Press.

Bujra, Janet. 1993. "Gender, Class and Empowerment: A Tale of Two Tanzanian Servants." *Review of African Political Economy* 56:68–78.

————. 1986. Urging Women to Redouble Their Efforts . . . Class, Gender, and Capitalist Transformation in Africa. In *Women and Class in Africa,* edited by Claire Robertson and Iris Berger. New York: Africana.

Bunch, Charlotte. 1993. Women's Subordination Worldwide: Global Feminism. In *Feminist Frameworks,* edited by Alison M. Jaggar and Paula S. Rothenberg. New York: McGraw-Hill.

Cagatay, Nilufer, Caren Grown, and Aida Santiago. 1986. "Nairobi Women's Conference: Toward a Global Feminism?" *Feminist Studies* 12 (Summer):401–412.

Caldwell, John C. 1982. *Theory of Fertility Decline.* New York: Academic Press.

Callaghy, Thomas M. 1994. "Africa: Falling Off the Map?" *Current History* (January):31–36.

Cameroon. Ministry of Information and Culture. 1985. *Agriculture in Cameroon.* Yaounde.

Carney, Judith A. 1988. Struggles Over Land and Crops in an Irrigated Rice Scheme: The Gambia. In *Agriculture, Women, and Land: The African Experience,* edited by Jean Davison. Boulder: Westview.

Cattell, Maria G. 1992. "Praise the Lord and Say No to Men: Older Women Empowering Themselves in Samia, Kenya." *Journal of Cross-Cultural Gerontology* 7:307–330.

Caulfield, Mina Davis. 1993. Imperialism, the Family, and Cultures of Resistance. In *Feminist Frameworks,* edited by Alison M. Jaggar and Paula S. Rothenberg. New York: McGraw-Hill.

Chakoadza, Austin M. 1993. *Structural Adjustment in Zambia and Zimbabwe: Reconstruction or Destruction?* Harare: Third World Publishing House.

"A Chance for Africa." 1991. *Africa News* 34 (May 20):1–3, 17.

Chanock, Martin. 1982. Making Customary Law: Men, Women, and Courts in Colonial Northern Rhodesia. In *African Women and the Law: Historical Perspectives,* edited by Margaret Jean Hay and Marcia Wright. Boston University Papers on Africa, no. 7. Boston: Boston University.

Charlton, Sue Ellen M. 1984. *Women in Third World Development.* Boulder: Westview.

Chazan, Naomi, Robert Mortimer, John Ravenhill, and Donald Rothchild. 1988. *Politics and Society in Contemporary Africa.* Boulder: Lynne Rienner.

Cheru, Fantu. 1989. The Role of the IMF and World Bank in the Agrarian Crisis of Sudan and Tanzania: Sovereignty vs. Control. In *The IMF, the World Bank and the African Debt: The Social and Political Impact.* Vol. 2. Edited by Bade Onimode. London: Zed.

Chibber, Ajay, and Stanley Fischer. 1991. Introduction. In *Economic Reform in Sub-Saharan Africa,* edited by Ajay Chibber and Stanley Fischer. Washington, DC: World Bank.

Clapham, Christopher. 1993. "Democratization in Africa: Obstacles and Prospects." *Third World Quarterly* 14:423–438.

Clark, Mari H. 1984. "Women-headed Households and Poverty: Insights from Kenya." *SIGNS* 10:338–354.

Cliffe, Lionel. 1982. Class Formation as an "Articulation" Process: East African Cases. In *Introduction to the Sociology of Developing Societies,* edited by Hamza Alavi and Teodor Shanin. New York: Monthly Review Press.

"Closing the Debt Gap." 1991. *Africa News* 34 (July 15):11.

Cloud, Kathleen. 1986. Sex Roles in Food Production and Distribution Systems in the Sahel. In *Women Farmers in Africa: Rural Development in Mali and the Sahel,* edited by Lucy E. Creevey. Syracuse, NY: Syracuse University Press.

Cloud, Kathleen, and Jane B. Knowles. 1988. Where Can We Go from Here? Recommendations for Action. In *Agriculture, Women, and Land: The African Experience,* edited by Jean Davison. Boulder: Westview.

Cohen, David Wm., and E. S. Atieno Odhiambo. 1992. *Burying SM: The Politics of Knowledge and the Sociology of Power in Africa.* Portsmouth, NH: Heinemann.

"Controversy Over African Aid Simmers." 1991. *Africa News* 35 (October 7):3–4.

Coole, Diana H. 1993. *Women in Political Theory: From Ancient Misogyny to Contemporary Feminism,* 2d ed. Boulder: Lynne Rienner.

Coontz, Stephanie. 1992. *The Way We Never Were.* New York: Basic Books.

Cordell, Dennis D., Joel D. Gregory, and Victor Piché. 1987. African Historical Demography: The Search for a Theoretical Framework. In *African Population and Capitalism: Historical Perspectives,* edited by Dennis D. Cordell and Joel W. Gregory. Boulder: Westview.

COSATU. 1992. "Resolutions on Women." *Review of African Political Economy* 56:124–125.

Cotran, E. 1989. The Future of Customary Law in Kenya. In *The S. M. Otieno Case: Death and Burial in Modern Kenya,* edited by J. B. Ojwang and J.N.K. Mugambi. Nairobi: Nairobi University Press.

Coughlin, Peter. 1990. Moving to the Next Phase? In *Manufacturing Africa: Performance & Prospects of Seven Countries in Sub-Saharan Africa,* edited by Roger C. Riddell. London: James Curey.

Courville, Cindy. 1994. Re-Examining Patriarchy as a Mode of Production. In *Theorizing Black Feminisms,* edited by Stanlie M. James and Abena P.A. Busia. New York: Routledge.

Crasson, G. 1982. *La Planification des Ressources Humaines dans les IVeme et Veme Plans de Développement Économique et Culturel de la République Unie de Cameroon.* Douala: Institut Panafricain pour le Développement.

Croll, Elizabeth J. 1986. Rural Production and Reproduction: Socialist Development Experiences. In *Women's Work,* edited by Eleanor Leacock, Helen I. Safa, et al. South Hadley, MA: Bergin & Garvey.

Crow, Ben. 1988. The Invidious Dilemmas of Capitalist Development. In Ben Crow, Mary Thorpe, et al., *Survival and Change in the Third World.* New York: Oxford University Press.

Cubbins, Lisa A. 1991. "Women, Men, and the Division of Power: A Study of Gender Stratification in Kenya." *Social Forces* 69 (June):1063–1083.

Cutrufelli, Maria R. 1983. *Roots of Oppression.* London: Zed.

da Costa, Peter. 1992. "The Capitalist Credo." *Africa Report* 37 (January–February):42–44.

Danaher, Kevin. 1993. Myths of African Hunger. In *Global Studies: Africa.* Institute of Food and Development. Reprint, Guilford, CT: Dushkin.

Dasgupta, Partha S. 1995. "Population, Poverty and the Local Environment." *Scientific American* (February):40–45.

Date-Bah, Eugenia. 1984. "Rural Women, Their Activities and Technology in Ghana: An Overview." In *Rural Development and Women in Africa.* Geneva: ILO.

Davison, Jean. 1988a. Land Redistribution in Mozambique and Its Effects on Women's Collective Production: Case Studies from Sofa Province. In *Agriculture, Women, and Land: The African Experience,* edited by Jean Davison. Boulder: Westview.

———. 1988b. Land and Women's Agricultural Production: The Context. In *Agriculture, Women, and Land: The African Experience,* edited by Jean Davison. Boulder: Westview.

———. 1988c. Who Owns What? Land Registration and Tensions in Gender Relations of Production in Kenya. In *Agriculture, Women, and Land: The African Experience,* edited by Jean Davison. Boulder: Westview.

"Debt Initiative May Be Lasting Summit Legacy." 1991. *Africa News* 34 (May 20):4, 18.

Dei, George J. Sefa. 1994. "The Women of a Ghanaian Village: A Study of Social Change." *African Studies Review* 37 (September):121–145.

Delphy, Christine. 1979. *A Materialist Analysis of Women's Oppression.* London: Women's Research and Resources Centre.

Dinan, Carmel. 1983. Sugar Daddies and Gold-Diggers: The White-Collar Single Women in Accra. In *Female and Male in West Africa,* edited by Christine Oppong. London: Allen & Unwin.

"Domestic Wrangle Sparks Off Women's Rights Debate." 1993. *Living On* (November/December):22.

Dorsey, Ellen. 1993. Securing Their Own Rights: The South African Women's Rights Charter Campaign. Paper presented at the 1993 Annual Meeting of the Southern Political Science Association, Savannah, GA.

Dunbar, Roberta Ann. 1983. Islamized Law and the Status of Women in Niger. Paper presented at the meeting of the Southeast Regional Seminar in African Studies, October 15, Charlottesville, VA.

Eisenstein, Zillah. 1989. *The Female Body and the Law.* Berkeley: University of California Press.

———. 1981. *The Radical Future of Liberal Feminism.* New York: Longman.

———, ed. 1979. *Capitalist Patriarchy.* New York: Monthly Review Press.

Eldridge, Elizabeth A. 1991. "Women in Production: The Economic Role of Women in Nineteenth-Century Lesotho." *SIGNS* 16 (Summer):707–731.

Elson, Diane. 1992. From Survival Strategies to Transformation Strategies: Women's Needs and Structural Adjustment. In *Unequal Burden: Economic Crisis, Persistent Poverty, and Women's Work,* edited by Lourdes Beneria and Shelley Feldman. Boulder: Westview.

————. 1989. The Impact of Structural Adjustment on Women: Concepts and Issues." In *The IMF, the World Bank and the African Debt: The Social and Political Impact.* Vol. 2. Edited by Bade Omimode. London: Zed.

Enabulele, Arlene Bene. 1985. The Role of Women's Associations in Nigeria's Development: Social Welfare Perspective. In *Women in Nigeria Today.* London: Zed.

Ernst and Young. 1988. *Private Enterprise Development: Gender Considerations.* Washington, DC: Bureau for Private Enterprise/USAID.

Evans, Peter. 1979. *Dependent Development: The Alliance of Multinational, State and Local Capital in Brazil.* Princeton, NJ: Princeton University Press.

"Fallacy of Income Generation." 1993. *Everyhome* 4:13.

Faludi, Susan. 1991. *Backlash: The Undeclared War Against American Women.* New York: Crown.

Fatton, Robert, Jr. 1992. *Predatory Rule: State and Civil Society in Africa.* Boulder: Lynne Rienner.

————. 1988. "Bringing the Ruling Class Back In: Class, State, and Hegemony in Africa." *Comparative Politics* 20:253–264.

Feinberg, Richard. 1991. "Reforming the Reformers." *Africa Report* 36 (September–October):33–36.

Flavin, Christopher, and John E. Young. 1993. Shaping the Next Industrial Revolution. In *State of the World 1993,* Lester R. Brown et al. New York: W. W. Norton.

Freeman, Donald. 1993. "Survival Strategy or Business Training Ground? The Significance of Urban Agriculture for the Advancement of Women in African Cities." *African Studies Review* 36 (December):1–22.

Funk, Ursula. 1988. Land Tenure, Agriculture, and Gender in Guinea-Bissau. In *Agriculture, Women, and Land: The African Experience,* edited by Jean Davison. Boulder: Westview.

Gabianu, A. Sena. 1990. The Susu Credit System: An Ingenious Way of Financing Business Outside the Formal Banking System. In *The Long-Term Perspective Study of Sub-Saharan Africa.* Vol. 2. Washington, DC: World Bank.

Gallin, Rita S. 1995. Engendered Production in Rural Taiwan: Ideological Bonding of the Public and Private. In *Engendering Wealth and Well-Being,* edited by Rae Lesser Blumberg, Cathy A. Rakowski, Irene Tinker, and Michael Monteon. Boulder: Westview.

García, Brígidia, and Orlandina de Oliveira. 1995. Gender Relations in Urban Middle-Class and Working-Class Households in Mexico. In *Engendering Wealth and Well-Being,* edited by Rae Lesser Blumberg, Cathy A. Rakowski, Irene Tinker, and Michael Monteon. Boulder: Westview.

Gatens, Moira. 1992. Power, Bodies and Difference. In *Destabilizing Theory: Contemporary Feminist Debates,* edited by Michele Barrett and Anne Phillips. Stanford, CA: Stanford University Press.

Gawanas, Bience. 1993. "Legal Rights of Namibian Women and Affirmative Action: The Eradication of Gender Inequalities." *Review of African Political Economy* 56:116–122.

Geiger, Susan. 1987. "Women in Nationalist Struggle: TANU Activists in Dar Es Salaam." *International Journal of African Historical Studies* 20:1–26.

Gellen, Karen. 1994a. "Expanding Women's Economic Knowledge." *African Farmer* (April): 10–11.

————. 1994b. "Unleashing the Power of Women Farmers." *African Farmer* (April):2–6, 42–43.

"Ghana Economy Gains Ground." 1991. *Africa News* (July 29):1–3.

"Girls Set to Prove Their Mettle in a Greasy Mechanics Course." 1993. *Living On* (November/December):23.

Gittinger, J. Price, with Sidney Chernick, Nadine R. Hornstein, and Katrene Saito. 1990. *Household Food Security and the Role of Women.* Washington, DC: World Bank.

Gladwin, Christine H., and Della McMillan. 1989. "Is a Turnaround in Africa Possible without Helping African Women to Farm?" *Economic Development and Cultural Change* 37 (January):345–369.

Goebel, Allison, and Marc Epprecht. 1995. "Women and Employment in Sub-Saharan Africa: Testing the World Bank and WID Models with a Lesotho Case Study." *African Studies Review* 38 (April): 1–22.

Goetz, Anne Marie. 1991. Feminism and the Claim to Know: Contradictions in Feminist Approaches to Women in Development. In *Third World Women and the Politics of Feminism,* edited by Chandra Mohanty et al. Bloomington: Indiana University Press.

Goheen, Miriam. 1991. The Ideology and Political Economy of Gender: Women and Land in Nso, Cameroon. In *Structural Adjustment and African Women Farmers,* edited by Christina H. Gladwin. Center for African Studies. Gainesville: University of Florida Press.

———. 1988. Big Men, Farm Women and Rural Self-Sufficiency: Land Concentration and the Subsistence Farm. Paper presented at the joint Cameroon Day-SERSAS Conference, April 7–9, Center for African Studies, University of Florida, Gainesville.

Gordon, April. 1995. "Gender, Ethnicity, and Class in Kenya: 'Burying Otieno' Revisited." *SIGNS* 20 (Summer):883–912.

———. 1994. "Class and Ethnicity in Kenya: The Otieno Case." *Journal of Asian and African Studies* 3:77–96.

———. 1992. "Capitalist Reforms in Sub-Saharan Africa." *Génève-Afrique* 30: 36–53.

———. 1991. "Economic Reform and African Women." *TransAfrica Forum* 8 (Summer):21–41.

Green, Cynthia P. 1994. *Sustainable Development: Population and the Environment.* Washington, DC: USAID.

Green, Daniel M. 1991. "Structural Adjustment and Politics in Ghana." *TranAfrica Forum* 8 (Summer):67–89.

Gregory, Joel W., and Victor Piché. 1983. "African Return Migration: Past, Present, and Future." *Contemporary Marxism* 7:169–183.

Grosz, Ron. 1988. *Developing a Women in Development Strategy for USAID/Tanzania.* PPC/WID:700W.

Guyer, Jane. 1987. Feeding Yaounde, Capital of Cameroon. In *Feeding African Cities,* edited by Jane I. Guyer. Bloomington: Indiana University Press.

———. 1986. Women's Role in Development. In *Strategies for African Development,* edited by Robert J. Berg and Jennifer Seymour Whitaker. Berkeley: University of California Press.

———. 1984. Family and Farm in Southern Cameroon. African Research Studies, no. 15. Boston: Boston University.

Haile, Daniel. 1985. Women, the Law and Convention. In *Women in Africa: Studies in Social and Economic Change,* edited by Nancy J. Hafkin and Edna G. Bay. Stanford, CA: Stanford University Press.

Harden, Blaine. 1990. Battle for the Body. In *Africa: Dispatches from a Fragile Continent.* Boston: Houghton Mifflin.

Harris, Joan. 1985. "Revolution or Evolution?" *Africa Report* 30 (March–April): 30–32.

Harris, Laurence. 1988. The IMF and Mechanisms of Integration. In Ben Crow, Mary Thorpe, et al., *Survival and Change in the Third World*. New York: Oxford University Press.

Harrison, Paul. 1990. Sustainable Growth in Africa Agriculture. In *The Long-Term Perspective Study of Sub-Saharan Africa*. Vol. 2. Washington, DC: World Bank.

Harsch, Ernest. 1994. "Freeing Markets: What Gains for Small-Scale Farmers?" *African Farmer* (April):29–29, 43.

Hartmann, Heidi. 1981. The Unhappy Marriage of Marxism and Feminism: Toward a More Progressive Union. In *Women and Revolution,* edited by Lydia Sargent. Boston: South End Press.

Hartmann, Heidi I., and Ann R. Markusen. 1980. "Contemporary Marxist Theory and Practice: A Feminist Critique." *Review of Political Economics* 12:87–94.

Hay, Margaret Jean. 1982. Women as Owners, Occupants, and Managers of Property in Colonial Western Kenya. In *African Women and the Law: Historical Perspectives,* edited by Margaret Jean Hay and Marcia Wright. Boston University Papers on Africa, no. 7. Boston: Boston University.

———. 1976. Luo Women and Economic Change During the Colonial Period. In *Women in Africa: Studies in Social and Economic Change,* edited by Nancy J. Hafkin and Edna G. Bay. Stanford, CA: Stanford University Press.

Helleiner, Gerald K. 1983. The Rise and Decline of the IMF. In *Banking on Poverty: The Global Impact of the IMF and World Bank,* edited by Jill Torrie. Toronto: Between the Lines.

Hellinger, Doug, and Ross Hammond. 1995. "Debunking the Myth." *Africa Report* 39 (November–December):52–55.

Hellinger, Stephen, Douglas Hellinger, and Fred M. O'Regan. 1988. *Aid for Just Development.* Boulder: Lynne Rienner.

Henderson, Hazel. 1994. Beyond GNP. In *Feminist Perspectives on Sustainable Development,* edited by Wendy Harcourt. London: Zed.

Henn, Jeanne K. 1988. The Material Basis of Sexism: A Mode of Production Analysis. In *Patriarchy and Class: African Women in the Home and the Workplace,* edited by Sharon B. Stichter and Jane L. Parport. Boulder: Westview.

———. 1983. "Feeding the Cities and Feeding the Peasants: What Role for Africa's Women Farmers?" *World Development* 11:1043–1055.

Herbst, Jeffrey. 1990. *State Politics in Zimbabwe.* Harare: University of Zimbabwe Publications.

Himbara, David. 1994. *Kenyan Capitalists, the State, and Development.* Boulder: Lynne Rienner.

hooks, bell. 1993. Black Women and Feminism. In *Feminist Frontiers III,* edited by Laurel Richardson and Verta Taylor. New York: McGraw-Hill.

House-Midamba, Bessie. 1990. *Class Development and Gender Inequality in Kenya, 1963–1990.* Lewiston, NY: Edwin Mellon.

Hultman, Tami. 1992. "I Am Woman." *Africa News* 36 (June 8–June 21):3.

Hyden, Goran. 1990a. The Changing Context of Institutional Development in Sub-Saharan Africa. In *The Long-Term Perspective Study of Sub-Saharan Africa,* edited by Laurel Richardson and Verta Taylor. Washington, DC: World Bank.

———. 1990b. Creating an Enabling Environment. In *The Long-Term Perspective Study of Sub-Saharan Africa.* Washington, DC: World Bank.

———. 1987. Capital Accumulation, Resource Distribution, and Governance in Kenya: The Role of the Economy of Affection. In *The Political Economy of Kenya,* edited by Michael G. Schatzberg. New York: Praeger.

———. 1983. *No Shortcuts to Progress*. Berkeley: University of California Press.

ILO (International Labor Organization). 1984. *Rural Development and Women in Africa*. Geneva: ILO.

Ingstad, Bendicte, Frank Bruun, Edwin Sandberg, and Sheila Tlou. 1992. "Care for the Elderly, Care by the Elderly: The Role of Elderly Women in a Changing Society." *Journal of Cross-Cultural Gerontology* 7:379–398.

International Socialist Organization Zimbabwe. 1994. "Abortion—A Woman's Right to Choose." *Living On* (May/April):8.

Isaacs, Dan. 1995. "Fulfilling a Dream." *Africa Report* 40 (January–February): 13–15.

Jacobson, Jodi L. 1993. Closing the Gender Gap in Development. In *State of the World 1993*, Lester R. Brown, et al. New York: W. W. Norton.

Jaggar, Alison M. 1983. *Feminist Politics and Human Nature*. Totowa, NJ: Rowman and Allanheld.

Joekes, Susan. 1987. *Women in the World Economy: An INSTRAW Study*. New York: Oxford University Press.

Joekes, Susan, Margaret Lycette, Lisa McGowan, and Karen Searle. 1988. Women and Structural Adjustment, Part I: A Summary of the Issues. Paper presented at the meeting of the Women in Development Expert Group of the OECD Development Assistance Committee, April 18, Paris.

Johnson, Pauline. 1994. *Feminism as Radical Humanism*. Boulder: Westview.

Johnson, Stanley P. 1987. *World Population and the United Nations: Challenge and Response*. New York: Cambridge University Press.

Johnson-Odim, Cheryl. 1991. Common Themes, Different Contexts: Third World Women and Feminism. In *Third World Women and the Politics of Feminism*, edited by Chandra Talpode Mohanty et al. Bloomington: Indiana University Press.

Kabira, Wanjiku M., and Elizabeth A. Nzioki. 1993. *Celebrating Women's Resistance: A Case Study of Women's Groups Movement in Kenya*. Nairobi: African Women's Perspective.

Kayongo-Male, Diane, and Philista Onyango. 1984. *The Sociology of the African Family*. New York: Longman.

Kennedy, Paul. 1988. *African Capitalism: The Struggle for Ascendancy*. Cambridge: Cambridge University Press.

Kettel, Bonnie. 1995. Gender and Environment: Lessons from WEDNET. In *Engendering Wealth and Well-Being: Empowerment for Global Change*, edited by Rae Lesser Blumberg et al. Boulder: Westview.

Kiondo, Andrew. 1992. The Nature of Economic Reform in Tanzania. In *Tanzania and the IMF: The Dynamics of Liberalization*, edited by Horace Campbell and Howard Stein. Boulder: Westview.

Kitching, Gavin. 1980. *Class and Economic Change in Kenya*. New Haven, CT: Yale University Press.

Knowles, Caroline. 1985. Women Under Development: Some Preliminary Remarks. In *Women in Nigeria Today*. London: Zed.

Koons, Adam S. 1988. Reaching Rural Women in the Northwest Province: A Presentation of More Ways in Which Women Are Not Men. Paper presented at the joint Cameroon Day-SERSAS Conference, Center for African Studies, April 7–9, University of Florida, Gainesville.

Laclau, E. 1971. "Feudalism and Capitalism in Latin America." *New Left Review* 67:19–38.

Laclau, Yannick. 1994. "Cairo Conference Showcases Work of NGOs." *Christian Science Monitor* (September 8):19.

Lall, Sanjaya. 1990. Structural Problems of Industry in Sub-Saharan Africa. In *The Long-Term Perspective Study of Sub-Saharan Africa*. Washington, DC: World Bank.

Langdon, Steven. 1987. Industry and Capitalism in Kenya: Contributions to a Debate. In *The African Bourgeoisie: Capitalist Development in Nigeria, Kenya, and the Ivory Coast*, edited by Paul M. Lubeck. Boulder: Lynne Rienner.

Langley, Phillip. 1983. A Preliminary Approach to Women and Development: Getting a Few Facts Right. In *The Roles of Women in the Process of Development*, edited by Gerard M. Ssenkoloto. Douala, Cameroon: Pan-African Institute for Development.

Leacock, Eleanor. 1986. Postscript: Implications for Organization. In Eleanor Leacock, Helen I. Safa, et al., *Women's Work: Development and the Division of Labor by Gender*. South Hadley, MA: Bergin & Garvey.

Leigh-Doyle, Sue. 1991. "Increasing Women's Participation in Technical Fields: A Pilot Project in Africa." *International Labor Review* 130:427–444.

Lele, Uma. 1991. Women, Structural Adjustment, and Transformation: Some Lessons and Questions from the African Experience. In *Structural Adjustment and African Women Farmers*, edited by Christina H. Gladwin. Gainesville: University of Florida Press (Center for African Studies).

Lewis, Barbara. 1982. Fertility and Employment: An Assessment of Role Incompatibility among African Urban Women. In *Women and Work in Africa*, edited by Edna G. Bay. Boulder: Westview.

Liatto-Katundo, Beatrice. 1993. "Women's Lobby and Gender Relations in Zambia." *Review of African Political Economy* 56:79–83.

Liebenow, J. Gus. 1986. *African Politics: Crises and Challenges*. Bloomington: Indiana University Press.

Lima, Teresa. 1994. "Women's Co-ops Spur Mozambican Farmers' Union." *African Farmer* (April):16–17.

Longwe, Sara H. 1990. From Welfare to Empowerment: The Situation of Women in Development in Africa: A Post–UN Women's Decade Update and Future Directions. Working paper no. 204 (March), Zambia Association for Research and Development.

Lonsdale, John. 1992a. The Moral Economy of Mau Mau. In Bruce Berman and John Lonsdale, *Unhappy Valley: Conflict in Kenya and Africa*. London: James Currey.

———. 1992b. African Pasts in Africa's Future. In Bruce Berman and John Lonsdale, *Unhappy Valley: Conflict in Kenya and Africa*. London: James Currey.

Lovell, Catherine H. 1989. *Breaking the Cycle of Poverty: The BRAC Strategy*. West Hartford, CT: Kumarian Press.

Lovett, Margot. 1989. Gender Relations, Class Formation, and the Colonial State in Africa. In *Women and the State in Africa*, edited by Jane L. Parpart and Kathleen A. Staudt. Boulder: Lynne Rienner.

Lubeck, Paul M., ed. 1987. *The African Bourgeoisie: Capitalist Development in Nigeria, Kenya, and the Ivory Coast*. Boulder: Lynne Rienner.

MacGaffey, Janet. 1988. Evading Male Control: Women in the Second Economy in Zaire. In *Patriarchy and Class: African Women in the Home and Workforce*, edited by Sharon B. Stichter and Jane L. Parpart. Boulder: Westview.

———. 1986. Women and Class Formation in a Dependent Economy. In *Women and Class in Africa*, edited by Claire Robertson and Iris Berger. New York: Africana Publishing.

MacGaffey, Janet, and Gertrude Windsperger. 1990. The Endogenous Economy. In *The Long-Term Perspective Study of Sub-Saharan Africa*. Vol 3. Washington, DC: World Bank.

MacGaffey, Wyatt. 1983. "Lineage Structure, Marriage, and the Family among the Central Bantu." *Journal of African History* 24:173–187.

Madlala, Nozizwe. 1994. "Women Fight On!" *Speak* (July):20–21.

Mahjoub, Azzam, ed. 1990. *Adjustment or Delinking? The African Experience.* London: Zed.

Mann, Kristen. 1991. "Women, Landed Property, and the Accumulation of Wealth in Early Colonial Lagos." *SIGNS* 16 (Summer):682–706.

———. 1982. Women's Rights in Law and Practice: Marriage and Dispute Settlement in Colonial Lagos. In *African Women & the Law: Historical Perspectives,* edited by Margaret Jean Hay and Marcia Wright. Boston University Papers on Africa, no. 7. Boston: Boston University.

Markovitz, Irving L. 1977. *Power and Class in Africa.* Englewood Cliffs, NJ: Prentice-Hall.

Marshall, Barbara L. 1994. *Engendering Modernity: Feminism, Social Theory and Social Change.* Boston: Northeastern University Press.

Mbilinyi, Marjorie, and Ruth Meena. 1991. "Reports from Four Women's Groups in Africa: Introduction." *SIGNS* 16 (Summer):846–848.

Meillassoux, Claude. 1981. *Meals and Money: Capitalism and the Domestic Community.* New York: Cambridge University Press.

Merry, Sally Engle. 1982. The Articulation of Legal Spheres. In *African Women & the Law: Historical Perspectives,* edited by Margaret Jean Hay and Marcia Wright. Boston University Papers on Africa, no. 7. Boston: Boston University.

Mies, Maria. 1988. Introduction to *Women: The Last Colony,* by Maria Mies, Veronika Bennholdt-Thomsen, and Claudia von Werlhof. London: Zed.

———. 1986. *Patriarchy and Accumulation on a World Scale: Women in the International Division of Labor.* London: Zed.

Mies, Maria, Veronika Bennholdt-Thomsen, and Claudia von Werlhof. 1988. *Women: The Last Colony.* London: Zed.

Milkman, Ruth. 1987. *Gender at Work: The Dynamics of Job Segregation by Sex during World War II.* Urbana: University of Illinois Press.

Moffett, George. 1994. "Women's Groups Coalesce in Cairo." *Christian Science Monitor* (September 8):1, 4.

Moghadam, Valentine M. 1995. Gender Dynamics of Restructuring in the Periphery. In *Engendering Wealth and Well-Being: Empowerment for Global Change,* edited by Rae Lesser Blumberg et al. Boulder: Westview.

———. 1994. Introduction: Women and Identity Politics in Theoretical and Comparative Perspective. In *Identity Politics and Women,* edited by Valentine M. Moghadam. Boulder: Westview.

———. 1993. *Modernizing Women: Gender and Social Change in the Middle East.* Boulder: Lynne Rienner.

Mohanty, Chandra T. 1991a. Introduction. In *Third World Women and the Politics of Feminism,* edited by Chandra Talpode Mohanty et al. Bloomington: Indiana University Press.

———. 1991b. Under Western Eyes: Feminist Scholarship and Colonial Discourses. In *Third World Women and the Politics of Feminism,* edited by Chandra Talpode Mohanty et al. Bloomington: Indiana University Press.

Molokomme, Athaliah. 1991. "Emang Basadi (Botswana)." *SIGNS* 16 (Summer): 848–851.

Molyneux, Maxine. 1985. "Mobilization Without Emancipation? Women's Interests, State and Revolution in Nicaragua." *Feminist Studies* 11(2):227–254.

Monshipouri, Mahmood. 1995. *Democratization, Liberalization, and Human Rights in the Third World.* Boulder: Lynne Rienner.

Monteon, Michael. 1995. Gender and Economic Crises in Latin America: Reflections on the Great Depression and the Debt Crisis. In *Engendering Wealth and Well-Being: Empowerment for Global Change,* edited by Rae Lesser Blumberg et al. Boulder: Westview.

Morna, Colleen Lowe. 1995. "Plus ça Change." *Africa Report* 40 (January–February):55–59.

———. 1994. "African Women Caught Between New Laws and Social Traditions." *Christian Science Monitor* (December 19):7.

———. 1991. "Ahead of the Opposition." *Africa Report* 36 (July–August):20–23.

Moser, Caroline. 1991. Gender Planning in the Third World: Meeting Practical and Strategic Needs. In *Gender and International Relations,* edited by Rebecca Grant and Kathleen Newland. Bloomington: Indiana University Press.

Mukarasi, Laeticia. 1991. *Post Abolished: One Woman's Struggle for Employment Rights in Tanzania.* Ithaca, NY: ILR Press.

Mullings, Leith. 1976. Women and Economic Change in Africa. In *Women in Africa: Studies in Social and Economic Change,* edited by Nancy J. Hafkin and Edna G. Bay. Stanford, CA: Stanford University Press.

Munyakho, Dorothy. 1994. "Kenyan Women Press for Land Rights." *African Farmer* (April):8–9.

Nafziger, E. Wayne. 1988. *Inequality in Africa: Political Elites, Proletariat, Peasants and the Poor.* New York: Cambridge University Press.

Nelson, Nici. 1988. How Women and Men Get By: The Sexual Division of Labor in the Informal Sector of a Nairobi Squatter Settlement. In *The Urbanization of the Third World,* edited by Josef Gugler. New York: Oxford University Press.

Newland, Kathleen. 1991. From Transnational Relationships to International Relations: Women in Development and the International Decade for Women. In *Gender and International Relations,* edited by Rebecca Grant and Kathleen Newland. Bloomington: Indiana University Press.

Newman, James L., and Russell Lura. 1983. "Fertility Control in Africa." *Geography Review* 73:396–406.

Ngugi wa Thiongo. 1982. *Devil on the Cross.* London: Heinemann.

Ninsin, Kwame A. 1990. Ghana Under the PNDC: Delinking or Structural Adjustment? In *Adjustment or Delinking? The African Experience,* edited by Azzam Mahjoub. London: Zed.

Nkwi, Paul. 1987. The Changing Role of Women and Their Contributions to the Domestic Economy in Cameroon. In *Transformations of African Marriage,* edited by David Parkin and David Nyamwaya. Manchester: Manchester University Press.

Novicki, Margaret A. 1995. "Interview: Nana Konadu Agyeman Rawlings." *Africa Report* 40 (January–February):52–54.

———. 1991. "A Cameroon Case Study." *Africa Report* 36 (September–October): 29–32.

Nyang'oro, Julius E. 1989. *The State and Capitalist Development in Africa: Declining Political Economies.* New York: Praeger.

Nzomo, Maria. 1989. "The Impact of the Women's Decade on Politics, Programs and Empowerment of Women in Kenya." *Issue: A Journal of Opinion* 17 (Summer):9–17.

Nzomo, Maria, and Kivutha Kibwana, eds. 1993. *Women's Initiatives in Kenya's Democratization.* Nairobi: The National Committee on the Status of Women.

Obbo, Christine. 1986. Stratification and the Lives of Women in Uganda. In *Women and Class in Africa,* edited by Clair Robertson and Iris Berger. New York: Africana.

———. 1980. *African Women: Their Struggle for Economic Independence.* London: Zed.

Obodina, Elizabeth. 1985. How Relevant Is the Western Women's Liberation Movement for Nigeria? In *Women in Nigeria Today.* London: Zed.

Oboler, Regina Smith. 1985. *Women, Power, and Economic Change.* Stanford, CA: Stanford University Press.

Ocholla-Ayayo, A.B.C. 1989. Death and Burial: An Anthropological Perspective. In *The S. M. Otieno Case: Death and Burial in Modern Kenya,* edited by J. B. Ojwang and J.N.K. Mugambi. Nairobi: Nairobi University Press.

Odera Oruka, H. 1989. Traditionalism and Modernization in Kenya: Customs, Spirits, and Christianity. *The S. M. Otieno Case: Death and Burial in Modern Kenya,* edited by J. B. Ojwang and J.N.K. Mugambi. Nairobi: Nairobi University Press.

Ojwang, J. B. 1989. Death and Burial in Modern Kenya. *The S. M. Otieno Case: Death and Burial in Modern Kenya,* edited by J. B. Ojwang and J.N.K. Mugambi. Nairobi: Nairobi University Press.

Okech-Owiti, M. D. 1989. Some Socio-Legal Issues. *The S. M. Otieno Case: Death and Burial in Modern Kenya,* edited by J. B. Ojwang and J.N.K. Mugambi. Nairobi: Nairobi University Press.

Okonjo, Kamene. 1976. The Dual-Sex Political System in Operation: Igbo Women and Community Politics in Midwestern Nigeria. In *Women in Africa: Studies in Social and Economic Change,* edited by Nancy J. Hafkin and Edna G. Bay. Stanford, CA: Stanford University Press.

Okoth-Okombo, D. 1989. Semantic Issues. *The S. M. Otieno Case: Death and Burial in Modern Kenya,* edited by J. B. Ojwang and J.N.K. Mugambi. Nairobi: Nairobi University Press.

Ollenburger, Jane C., and Helen A. Moore. 1992. *A Sociology of Women: The Intersection of Patriarchy, Capitalism and Colonization.* Englewood Cliffs, NJ: Prentice Hall.

Olofin, S. 1991. The Prospects for an Outward Looking Industrialization Strategy Under Adjustment in Sub-Saharan Africa. In *Economic Reform in Sub-Saharan Africa,* edited by Ajay Chibber and Stanley Fischer. Washington, DC: World Bank.

Onimode, Bade. 1989. The IMF and World Bank Programmes in Africa. In *The IMF, the World Bank and the African Debt: The Economic Impact.* Vol. 1. edited by Bade Onimode. London: Zed.

Oppong, Christine. 1981. *Middle Class African Marriage.* London: George Allen & Unwin.

Orvis, Stephen. 1993. "The Kenyan Agrarian Debate: A Reappraisal." *African Studies Review* 36 (December):23–48.

Otero, Maria. 1987. *Gender Issues in Small-Scale Enterprise.* Washington, DC: USAID.

Owoh, Kenna. 1995. Gender and Health in Nigerian Structural Adjustment: Locating Room to Maneuver. In *Engendering Wealth and Well-Being: Empowerment for Global Change,* edited by Rae Lesser Blumberg et al. Boulder: Westview.

Pala Okeyo, Achola. 1981. "Reflection on Development Myths." *Africa Report* 26 (March–April):7–10.

———. 1980. Daughters of the Lakes and Rivers: Colonization and the Land Rights of Luo Women. In *Women and Colonization: Anthropological Perspectives,* edited by Mona Etienne and Eleanor Leacock. New York: Praeger.

Palmer, Ingrid. 1991. *Gender and Population in the Adjustment of African Economies: Planning for Change.* Geneva: ILO.

Pankhurst, Donna, and Susie Jacobs. 1988. Land Tenure, Gender Relations, and Agricultural Production. In *Agriculture, Women, and Land: The African Experience,* edited by Jean Davison. Boulder: Westview.

Parkin, David. 1978. *The Cultural Definition of Political Response: Lineal Destiny Among the Luo.* London: Academic Press.

Parpart, Jane L. 1988. Women and the State in Africa. In *The Precarious Balance: State and Society in Africa,* edited by Donald Rothchild and Naomi Chazan. Boulder: Westview.

Parpart, Jane L., and Kathleen A. Staudt. 1989. Women and the State in Africa. In *Women and the State in Africa,* edited by Jane L. Parpart and Kathleen A. Staudt. Boulder: Lynne Rienner.

Pateman, Carole. 1989. *The Disorder of Women.* Cambridge: Polity Press.

Paukert, Felix. 1973. "Income Distribution at Different Levels of Development: A Survey of Evidence." *International Labor Review* 108 (2–3):97–125.

Payer, Cheryl. 1983. Researching the World Bank. In *Banking on Poverty: The Global Impact of the IMF and World Bank,* edited by Jill Torrie. Toronto: Between the Lines.

Pearson, Ruth. 1988. Female Workers in the First and Third Worlds: The Greening of Women's Labour. In *On Work: Historical, Comparative, and Theoretical Approaches,* edited by R. A. Pahl. Oxford: Blackwell.

Peil, Margaret. 1981. *Cities and Suburbs: Urban Life in West Africa.* New York: Africana.

"People Power: 'Unstoppable.'" 1992. *Africa News* 35 (December 23–January 6):2.

Perchenock, Norma. 1985. Double Oppression: Women and Land Matters in Kaduna State. In *Women in Nigeria Today.* London: Zed.

Phillips, Anne. 1992. Universal Pretensions in Political Thought. In *Destabilizing Theory: Contemporary Feminist Debates,* edited by Michele Barrett and Anne Phillips. Stanford, CA: Stanford University Press.

Pinckney, Robert. 1994. *Democracy in the Third World.* Boulder: Lynne Rienner.

Pittin, Renee. 1985. Organizing for the Future. In *Women in Nigeria Today.* London: Zed.

Poats, S., J. Gearing, and S. Russo. 1989. *Executive Summary of Gender Issues in Farming Systems Research and Extension: A Survey of Current Projects.* Washington, DC: WID/AID.

Press, Robert M. 1994. "An Ancient African Custom Comes Under Fire." *Christian Science Monitor* (December 30):6.

Pringle, Rosemary, and Sophie Watson. 1992. Women's Interests. In *Destabilizing Theory: Contemporary Feminist Debates,* edited by Michele Barrett and Anne Phillips. Stanford, CA: Stanford University Press.

Putterman, Louis. 1994. "Tanzanian Markets 'as Unpredictable as the Rains.'" *African Farmer* (April):30–31.

Qadir, Shahid, Christopher Clapham, and Barry Gills. 1993. "Sustainable Democracy: Formalism vs. Substance." *Third World Quarterly* 14:415–422.

Rakowski, Cathy A. 1995. Conclusion: Engendering Wealth and Well-Being— Lessons Learned. In *Engendering Wealth and Well-Being: Empowerment for Global Change,* edited by Rae Lesser Blumberg et al. Boulder: Westview.

Rashid, Sadig. 1994. Africa at the Doorstep of the Twenty-First Century: Can Crisis Turn to Opportunity? In *Africa Within the World: Beyond Dispossession and Dependence,* edited by Adebayo Adedeji. London: Zed.

Redding, Sean. 1993. "Legal Minors and Social Children: Rural African Women and Taxation in the Transkei, South Africa." *African Studies Review* 36 (December):49–74.

Renzetti, Claire M., and Daniel J. Curran. 1986. "Structural Constraints on Legislative Reform: Guinean Women and the Promise of Liberation." *Contemporary Crises* 10:137–155.

Riddell, Roger, ed. 1990. *Manufacturing Africa.* London: James Currey.

Roberts, Penelope A. 1988. Rural Women's Access to Labor in West Africa. In *Patriarchy and Class: African Women in the Home and the Workplace,* edited by Sharon B. Stichter and Jane L. Parpart. Boulder: Westview.

Robertson, Claire. 1995. Trade, Gender, and Poverty in the Nairobi Area: Women's Strategies for Survival and Independence in the 1980s. In *Engendering Wealth and Well-Being: Empowerment for Global Change,* edited by Rae Lesser Blumberg et al. Boulder: Westview.

———. 1988. "Invisible Workers: African Women and the Problem of the Self-Employed in Labour History." *Journal of Asian and African Studies* 23 (January and April):180–198.

———. 1986. Women's Education and Class Formation in Africa, 1950–1980. In *Women and Class in Africa,* edited by Claire Robertson and Iris Berger. New York: Africana.

———. 1984. *Sharing the Same Bowl: A Socioeconomic History of Women and Class in Accra, Ghana.* Bloomington: Indiana University Press.

Robertson, Claire, and Iris Berger, eds. 1986. *Women and Class in Africa.* New York: Africana.

Rosaldo, Renato. 1989. *Culture and Truth: The Remaking of Social Analysis.* Boston: Beacon Press.

Rowland, Barbara M., and Peregrine Schwartz-Shea. 1989. Empowering Women: Self, Autonomy, and Responsibility. Paper presented at the American Political Science Association meeting, August 31–September 3, Atlanta.

Russo, Ann. 1991. We Cannot Live Without Our Lives. In *Third World Women and the Politics of Feminism,* edited by Chandra Talpode Mohanty et al. Bloomington: Indiana University Press.

Russo, Sandra, Jennifer Bremer-Fox, Susan Poats, and Laurence Graig. 1989. *Gender Issues in Agriculture and Natural Resource Management.* Washington, DC: WID/AID.

Safa, Helen I. 1995. Gender Implications of Export-Led Industrialization in the Caribbean Basin. In *Engendering Wealth and Well-Being: Empowerment for Global Change,* edited by Rae Lesser Blumberg et al. Boulder: Westview.

———. 1986. Runaway Shops and Female Unemployment: The Search for Cheap Labor. In *Women's Work: Development and the Division of Labor by Gender,* by Eleanor Leacock, Helen I. Safa, et al. South Hadley, MA: Bergin & Garvey.

Safilios-Rothschild, Constantina. 1990. Women's Groups: An Underutilized Grassroots Institution. In *The Long-Term Perspective Study of Sub-Saharan Africa.* Vol. 3. Washington, DC: World Bank.

Said, Edward. 1978. *Orientalism.* New York: Pantheon.

Samoff, Joel. 1992. Theory and Practice in the Analysis of Tanzanian Liberalization: A Comment. In *Tanzania and the IMF: The Dynamics of Liberalization,* edited by Horace Campbell and Howard Stein. Boulder: Westview.

Sandbrook, Richard L. 1993. *The Politics of Africa's Economic Recovery.* Cambridge: Cambridge University Press.

———. 1985. *The Politics of Africa's Economic Stagnation.* Cambridge: Cambridge University Press.

Sangmpam, S. N. 1993. "Neither Soft nor Dead: The African State Is Alive and Well." *African Studies Review* 36 (September):73–94.

Sangree, Walter H. 1992. "Grandparenthood and Modernization: The Changing Status of Male and Female Elders in Tiriki, Kenya, and Irigwe, Nigeria." *Journal of Cross-Cultural Gerontology* 7:331–361.

Schatz, Sayre P. 1987. Postimperialism and the Great Competition. In *Postimperialism: International Capitalism and Development in the Late Twentieth Century,* by David G. Becker, Jeff Frieden, Sayre P. Schatz, and Richard L. Sklar. Boulder: Lynne Rienner.

Schildkrout, Enid. 1982. Dependence and Autonomy: The Economic Activities of Secluded Hausa Women in Kano, Nigeria. In *Women and Work in Africa,* edited by Edna G. Bay. Boulder: Westview.

Schmidt, Elizabeth. 1991. "Patriarchy, Capitalism, and the Colonial State in Zimbabwe." *SIGNS* 16 (Summer):732–756.

Schoepf, Brooke G. and Claude Schoepf. 1988. Land, Gender, and Food Security in Eastern Kivu, Zaire. In *Agriculture, Women, and Land: The African Experience,* edited by Jean Davison. Boulder: Westview.

Schuster, Ilsa. 1982. Marginal Lives: Conflict and Contradiction in the Position of Female Traders in Lusaka, Zambia. In *Women and Work in Africa,* edited by Edna G. Bay. Boulder: Westview.

Scott, Catherine V. 1995. *Gender and Development: Rethinking Modernization and Dependency Theory.* Boulder: Lynne Rienner.

Senghore, Ismaila, and Amie Bojang-Sissoho. 1994. "Women's 'Wisdom': Banking on Themselves." *African Farmer* (April):7.

Sennett, Richard. 1970. *Families Against the City.* New York: Vintage.

Shaw, Timothy M. 1994. Africa in the New World Order: Marginal and/or Central? In *Africa Within the World: Beyond Dispossession and Dependence,* edited by Adebayo Adedeji. London: Zed.

Shepherd, Anne. 1992. "The Lost Decade," *Africa Report* 37 (January–February): 36–38.

Shipton, Parker. 1992. "Debts and Trespasses: Land, Mortgages, and the Ancestors in Western Kenya." *Africa* 62:357–388.

————. 1984. "Lineage and Locality as Antithetical Principles in East African Systems of Land Tenure." *Ethnology* 23 (April):117–132.

Shipton, Parker, and Mitzi Goheen. 1992. "Understanding African Land-Holding: Power, Wealth, and Meaning." *Africa* 62:307–325.

Shivji, Issa G. 1992. The Politics of Liberalization in Tanzania: The Crisis of Ideological Hegemony. In *Tanzania and the IMF: The Dynamics of Liberalization,* edited by Horace Campbell and Howard Stein. Boulder: Westview.

————. 1990. Tanzania: The Debate on Delinking. In *Adjustment or Delinking: The African Experience,* edited by Azzam Mahjoub. London: Zed.

Skinner, Elliott P. 1985. Labor Migration and National Development in Africa. In *African Migration and National Development,* edited by Beverly Lindsay. University Park: Pennsylvania State University Press.

Sklar, Richard L. 1991a. Beyond Capitalism and Socialism in Africa. In *African Politics and Problems in Development,* by Richard L. Sklar and C. S. Whitaker. Boulder: Lynne Rienner.

————. 1991b. Developmental Democracy. In *African Politics and Problems in Development,* by Richard L. Sklar and C. S. Whitaker. Boulder: Lynne Rienner.

————. 1991c. The Nature of Class Domination in Africa. In *African Politics and Problems in Development,* by Richard L. Sklar and C. S. Whitaker. Boulder: Lynne Rienner.

―――. 1987. Postimperialism: A Class Analysis of Multinational Corporate Expansion. In *Postimperialism: International Capitalism and Development in the Late Twentieth Century*, by David G. Becker, Jeff Frieden, Sayre P. Schatz, and Richard L. Sklar. Boulder: Lynne Rienner.

Sklar, Richard L., and C. S. Whitaker. 1991. *African Politics and Problems in Development*. Boulder: Lynne Rienner.

Skolnick, Arlene. 1991. *Embattled Paradise: The American Family in an Age of Uncertainty*. New York: Basic Books.

Smith, Dorothy. 1987. *The Everyday World as Problematic*. Boston: Northeastern University Press.

Smith, Joan. 1994. The Creation of the World We Know: The World Economy and the Re-Creation of Gendered Identities. In *Identity Politics and Women*, edited by Valentine M. Moghadam. Boulder: Westview.

Sottas, Beat. 1992. "Aspects of a Peasant Mode of Production: Exchange and the Extent of Sufficiency Among Smallholders in Western Lakipia, Kenya." *Journal of Asian and African Studies* 27:271–295.

Stamp, Patricia. 1991a. "Burying Otieno: The Politics of Gender and Ethnicity in Kenya." *SIGNS* 16 (Summer):808–845.

―――. 1991b. "The Politics of Dissent in Kenya." *Current History* 90 (May): 205–208, 227–229.

―――. 1989. *Technology, Gender, and Power in Africa*. Ottawa: International Development Research Centre.

―――. 1986. Kikuyu Women's Self-Help Groups: Toward an Understanding of the Relation Between Sex-Gender System and Mode of Production in Africa. In *Women and Class in Africa*, edited by Claire Robertson and Iris Berger. New York: Africana.

Staudt, Kathleen. 1987. Women's Politics, the State, and Capitalist Transformation in Africa. In *Studies in Power and Class in Africa*, edited by Irving L. Markovitz. New York: Oxford University Press.

―――. 1986. Stratification: Implications for Women's Politics. In *Women and Class in Africa*, edited by Claire Robertson and Iris Berger. New York: Africana.

―――. 1982. Women Farmers and Inequities in Agricultural Services. In *Women and Work in Africa*, edited by Edna G. Bay. Boulder: Westview.

Steady, Filomina Chioma. 1985. "African Women at the End of the Decade." *Africa Report* 30 (March–April):4–8.

Stichter, Sharon. 1987. Women and the Family: The Impact of Capitalist Development in Kenya. In *The Political Economy of Kenya*, edited by Michael G. Schatzberg. New York: Praeger.

Stone, M. Priscilla, Glen Davis Stone, and Robert M. Netting. 1990. The Sexual Division of Labor in Kofyar Agriculture. Paper presented at the November meeting of the African Studies Association, Chicago, IL.

Stucki, Barbara R. 1992. "The Long Voyage Home: Return Migration among Aging Cocoa Farmers in Ghana." *Journal of Cross-Cultural Gerontology* 7: 363–378.

Swainson, Nicola. 1987. Indigenous Capitalism in Postcolonial Kenya. In *The African Bourgeoisie. Capitalist Development in Nigeria, Kenya, and the Ivory Coast*, edited by Paul M. Lubeck. Boulder: Lynne Rienner.

TAMWA (Tanzanian Media Women's Association). 1993. "Violence Against Women in Tanzania." *Review of African Political Economy* 56:111–116.

Tandon, Yash. 1990. Zimbabwe and Uganda: A Contrasting Record. In *Adjustment or Delinking? The African Experience,* edited by Azzam Mahjoub. London: Zed.

Taylor, John G. 1979. *From Modernization to Modes of Production: A Critique of the Sociology of Development and Underdevelopment.* London: Macmillan.

Thomas-Slaytor, Barbara P. 1992. "Class, Ethnicity, and the Kenyan State: Community Mobilization in the Context of Global Politics." *International Journal of Politics, Culture, and Society* 4:301–321.

Tiano, Susan. 1987. Gender, Work, and World Capitalism: Third World Women's Role in Development. In *Analyzing Gender: A Handbook of Social Science Research,* edited by Beth B. Hess and Myra Mark Ferree. Newbury Park, CA: Sage.

Transafrica Forum Seminar. 1987. "Development Policy: Black Female Perspectives." *Transafrica Forum* 4 (Spring):69–106.

Tripp, Aili Mari. 1992. The Impact of Crisis and Economic Reform on Women in Urban Tanzania. In *Unequal Burden: Economic Crises, Persistent Poverty, and Women's Work,* edited by Lourdes Beneria and Shelley Feldman. Boulder: Westview.

———. 1991. Women and Democratization in Africa: Reflections on the Tanzanian Case. Paper presented at the November 23–26 meeting of the African Studies Association, St. Louis, MO.

Urdang, Stephanie. 1985. The Last Transition? Women and Development. In *The Difficult Road to Socialism in Mozambique,* edited by John Saul. New York: Monthly Review Press.

Valverde, Mariana. 1985. *Sex, Power, and Pleasure.* Toronto: Women's Press.

Van Allen, Judith. 1976. "Aba Riots" or Igbo "Women's War?" Ideology, Stratification, and the Invisibility of Women. In *Women in Africa: Studies in Social and Economic Change,* edited by Nancy J. Hafkin and Edna G. Bay. Stanford, CA: Stanford University Press.

Van Doren, J. W. 1989. African Tradition and Western Common Law: A Study in Contradiction. *The S. M. Otieno Case: Death and Burial in Modern Kenya,* edited by J. B. Ojwang and J.N.K. Mugambi. Nairobi: Nairobi University Press.

Vellenga, Dorothy D. 1986. Matriliny, Patriliny, and Class Formation among Women Cocoa Farmers in Two Rural Areas of Ghana. In *Women and Class in Africa,* edited by Claire Robertson and Iris Berger. New York: Africana.

Venema, Bernhard. 1986. The Changing Role of Women in Sahelian Agriculture. In *Women Farmers in Africa: Rural Development in Mali and the Sahel,* edited by Lucy E. Creevey. Syracuse, NY: Syracuse University Press.

ver Eecke, Catherine. 1989. "From Pasture to Purdah: The Transformation of Women's Roles and Identities among the Adamawa Fulbe." *Ethnology* 28 (January):53–73.

Vock, Jane. 1988. Demographic Theories and Women's Reproductive Labor. In *Patriarchy and Class: African Women in the Home and the Workforce,* edited by Sharon B. Stichter and Jane L. Parpart. Boulder: Westview.

von Bulow, Dorthe, and Anne Sorensen. 1993. "Gender and Contract Farming: Outgrower Schemes in Kenya." *Review of African Political Economy* 56:38–52.

von Werlhof, Claudia. 1988a. The Proletariat Is Dead: Long Live the Housewife! In *Women the Last Colony,* by Maria Mies, Veronika Bennholdt-Thomsen, and Claudia von Werlhof. London: Zed.

————. 1988b. Women's Work: The Blind Spot in the Critique of Political Economy. In *Women the Last Colony,* by Maria Mies, Veronika Bennholdt-Thomsen, and Claudia von Werlhof. London: Zed.

Vuorela, Ulla. 1992. The Informal Sector, Social Reproduction, and the Impact of the Economic Crisis on Women. In *Tanzania and the IMF: The Dynamics of Liberalization,* edited by Horace Campbell and Howard Stein. Boulder: Westview.

Walby, Sylvia. 1992. Post-Post-Modernism? In *Destabilizing Theory: Contemporary Feminist Debates,* edited by Michele Barrett and Anne Phillips. Stanford, CA: Stanford University Press.

————. 1990. *Theorizing Patriarchy.* Cambridge: Basil Blackwell.

————. 1986. *Patriarchy at Work.* Minneapolis: University of Minnesota Press.

Ward, Kathryn. 1990. Introduction and Overview. In *Women Workers and Global Restructuring,* edited by Kathryn Ward. Ithaca, NY: ILR Press.

————. 1984. *Women in the World-System: Its Impact on Status and Fertility.* New York: Praeger.

Watson, William. 1958. *Tribal Cohesion in a Money Economy.* Manchester: Manchester University Press.

Weeks-Vagliani, Winifred. 1985. Women, Food, and Rural Development. In *Crisis and Recovery in Sub-Saharan Africa,* edited by Tore Rose. Paris: Organization for Economic Co-operation and Development.

Wells, Julia. 1982. Passes and Bypasses: Freedom of Movement for African Women under the Urban Areas Act of South Africa. In *African Women and the Law: Historical Perspectives,* edited by Margaret Jean Hay and Marcia Wright. Boston University Papers on Africa, no. 7. Boston: Boston University.

Whitaker, C. S. 1991. Doctrines of Development and Precepts of the State: The World Bank and the Fifth Iteration of the African Case. In *African Politics and Problems in Development,* by Richard L. Sklar and C. S. Whitaker. Boulder: Lynne Rienner.

WID. 1989. *(A Report to Congress) Planning for the Next Decade: A Perspective of Women in Development.* Washington, DC: AID.

Wilson, Francille Ruson. 1982. Reinventing the Past and Circumscribing the Future: Authenticité and the Negative Image of Women's Work in Zaire. In *Women and Work in Africa,* edited by Edna G. Bay. Boulder: Westview.

*Women in Nigeria Today.* 1985. London: Zed.

Woods, Dwayne. 1992. "Civil Society in Europe and Africa: Limiting State Power Through a Public Sphere." *African Studies Review* 35 (September):77–100.

World Bank. 1994a. *Adjustment in Africa.* New York: Oxford University Press.

————. 1994b. *World Development Report.* New York: Oxford University Press.

————. 1992. *World Development Report.* New York: Oxford University Press.

————. 1991. *World Development Report.* New York: Oxford University Press.

————. 1990a. *Report on Adjustment Lending II: Policies for Recovery of Growth.* (Internal report.) Washington, DC: World Bank.

————. 1990b. *Women in Development: A Progress Report on the World Bank Initiative.* Washington, DC: World Bank.

————. 1989a. *Kenya: The Role of Women in Economic Development.* Washington, DC: World Bank.

————. 1989b. *Sub-Saharan Africa: From Crisis to Sustainable Growth.* Washington, DC: World Bank.

————. 1986. *Population Growth and Policies in Sub-Saharan Africa.* Washington, DC: World Bank.

————. 1984. *Toward Sustained Development in Sub-Saharan Africa: A Joint Program of Action.* Washington, DC: World Bank.

————. 1981. *Accelerated Development in Sub-Saharan Africa: An Agenda for Action.* Washington, DC: World Bank.

Wright, Marcia. 1982. Justice, Women, and the Social Order in Abercorn, Northern Rhodesia, 1897–1903. In *African Women and the Law: Historical Perspectives* edited by Margaret Jean Hay and Marcia Wright. Boston University papers on Africa, no. 7. Boston: Boston University.

Young, Crawford. 1982. *Ideology and Development in Africa.* New Haven, CT: Yale University Press.

Yuval-Davis, Nira. 1994. Identity Politics and Women's Ethnicity. In *Identity Politics and Women*, edited by Valentine M. Moghadam. Boulder: Westview.

# ▲
# Index

Empowerment of women, 72, 89, 90, 92, 98, 120, 157, 182

Entrepreneurship, 23, 33, 36, 37, 39, 43, 53, 55, 56, 70, 86, 89, 98, 99, 121, 126, 127, 131, 142, 143, 154, 166, 167, 188; capitalist, 38; in the informal sector, 8; in the private sector, 2; in development, 5, 125; of women, 96, 97, 145, 155

Environment, 185; degradation of, 40, 185, 186; problems with, 69

Ethiopia, 114

Ethnicity, 10, 21, 24, 25, 26, 37, 42, 81, 121, 124, 163, 165, 168, 171

Exploitation: economic, 78, 79; sexual, 84; of women, 6, 21; of workers, 39

Exports, 51, 53, 60, 143; crops, 35, 41, 49, 56, 69, 85, 138, 182; in developing countries, 2; industries, 73; labor force for, 40; prices, 57

Extended family, 29, 42, 43, 47, 124, 169, 170, 174, 186, 190n5

Extension services, 40, 41, 161n6, 168, 179

Factories, 22, 48, 153

Factory jobs, 34, 35

Familial mode of production, 21, 25, 32, 33, 34, 35, 36, 37 38, 39, 42, 44, 47, 48, 49, 54, 58–61, 67, 74, 85, 100, 102, 110, 111, 115, 116, 120, 122–126, 135, 138, 139, 141, 149, 155, 163, 165, 167, 169, 170, 172, 179, 184, 186

Family, 15, 163; extended, 29, 42, 43, 47, 124, 169, 170, 174, 186, 190n7; middle-class, 174; nuclear, 34, 43, 170–175, 179, 180, 189n4; -owned land, 30, 42, 173; production system, 30; values, 61, 83, 95, 116

FAO. *See* Food and Agriculture Organization

Farming, 34, 35, 48, 49, 51, 55, 68, 83, 87, 143, 173, 181, 182; by women, 40, 68, 69, 95–97, 102, 103, 137, 138, 141, 146, 147, 153, 175, 181; collectively, 156; commercial, 7, 43, 53, 139, 151, 155; peasant, 142, 164; small-holder, 56, 69, 147, 166, 174, 182; subsistence, 31

FDEA. *See* Femme Développement Enterprise en Afrique

Female: circumcision, 16, 18, 99, 107, 117; migration, 62

Feminism, 77, 78, 81, 82, 91, 106, 120; liberal, 79; postmodernist, 15, 25, 26, 28,

78; radical, 16, 18, 19, 42; Western, 13, 15, 78, 84

Feminist: political economy, 17; politics, 20, 28, 93, 101, 126, 130, 182; theory, 6, 9, 20, 22, 25–27, 78, 80

Feminists, 10, 141; scholars, 13, 27, 28, 129

Femme Développement Enterprise en Afrique (FDEA) (Senegal), 181

Fertility, 40, 43, 76, 186

Financial institutions, 32; in capitalist industrial nations, 2; International Monetary Fund (IMF), 2, 4, 55, 84, 122, 131, 142–44; World Bank, 2–4, 8, 14, 40, 49, 51, 52, 54, 55, 94, 96, 122, 123, 128, 131, 161n5, 180, 183, 185, 186, 190n6

Food, 65, 104; processing, 86, 143, 153, 179; production, 40, 58, 59, 85, 95, 116, 137, 146; subsidies, 2

Food and Agriculture Organization (FAO), 136

Food crops, 30, 41, 56, 103, 114, 139, 150, 182; for export, 69

Foreign investment, 51, 142; in Africa, 4, 9, 38, 140

Formal sector, 70, 88, 97, 136, 145

Free markets, 20, 36, 41, 48, 49

Free trade policies, 2

FRELIMO party, 54

Ga, 62

Gabon, 123

GAD. *See* Gender and Development

Gambia, The, 68, 97, 125, 151

GATT. *See* General Agreement on Tariffs and Trade

Gender: bias, 41, 72, 98, 116, 149, 152, 153; discrimination, 15, 20, 41, 42, 73, 78, 84, 124, 130, 147, 158, 169; equality, 9, 17, 24, 26, 28, 72, 75, 79, 82, 83, 93, 101, 103, 113, 118, 120, 121, 124, 157, 179, 181, 183, 184, 186; inequity, 5, 6, 8, 19, 25, 40, 42, 43, 57, 61, 78, 82, 104; issues, 10, 42, 85, 92, 93, 111, 140, 147, 181, 183, 189; roles, 24, 99, 105, 112, 113, 116, 120

Gender and Development (GAD), 159. *See also* Women in Developemnt (WID)

Gender relationships, vii, 6, 7, 8, 11, 18, 19, 21, 23–25, 30, 36, 57, 59, 61, 65, 69, 72, 73, 102, 103, 105, 114, 115, 120, 141, 175, 176, 181, 183; precapitalist, 35; patriarchal, 83, 110

# ▲
# About the Book

Using insights from feminist theory and political economy, Gordon examines the implications for women of current economic and political reform efforts in Africa.

Much of the work on women in Africa argues that patriarchy and capitalism have collaborated in the exploitation and control of women to support dependent capitalist development; therefore, both are antithetical to the interests of women. Dependent capitalist development, however, has been a failure. And now, Gordon contends, the interests of patriarchy—in its current form in Africa—and capitalism no longer coincide. Further capitalist expansion requires improving the status of women, who now have a chance to improve their opportunities and alter patriarchal structures.

Nevertheless, the mutuality of capitalist and feminist interests is only partial. Gordon points out that if women are to avoid merely substituting one form of patriarchy for another (i.e., that typical of Western capitalist societies), they must develop new strategies and alliances to shape a future beyond dependent capitalist and patriarchal inequalities.

*April A. Gordon* is associate professor of sociology and director of the Women's Studies Program at Winthrop University. She is coeditor of *Understanding Contemporary Africa.*